20.95

# The Idea of a Town

D1067194

OAKVILLE GALLERIES
1306 LAKESHORE ROAD EAST
OAKVILLE, ONTARIO L6J 1L6

Marble panel showing two men dressed in togas guiding a yoke of two oxen (bulls?) with four
similarly dressed figures following. 3rd century A.D. Found at Aquilea.
    As the toga is hardly peasant's working dress, this relief was taken to represent a ritual scene
by its discoverer, in fact **the drawing of the 'sulcus primigenius',** even though the manner of
wearing the toga (the heads are not covered) does not conform to the descriptions of the rite.
*'Notizie Scavi', 1931, p. 472 ff.; 'Archäologischer Anzeiger' 1932, p. 454*
*Museo Civico, Aquilea*

Joseph Rykwert

# The Idea of a Town

The Anthropology of Urban Form in Rome, Italy
and the Ancient World

*The MIT Press*
*Cambridge, Massachusetts*
*London, England*

First MIT Press edition 1988
Published by arrangement with Princeton University Press, Princeton, New Jersey

This book was set by Asco Trade Typesetting Ltd., Hong Kong and printed and bound by Halliday Lithograph in the United States of America.

Library of Congress Cataloging-in-Publication Data

Rykwert, Joseph, 1926–
    The idea of a town: the anthropology of urban form in Rome, Italy  and the ancient world/Joseph Rykwert.—1st MIT ed. p.     cm.
    Includes bibliographical references and index.
    ISBN 0-262-68056-4 (pbk.)
    1. City planning—History.   2. Cities and towns, Ancient.
I. Title.
[HT166.R94   1988]
307.1′2′093—dc19

to A & A & A  and to the memory of Michael Ayrton

## Preface to the Paper Edition

In the thirty years since the book was first conceived and written, much has changed. Archeologists have been busy in Rome, in Latium and Etruscan settlements; there has also been much historical and philological work of which some account must be taken. But most important, the context in which the book will be read is entirely different. I will therefore address this question first.

The book is very timely again. When it first appeared, as a special issue of the Dutch review *Forum*, its editor, Aldo van Eyck, suggested that it would serve as a reminder to architects of something which they seemed to have forgotten: that the city was not just a rational solution to the problems of production, marketing, circulation and hygiene—or an automatic response to the pressure of certain physical and market forces—but that it also had to enshrine the hopes and fears of its citizens.

The image of the city responding by some instinct unreflectively to external and internal pressures was much favoured by urban theorists. If the city was a 'natural' product, it followed that the discovery and observance of the 'laws' of technical growth, of market forces in land value, or of traffic flow, absolved planners and architects from the responsibility of intention, and therefore of value judgement—and of artifice; they were not to worry about the 'rules' of any art.

At that time, 'housing' was the primary concern of those who planned and built in cities, and the conviction that building was about 'housing' and that 'housing' inevitably meant point or slab blocks was virtually unquestioned. During the great building euphoria of the sixties a number of more or less avant-garde architects (which meant those who drew a lot and built very little) produced a plethora of projects which presumed on an exponential growth of production and technics. The Dutch painter-utopian, Constant Niewenhuis, Yona Friedman, who was working in Paris, and the Soviet NER group separately pioneered this approach. At the same time, major 'established' architects such as Kenzo Tange and Paul Rudolph—and later, even 'commercial' offices—did projects in this vein. Since any such realizations would inevitably have called on highly industrialized prefabrication, such projects appealed to the building industry. The English group Archigram and its followers flooded the world with a frenzy of drawings for urban complexes put together out of mains-fed capsules. 'Plug-in City', 'Walking City', became slogans as much as projects. Almost equally influential, the Japanese Metabolists wanted the city-plan to be a programme for a process of constant change, as the name of the group implied. They too attempted to reduce dwelling to the individual capsule; yet in spite of that, their drawings suggested units clustered into arbitrary and almost aggressively shaped structures. All this was heady stuff, and young architects all over the world turned out great quantities of similar projects.

In such an atmosphere, the idea that town planning could in any sense be called an 'art' was thought ridiculously *passé*, while the notion that there might be anything 'symbolic' about the fabric of the city seemed almost offensively frivolous. The town was a complicated piece of machinery, producing and functioning in the same way as organisms described and studied by some biologists. All those plug-in and robotic images figured and represented that vision exactly.

In order to be seen to work, the city had not only to look like an engine, but its different functions had to be ordered, classified, parcelled out into zones into which they were separated for more efficient working. According to the most popular of such schemes, devised in the late nineteen-thirties by the International Congress of Modern Architecture (CIAM), they were dwelling, recreation, working and transport. Following this analysis, any number of plans were applied to existing towns with devastating results, and many urban projects were built on these lines during the nineteen-forties, fifties and sixties in which segregation was achieved most simply, and therefore most commonly, by stacking the zone of dwellings into high-rises while other functions remained on the ground. This, of course, meant that dwelling was isolated from public space, with the exception of the high-level corridor-street, which was allowed to replace the internal corridors of older housing; while the buildings for work, but above all those for recreation—which, after all, meant churches, libraries and even law-courts as well as theatres and swimming pools—were dwarfed by housing. Oddly enough, Le Corbusier, who was one of the main movers in CIAM and a promoter of the zoning proposals, broke these rules in his famous housing block in Marseilles, for he included a high-level shopping street halfway up the height of the block and placed a nursery school and a theatre on the roof. His were token moves, and isolated—they were not regarded with any sympathy by administrators or by his colleagues.

A number of disparate events shook these convictions, or at any rate put them to the question, even before the tide of users' disillusionment with high-rise public housing reached the present level of discontent. The economic and energy crisis provoked by the June 1967 Six-Day War in the Near East and the fear of energy shortages (which proved unfounded in the event) did trigger a reaction of distrust in the positive ideology of industrial building and technical improvement as a solution to the ills of the city. More generally, the conviction grew that economic growth was not the unmitigated social blessing it had been believed to be. These sentiments were best summed up in Ernst Schumacher's book *Small Is Beautiful*, which first appeared in the year he died, 1977.

Great movements in the 'outside' world coincided with a rejection of the planners' efforts by the very clients who were deemed to have benefitted from them. The mechanic/organic model had implied a decisive dismissal of history as irrelevant to the planners' business; they worked, after all, with the conviction that methods of statistical and other social enquiry allowed them to project the citizens' present needs into a foreseeable future. The assumption that social functions could be studied mechanically, or at any rate 'modelled', was based on the premise that needs were a function of, were 'felt' by, the whole social body. In fact, needs which are 'felt' can only be known as part of the individual experience of each citizen. Now such experience can only be described narratively, it cannot be usefully tabulated or seized in diagrammatic form. And the narration is always, however small the narrator's scale, historical. The rejection of history as a method for the study of the urban fabric, and the postulation of an efficient, conflictless city, was projected into a historical future tense, in which the experience of pain and distress, the inevitable common fate of human kind, found no accommodation or acknowledgement in the zoned and smoothly running city.[1]

Among the professionals, Christopher Alexander's paper 'The City Is Not a Tree' showed the flaw of considering urban complexity in terms of simplistic mathematical modelling. The research directed at Cambridge by Lionel March demonstrated that the choice of high-rise over low-rise housing was based on a mistaken assumption about the saving in space which could be obtained by concentrating housing in high-rise accommodation. Kevin Lynch began to investigate the image of the town which its inhabitants formed, as it were, intersubjectively. The study of architectural typology and urban morphology—terms and endeavours associated with Aldo Rossi—concentrated on the detailed study of the invariant configurations of the units in which citizens lived, and on the texture which these units made up in their cities, but did not consider the tension between the edge of the city and its centre. A number of sociologists, such as Peter Wilmot in England and later, but much more radically, Erving Goffman in the United States, were concerned about the relation between social pattern and physical dwelling structures.

All such ways of criticising the present urban situation—which appeared the more glaring the more integrated and 'holistic' they were—had one disadvantage: they were all descriptive and analytic. They were oriented towards explaining where the city failed to work and what its drawbacks were. There was no mediation, however, no rational discourse which would allow the planner to proceed from past failure to future success. The writers who did attempt a general and positive account of the whole complex urbanistic phenomenon were very rare and very depressing: one of them—who had better remain nameless here—complained in about 1980 'that much of the literature on city form is outstanding for its stupefying dullness'. 'That urban theory is so boring is more than discouraging. It must be a sign of deeper difficulties', he added. 'City planning has stagnated', another prominent theorist had written twenty years earlier: 'it bustles, but it does not advance'.

The boredom was due, in part at least, to theoretical abstraction—or perhaps more accurately, to a detachment which concealed the sense of incurable impotence. For several decades, during the fifties, sixties and seventies (the custom may still persist here and there) designers of the most banal urban complexes would lecture on their projects—which were usually produced by merely manipulating commercial and 'market' pressures with more or less skill—yet in the course of the lecture show slides of 'ideal' or 'timeless' urban situations: St Mark's Square in Venice, Dubrovnik or any one of a number of Italian hill towns or Greek island villages (all places where town-planners often repaired for their vacations) to justify some aspect of their plan or procedure. There was no way of either acceding to or dismissing such parallels, since the planners' language was made up entirely of platitudes, which could (inevitably) apply to both their own projects and to the examples which they chose to illustrate. Contradiction or dispute seemed ill-mannered, or even in bad faith. Discussions of historical plans in books on urbanism were also disturbing: Pierre-Charles L'Enfant's use of a mixed layout—grid structure of roads cut by diagonal avenues—in his plan for Washington, for instance, was blamed for that city's lackluster urban life while the same mixed layout was considered the secret of Idelfonso Cerda's all-too-great success in achieving the development of Barcelona within his *ensanche*.

This absence of any agreement about how to link social and economic theories to the physical fabric is only one aspect of the monumental dullness complained of in my quotations. A much more serious problem was the planners' conviction that planning was not only an *a*historical but also an *a*political process. Inescapably, the growth of the physical fabric over the last century was setting the planner problems against which he was not armed at all.

The greatest change of approach in urbanism developed from a growing appreciation that the physical structure of a city could not be discussed in plan terms any longer. The skyline had become the most important configuration in our vision of the city, yet planning theories had so far not taken any coherent account of it. Montgomery Schuyler, the most perceptive American architectural critic of his time, pointed the problem out nearly a century ago when he said of the New York skyline that '. . . it was not an architectural vision, but it does, most tremendously, look like business . . .'[2]

This aspect of the city had been recognized by designers for some time, even if it had not entered theoretical discourse. Le Corbusier, in some early schemes, notably the huge project for Algiers, alluded to it, but it was approached more explicitly by Louis Kahn in his various schemes for Philadelphia. Hans Hollein and his Viennese colleagues were inspired by the enigmatic and sinister metaphoric power of large structures set in a rural or a wild landscape. Several attempts were made to construct fragments of a three-dimensional city, of which *Habitat* (designed by Moshe Safdie for the Montreal exhibition of 1967) and the city-centre in Cumbernauld, designed by a team led by Geoffrey Copcutt, were the most conspicuous; but they have not been unqualifiedly successful, either socially or economically. Meanwhile several European highways have been spanned by large and complex buildings (the Berlin Congress Centre is an instance) in which complicated internal relations are made between various forms of movement, as yet without art. Yet it seems to me that this is the realm where the architect-planner must really intervene.

This book was first conceived in the nineteen-fifties, at the height of the postwar building boom and of the planners' professional arrogance. It set out polemically to provide some rational account of the structure and intentions of the builders of those Italian towns whose beauties picturesquely oriented Anglo-American theorists displayed in nostalgic, lyrical travelogue and over-contrast photographs. It was to have been part of a much larger publication, which was to describe the rise and transformation of the cities over the centuries, which I had intended to write in collaboration with the Italian sociologist, Carlo Doglio.

The natural starting point for such a book was Numa Fustel de Coulanges' *La Cité Antique*, which was first published in 1859. It seemed strange then that no later attempt had been made to develop his approach and examine the notional structure of the ancient town, and how that structure might be transmitted and understood by its citizens. That is what I determined to write. At that time I happened also to read *Tristes Tropiques*, Claude Lévi-Strauss' account of his journeyings to and in the Amazon basin, and was struck by his description of the unity between village plan, kinship system and the world-picture of the Bororo, a people of the poorest material culture, and by the way each aspect of this picture mastered much of their thinking and action.[3] I also came across John Neihardt's *Black Elk Speaks, Being the Life Story of a Holy Man of the Oglala Sioux*, which described the shaman-visionary's dismay at the way in which the white man had managed to destroy all his people's power by making them live in square houses, so that they were cut off from the health and vigour which they drew from the harmony between their physical surroundings and their circular world-picture: '. . . Our tepees were round like the nests of birds, and these were always set in a circle, the nation's hoop, a nest of many nests, where the Great Spirit meant us to hatch our children . . .'[4] Such readings were framed for me in the chapter on sacred space in Mircea Eliade's *Treatise on the History of Religion*,[5] which, for all the criticisms it has received, remains the most extensive and persuasive study of such matters. Much recent thinking about the nature of symbolism, myth, ritual and their interrelation has not led me to modify this view.

The revision of the text for the much extended second edition was done in the sixties. Much light has been thrown on the theoretical background of this essay by some recent studies. Mary Douglas' *Natural Symbols*, for instance, and Basil Bernstein's closely related *Class, Codes and Control*[6] attempt a kind of historical economy of symbol, which would say something about the way we understand our own bodies—and how that understanding, and indeed every acceptance and construing of a linguistic or any other message, is conditioned by the way we perceive our role in a social context. Jean Baudrillard's books,[7] though written from an entirely different point of view from mine, raised many issues for me about the nature of symbolism in mass culture. In *Rethinking Symbolism* Dan Sperber makes an explicit critique of Lévi-Strauss' semiotic approach to symbols as counters in a closed system which I find wholly sympathetic;[8] he suggests that semiology is an inappropriate method for examining symbolism, since:

> Symbols are not signs . . . their interpretations are not meanings . . . The data an individual uses in learning symbolism do not constitute a sample of a fixed set similar to the sentences of a language . . . A corollary of this cognitive nature is that there is no multi-symbolism analogous to multi-lingualism . . . symbolic data,

no matter what their origin, integrate themselves into a single system within a given individual . . .

Sperber's view of symbolism, that it is both cognitive and evocative at the same time, yet closed to any semiotic reading, is the view taken in this book.

In a meditation on Livy's account of the earliest Rome, which he himself had wanted to subtitle the 'philosophy of bodies in a mix', Michel Serres[9] also seems to take just such a view of symbolism, and presents the city as a palimpsest of superimposed 'readings' in which the grid of urban texture makes a matrix of evocations through the city's history and the repeated patterns of its murders and of violence. Those critics who reproached me with presenting too idyllic a view of the ancient city were justified only in so far as my aim was to show how the city founders went about their business and also how they rationalized it. I was not here concerned with how their plans might have failed partially or even totally.

Inevitably perhaps, the city in ancient literature had no better press than in the modern. And that has always been a part of the urban ethos:

God the first Garden made, and the first City, *Cain*.[10]

Like Cain, Romulus was a fratricide, and the founder's crime was only the first of the many with which the city was ever stained. I recall this exemplar to make two disclaimers.

First, I need to remind the readers that to Roman poets and moralists the city was a bad place: crowded, dirty, smelly, noisy, violent, corrupt. In that it was like the modern city of literature. Cicero, Horace, Ovid, Pliny the Younger, Juvenal, Martial, descant on this theme constantly. It is not because the ancient city is being presented as an ideal environment that ancient urbanophobia has no place in this book. That was not my aim at all. Of course the ancient city was full of pain, vice and evil. Of course its citizens often resented, hated and despised it. My point was that it was designed to absorb all that without breaking, though in fact a study of ancient anti-urbanism, analogous to Morton and Lucia White's study of the phenomenon in the United States remains to be done.[11]

Second, I must make it quite clear that the book does not advocate a return to an ancient order. I am quite aware that the gap between the 'closed' city of antiquity and the 'open' one of my own time is unbridgeable. I am definitely a consenting citizen of the open city, and my view of the matter is not very different from Harvey Cox's theologically justified acceptance of the de-sacralized society of our time.[12]

I will therefore summarize here what the reader will find clearly (if briefly) stated in the last paragraph of the book, since some of my critics may consider my disclaimer insincere. In spite of its otherness, and its failures, the modern planner still has one important lesson to learn from ancient precedent: namely, that any 'pattern' which the city has to offer, however it is achieved, must be strong enough to survive all its inevitable disorders and other vicissitudes and structure the urban experience; and that it must be of such a nature as to allow the citizen to 'read' it through the sort of imagery which Kevin Lynch deduced from his fellow-citizens' response to the city of Boston,[13] though the planner must learn to offer the citizen more grip on his town than Lynch's subjects had been offered by chaotic Boston.

The book is being re-issued at a time when history has come back into vogue. Studies of inert 'types' and motiveless morphologies are multiplying. Books on history abound in architectural bookshops. However, the history which is being presented for the use of architects and urbanists is not of the kind which historians make and read. It is a catalogue-history, devoid of narration, in which the phenomenal past is digested to a set of timeless motifs on which the designer can call to deck out his project in a garb which will produce, so it is generally thought, the right kind of denotative response in the public. While market forces, the traffic engineer and the planning administrators operate as before, their sins are now covered by a skin of ornament borrowed from the history books. It would be a grotesque situation were it not also sinister, since again the pattern of the city is forgotten. Whereas the sins of the immediate past were the imposition of an excessive ordering and a concentration on housing, the current trend is to treat the building (particularly the administrative or speculative building) as an isolated 'architectural' object without reference to the texture of the town. In the fifties and sixties the grid oppressed and emasculated the object. In the seventies and eighties the unruly object is deforming and eroding the grid.

The reminder which seems to matter most now is about pattern and texture. If the city is to be known to its citizens as a 'legible' one, they must be able to read it as at least one, but preferably several, superimposed and easily recognizable patterns. Within these patterns a mix and swirl should find public open space for its deployment. The city must also show itself to the citizen in institutions which are conspicuous, even flagrant parts of public space. It is very probable that this can only be done in the late twentieth century if the city is treated as a three-dimensional entity. The skyline must no longer 'most tremendously' in Montgomery Schuyler's words, 'look like business' which has pushed up through the arbitrary grid of the street pattern: it must become 'an architectural vision'.

Such a suggestion can only be advanced here for further discussion. This book was primarily concerned with ancient Rome and some recent excavation and research has modified some of the emphasis of my statements. The most important excavation has been that of the archaic sanctuary by the old church of St Ombono near the Roman Forum, which has now been identified as that of the twin temples of Mater Matuta and Fortuna, founded, according to the chroniclers and annalists, by King Servius Tullius (who reigned 577–534 B.C.) and reconstructed more splendidly by Tarquin the Proud (who reigned 534–509 B.C.). The radio-carbon examination of the wood on the site has vindicated the annalists' dating.[14]

Almost as important has been the re-examination of the remains of the *Regia* on the Roman Forum, the reputed house of King Numa, by its excavator, Frank Brown, who has indeed modified the picture of the earliest building in the way I suggested in the caption to fig. 82.[15] It now seems that the first wooden huts on the site were buried towards the end of the seventh century, after a flood. A radiocarbon examination of the wood gives a date of about 680 B.C. for the cutting of the trees. This is within the traditional reign of King Numa (713–679 B.C.) according to the chronicles. After the flood, there follow four stages of the building under the Monarchy when the *Regia* seems to have held a double sanctuary, though not one rigorously orientated (apart from its southern wall). The great circular hearth was indeed placed in its present position at the beginning of the Republican period, when the *Regia* was completely re-built about 510 B.C.

Apart from the *Regia* itself, a number of changes in the realignment and identity of certain buildings on the Forum Romanum[16] have been recorded in a recent study by Filippo Coarelli. The *Lapis Niger*, which I had considered tentatively as one possible 'Tomb of Romulus', is named as the Volcanal by him; though, since any 'tomb' of Romulus had to be figurative, because traditions agree that after his disappearance he was 'assumed among the gods' or deified as Quirinus, it is more appropriate to call it here the *heroon*, the place where the putative murder of Romulus took place.

The paving of the *Lapis Niger*, which was probably put down at the time of Sulla, was contemporary with an enlargement and realignment of the Roman Forum, and the removal of the presumed circular *comitium*. The fragments of an unusually fine Attic black-figure vase (fairly precisely datable to 570–560 B.C) provides a date *ante quem* for the setting up of the little shrine in the form buried under the *Lapis*.[17]

There is much comparative material discovered since my publication. The site of the twelve altars at Lavinium, where Roman magistrates sacrificed on laying down office, has been found to contain a *heroon*, in the form of a circular tumulus probably laid down 675–650 B.C., of the kind I have discussed in Paestum and Kyrene. It may well be the *heroon* of Aeneas, to which Dionysius of Halicarnassus had alluded.[18] An *auguraculum*, more impressive than the fragmentary one at Cosa, was found at Bantia (now S. Maria di Banzia, near Venosa in Lucania),[19] and the remains of the Roman augurs' eyrie or *templum* have been tentatively identified on the Capitol Hill. It now seems that the points of the augurs' compass were linked to definite landmarks, and that there were several such eyries in Rome, perhaps all placed without the *pomoerium*, which bounded the city site as *liberatum et effatum*.[20] Outside Rome proper, the plan of Cosa has been given a much more definite form, and the development of the town traced by Frank Brown, whom I have already mentioned as the excavator of the Roman Forum.[21]

I have nothing new to report on the larger issues: Etruscan origins, the Etruscan language, the relative debt of the Romans to the Greek and Etruscan traditions. The 'Etruscan Year', 1985, saw a number of more or less important exhibitions and publications, which have shown the problems in greater detail but have not brought resolutions.[22] Although it is possible to compile a small Etruscan vocabulary, and there is an outline of syntax, the grammar remains obscure. It is clear that it is neither an

Indo-European nor a Semitic language. It seems to belong to some proto-Mediterranean group of languages—of which precious little is still known.[23] Until more is discovered, the linguistic question will not help with the problem of Etruscan origins.[24]

Although the Greek contribution to Rome was great, the excavation report about one of the earliest, if not the earliest Greek colony in Sicily, Megara Hyblaea north of Syracuse, shows that certainly at Megara the layout was not *quadratus*; centered as it is from the outset on an explicit *agora*, and further distinguishing primary from secondary streets (which are differently orientated), it has thrown the difference between Greek and Etruscan layout methods into relief.[25]

The Greek and Latin languages make this distinction quite explicit: the very word *urbs* is probably of Etruscan origin, and it is only obliquely related to *civitas*, which is the collective noun for a group of *cives*. *Civis* is usually translated, quite rightly as 'citizen', but it means more: a free man, the head of a household. *Urbs* indicates the way in which the city was physically, ritually and legally made. The Greek word *polis*, on the other hand, means a defensible place, and *polites* are those who live within the walls. The words for city and citizen are therefore quite differently related in Greek and Latin: and that is partly due to the way the Etruscan-derived *urbs* replaced the older Indo-European word, *tota* for city, which survived in the neighbouring Oscan language.[26]

The relation between Roman and Greek city foundations and their founders remains one most interesting question which is still outstanding. Although the names of the hero-founders and re-founders of Greek towns are known in plenty, information about what they actually did, ritually, is quite hard to come by.[27] The opposite is true of the Romans. Where city- (or at any rate colony) founders are well-known, they are not revered, and never heroized. It is almost as if the founding and re-founding of the Greek city was the work of an independant divinely inspired figure whereas that of the Roman city was always a substitution, a vicarious action.[28] Every Roman town-founder was always a stand-in for Romulus: because every town, every foundation, was a reiteration of Rome. Had Plutarch devoted one of his *Roman Questions* to this conundrum, we would probably not have been very much the wiser; but though he may not have enlightened us fully, he could at least have given a lead.

Were I to write the book now, it would, I dare say, have been better, or at least better informed, but I doubt if it would be very different, in spite of my critics. I might have been much more acutely aware of the role and appreciation of cunning as a technical accomplishment, even in ritual and divination,[29] for instance, but my approach would still be synchronic, since throughout the social and economic changes of the Republic and Empire certain religious notions, transmitted through ritual behaviour, suffered little change, although they were put to different political and even social uses.[30] As with myth, so with ritual—its origin is out of reach; it is its transmission which matters. The way myth and ritual shape, even create, the man-made environment and the way in which they rationalize and explain it are what concerns me here.

1   A brief but valuable essay on this problem in Richard Sennett's *The Uses of Disorder: Personal Identity and City Life*, New York 1971, pp. 96 ff.

2   In 'The Sky-line of New York, 1881–1897', *Harper's Weekly*, March 20, p. 295; see William Taylor, 'New York et l'Origine du Skyline', *Urbi* III, March 1980, pp. XIIf, and T. A. P. van Leeuwen, *The Skyward Trend of Thought*, The Hague, 1986, pp. 84f.

3   Paris, 1955, pp. 227ff, 249ff. In *Anthropologie Structurale* (Paris, 1958, pp. 147ff.) Claude Lévi-Strauss concentrates his attention on the parallels to Bororo organization to show their essentially dual character, which he considers a fundamental characteristic of all social organization—see, however, R. Caillois, *L'Homme et le Sacré*, Paris, 1950, pp. 8off.

4   Lincoln, Nebraska, 1932; pp. 198ff.

5   *Traité d'Histoire des Religions*, Paris, 1953, pp. 315ff. Developed in *Images et Symboles*, Paris, 1952, pp. 48ff; *Mythes, Rêves et Mystères*, Paris, 1957, pp. 206ff.

6   London, 1973, esp. pp. 27ff, 94ff; St Alban's, 1973, esp. pp. 193ff. See a discussion of this problem by S. C. Humphreys, *Anthropology and the Greeks*, London, 1978, pp. 265ff.

7   *Système des Objets*, Paris, 1968; *Pour une Critique de l'Economie Politique du Signe*, Paris, 1972.

8   Cambridge, 1975; pp. 85ff.

9   *Rome, le Livre des Fondations*, Paris, 1983.

10  A. Cowley, 'The Garden', *Works*, London, 1710, p. 735.

11  Morton and Lucia White, *The Intellectual versus the City*, Cambridge, Mass., 1962.

12  *The Secular City*, Harmondsworth, 1968; see also *Herméneutique de la Sécularisation*, ed. by Enrico Castelli, Paris, 1976.

13  *The Image of the City*, Cambridge, Mass., 1960.

14  Antonio M. Collini and others, 'L'Area Sacra di S. Ombono', in *La Parola del Passato* XXXII, Naples, 1977, pp. 9ff; summed up by F. Coarelli, *Roma Sepolta* Rome, 1984, pp. 8ff.

15  Frank E. Brown, 'La Protostoria della Regia', *Rendiconti della Pontificia Accademia di Archeologia* XLVII, Rome, 1974–5, pp. 8ff. On the dating of the timber, see p. 19. Brown assumes (p. 35) that the two sanctuaries had the same dedications as those of the later *Regia*, to Mars and Ops Consiva. It was, in any case, never regarded as the king's palace: the private addresses of the Roman kings, including Numa were given by various authors. See Brown, p. 36, n. 15, and Filippo Coarelli, *Il Foro Romano*, Rome, 1986, vol. I (2nd ed.; vol. II, 1985), pp. 57ff.

16  The Volcanal/*Lapis Niger*/Tomb of Romulus is discussed by F. Coarelli, *op. cit.*, 1986/5, vol. I, pp. 161ff.

17  F. Coarelli, *op. cit.* 1985/6, pp. 177f.

18  Dion. Hal., I, 37. See Geneviève Dury Moyaers, *Enée et Lavinium*, Brussels, 1981. On Greek influence in Latium, see E. La Rocca and M Torelli 'Territorio Laziale e Gravisca', *La Parola del Passato* XXXII, Naples, 1977, pp. 375ff. On Etruscan influence, see Larissa Bonfante, *Out of Etruria: Etruscan Influence North and South*, BAR Series, 103.

19  M. Torelli, 'Un Templum Augurale d'Età Republicana a Bantia', in *Rendiconti dell'Accademia dei Lincei* XXII, 1966, pp. 293ff.

20  Frank E. Brown, *Cosa: The Making of a Roman Town*, Ann Arbor, Mich., 1980.

21  *Scrivere Etrusco: Della Legenda alla Conoscenza*, Milan, 1985; G. Colonna, *Santuari d'Etruria*, Florence, 1985. On the legend of the Etruscans, see G. Morolli, '*Vetus Etruria*', Florence, 1985.

22  F. Coarelli, *op. cit.* (1986/5) vol. I, pp. 100ff., and A. Magdelain, 'L'Auguraculum de l'Arx à Rome et dans d'Autres Villes', *Revue des Etudes Latines* XLVII, 1969, pp. 253ff.

23  For a summary of evidence and vocabulary, see R. Staccioli, *La Lingua degli Etruschi*, Rome, 1969. For a brief review, see Alain Hus, *Les Etrusques et Leur Destin*, Paris, 1980, pp. 152ff.

24  See Luciana Aigner Foresti, *Tesi, Ipotesi e Considerazioni sull'Origine degli Etruschi*, Vienna, 1974; Gertrud Kahl-Furthmann, *Die Frage nach dem Ursprung der Etrusker*, Meisenheim am Glan, 1976.

25  G. Vallet, François Villard, and Paul Auberson, *Megara Hyblaea: I. Le Quartier de l'Agora Archaique*, Rome, 1976. Further reflections on this problem, on the introduction of a Greek round-shaped *comitium* (whence the *Graecostasis* on the Roman Forum) in F. Coarelli, *op. cit.*, 1985/6, vol. I, pp. 138ff. On the protohistory of Graeco-Italic contacts, see Dominique Briquel, *Les Pélasges en Italie: Recherches sur l'Histoire de la Légende*, Rome & Paris, 1984.

26  E. Benveniste, *Le Vocabulaire des Institutions Indo-Européennes*, Paris, 1969, vol. I, pp. 335ff.

27  C. Berard 'L'Héroisation et la Formation de la Cité: Un Conflit idéologique', *Architecture et Société*, Paris, 1983, pp. 43ff. François de Polignac, *La Naissance de la Cité Grecque*, Paris, 1984, esp. pp. 118ff.

28  It is interesting that the Emperor Hadrian was heroized as a Greek-type *ktistes* in Athens. That was the implication both of the inscription on the Arch of Hadrian by the Olympeion, and by his appearing as the eponym of a tribe. See Paus., I, 5, v., who mentions two other 'modern' tribes.

29  Marcel Detienne and Jean-Pierre Vernant, *Cunning Intelligence in Greek Culture and Society*,
    Hassocks, Sussex, 1978. But see M. Schofield, 'Cicero for and Against Divination', *JRS*
    LXXVI, 1986, pp. 47ff.

30  I owe this formulation to Mary Beard: 'The Sexual Status of Vestal Virgins', *JRS* LXX,
    1980, pp. 12ff. The situation of Roman mythography is illustrated by Georges Dumézil's
    reiteration of his account of the earliest history of Rome as a mythographic fabrication in
    *Mythe et Epopée*, Paris, 1968–73, vol. I, pp. 261ff., vol. III, pp. 93ff. I cannot add biblio-
    graphy on comparative material here, simply because it is now too extensive. On the Islamic
    city, Oleg Grabar's chapters on the city in his *Formation of Islamic Art*, New Haven and
    London, 1973, and Paolo Cuneo, *Storia dell'Urbanistica: Il Mondo Islamico*, Rome, 1986; on
    the Renaissance figuration of the city, Paolo Marconi (ed.) *La Città come Forma Symbolica*,
    Rome, 1973, should, however, be mentioned.

The Idea of a Town

# Contents

Contents

# Illustrations

# Acknowledgements

I would like first to record my continued gratitude to Mr Simon Nowell-Smith, who made the writing of this book possible and has continued to help me at all stages. In its first form, the manuscript was read by Professor Christopher Cornford, Mr Eric John, Dr Christopher Ligota, Countess Benita de'Grassi and Mrs Agatha Sadler, to whom I continue to be indebted. Professor Aldo van Eyck published it in its original form as a special issue of the magazine *Forum* of which he was then editor, and welcomed it with a most generous preface. Mr Jurriaan Schröfer was the enthusiastic and sympathetic designer of the original publication.

The matter of this book had been discussed with Dr Franz Elkisch, Professor Sigfried Giedion, Professor Colin Rowe and Mr Edward Wright. Mr Michael Ayrton has given me much help and encouragement. Unfortunately, I did not avail myself of W. F. Jackson-Knight's unique insight into the world of the Aeneid until the last year of his life. Professor Frank E. Brown allowed me to work with him for two summers at the American Academy in Rome. Professor G. A. Mansuelli, Soprintendente alle Antichità Bologna, has been most generous with his material concerning the excavation at Marzabotto. Various points have been discussed with Professor Richard Brilliant, Dr Gordon Brotherston, Dr Anthony Bulloch, Professor William L. MacDonald, Professor Mario Napoli, Mr Lawrence Nield, Professor G. Vallet, Dr Dalibor Vesely and Dr Giuseppe Vosa. The staffs of various libraries—the Warburg Institute, the Hellenic and Roman Societies, the London Library, the University of Essex and the American Academy in Rome—have been helpful, and often forbearing. Princess Margharita Rospigliosi smoothed many rough places in Rome.

The Nonesuch Press have very kindly allowed me to quote the translation of Pindar's fourth Pythian ode by H. T. Wade-Gray and C. M. Bowra; the Manchester University Press a passage from A. J. Graham's *Colony and Mother City*; and Sigmund Freud Copyrights Ltd., the Institute of Psycho-Analysis, The Hogarth Press Ltd. and the Liveright Publishing Corporation a passage from the *Five Lectures* on Psycho-Analysis by Sigmund Freud, revised and edited by James Strachey.

The illustrations of Wang-Ch'eng and Hsiao-T'un are reproduced from *The Pivot of the Four Quarters* by P. Wheatley by permission of Edinburgh University Press, and the Dogon blanket from *La Parole chez les Dogon* by G. Calame-Griaule by permission of Messrs. Gallimard; the fragments of the map of Orange and the diagrams by permission of *Gallia* from the supplementary volume by A. Piganiol, and the reconstructions of the Agora at Cyrene by permission of L'Erma di Bretschneider from *L'Agora di Cirene* by Sandro Stucchi.

Mrs Sybilla Haynes and Mr Andrew Saint have very kindly read the final manuscript and purged some of its grosser errors. The continuation of my first studies was helped by a grant from the Phoenix Trust and from the Bollingen Foundation.

I should like to thank Mr Giles de la Mare and Mrs Valerie Griffiths for their exemplary editing, and Mr Eugene Sandersley whose patience, has preserved me from many slips and mistakes.

All married authors owe something to their wives with each book published. Few can have been as much indebted as I have been, with the appearance of this one.

# Abbreviations

## I Periodicals and Books of Reference

| | |
|---|---|
| *Abhandlungen der Heidelberger Akademie der Wissenschaften, Philosophisch-Historische Klasse* | *Abh.Heid.Ak.Wiss. Ph.-Hist.Kl.* |
| *American Journal of Archaeology* | *A.J.A.* |
| *American Journal of Philology* | *A.J.P.* |
| *American Academy in Rome* | *Am.Ac.Rome* |
| *Bibliothèque des Écoles Françaises d'Athènes et de Rome* | *Bibl.des Ec.Fr.d'Ath.et Rome* |
| *Bullettino della Commissione Archeologica di Roma* | *Bull.Com.* |
| *Bullettino dell'Istituto Storico dell'Arma del Genio* | *Bull.Ist.Stor.* |
| *Corpus Inscriptionum Latinarum* | *C.I.L.* |
| *Classical Review* | *C.R.* |
| C.O.D. Du Cange, *Glossarium ad Scriptores Mediae et Infimae Latinitatis*, Frankfurt-am-Main, 1681 ff. | Du Cange |
| *Journal of Roman Studies* | *J.R.S.* |
| *Kritische Beiträge* | *Krit.Beitr.* |
| *Memoirs of the American Academy in Rome* | *Mem.Am.Ac.Rome* |
| *Mitteilungen des Deutschen Archäologischen Institut, Römische Abteilung* | *Mitt.Deutsc.Arch.Inst.Röm.* |
| *Notizie degli Scavi di Antichità* | *Not.Scav.* |
| *Papers of the British School in Rome* | *Papers, Brit.Sch.* |
| *Revue d'Assyriologie* | *R.d'Ass.* |
| Paulys *Real-Encyclopädie der Klassischen* ed. Georg *Altertumswissenschaft*: new edn., Wissowa, Stuttgart, 1894 ff. | *R.E.* |
| *Revue de l'Histoire des Religions* | *R.Hist.Rel.* |
| *Rheinishes Museum der Philologie* (Neue Folge) | *Rh.M.*(N.F.) |
| *Sonder-Bericht* | *S.B.* |
| *Supplementum Epigraphicum Graecum*, ed. J. J. E. Hondius et al., Leyden, 1934 ff. | *S.E.G.* |
| *Studi Etruschi* | *St.Etr.* |
| *Studi Materiali per la Storia delle Religioni* | *St.M.St.R.* |
| *Transactions of the American Philological Association* | *T.A.P.A.* |

## II Sources

| | |
|---|---|
| Ammianus Marcellinus, *The Histories* | Amm.Marc. |
| Apollodorus, *Bibliotheca* | Apollod. |
| Apollonius Rhodius, *The Argonautica* | Apol.Rhod. |
| Appian of Alexandria, *Roman History* | App. |
| Aristotle, *Politics* | Aristotle, *Pol.* |
| Arnobius Afer, *Against the Gentiles* | Arnob.*Adv.Gent.* |
| Aulus Gellius, *The Attic Nights* | Aul.Gell. |
| M. Aurelius Augustinus (St. Augustine), *The City of God* | Aurel.Aug.*de Civ.Dei.* |
| M. Porcius Cato, the Censor, *On Agriculture* | Cato, *de R.R.* |
| M. Tullius Cicero, *Speech against Publius Vatinius* | Cic. *in P.Vatin.* |
| *Philippics against Mark Antony* | *Philipp.* |
| *Letters to T. Pomponius Atticus* | *ad Attic.* |
| *On Divination* | *de Div.* |
| *On the Laws* | *de Leg.* |
| *On the Nature of the Gods* | *de Nat.Deor.* |
| *On Offices* | *de Off.* |
| *On the Republic* | *de Rep.* |

| | |
|---|---|
| *Laelius*, or *On Friendship* | *Lael.* |
| L. Junius Modestus Columella, *On Agriculture* | Col.*de R.R.* |
| *Corpus Agrimensorum Romanorum*, ed. C. Thulin, vol. I, pt. I, 'Opuscula Agrimensorum Veterum', Leipzig, 1913 | *Corp.Agr.Vet.* |
| *Culex*, *The Gnat* (attr. Virgil) | Culex |
| Diodorus Siculus, *The Historical Anthology* | Diod.Sic. |
| Dio Cassius, *The Roman History* | Dio Cass. |
| Dionysius of Halicarnassus, *The Early History of Rome* | Dion.Hal. |
| Quintus Ennius, *The Annals* | Ennius |
| Sextus Pompeius Festus, *On the Meaning of Words*, with the Epitome of Paul the Deacon (*Sexti Pompei Festi de Verborum Significatu . . . cum Pauli Epitome*, ed. Wallace M. Linday, Leipzig, 1913) | Fest. |
| F. Jacoby, *Die Fragmente der Griechischen Historiker*, Berlin and Leyden, 1923–58 | *F.G.H.* |
| Flavius Vegetius Renatus, *On Strategy* | Flav.Veg. |
| Sextus Julius Frontinus, *On Strategy* | Front.*Strat.* (see also Jul.Front.) |
| Herodotus, *The Histories* | Herod. |
| Hippocrates, *Aphorisms* | Hippocr.*Aphor.* |
| Homer, *The Homeric Hymns* | Hom.*Hymn.* |
| *The Iliad* | *Il.* |
| *The Odyssey* | *Od.* |
| Q. Horatius Flaccus, *Odes* | Hor.*Car.* |
| *On The Art of Poetry* | *de Ar.Poet.* |
| *Epodes* | *Epod.* |
| *Satires* | *Sat.* |
| Hyginus Gromaticus (in *Corp.Agr.Vet.*) | Hyg.Grom. |
| *On Military Camps* | *de Castr.* |
| *On the Drawing of Borders* | *de Const.Limit.* |
| *On the Fortification of Camps* | *de Munit.Castr.* |
| *The Fables* | *Fab.* |
| Isidore of Seville, *Origins*, or *On Etymology* | Isid. |
| Julius Frontinus (in *Corp.Agr.Vet.*), *On Disputes about Land* | Jul.Front. (see also Front.*Strat.*) |
| M. Junius Justinus, *History* (abridging Trogus Pompeius) | Justin |
| T. Livius Patavinus, *History of the City Since its Foundation* | Livy |
| Gaius Ennius Lucilius, *The Satires* | Lucil. |
| Aurelius Theodosius Macrobius, *Saturnalia* | Macrob.*Sat.* |
| *The Architecture of Mānasāra*, ed. K. P. Acharya, London, 1933 ff. | *Manasara* |
| Martianus Capella, *The Satyricon, On The Marriage of Philology and Mercury* | Mart.Cap. |
| Nonnius Marcellus, *Knowledge in Brief* | Nonnius |
| Xenophon, *Economics* | *Oecon.* |
| Publius Ovidius Naso, *On the Art of Love* | Ovid.*de A.A.* |
| *Fasti* | *Fasti* |
| *The Metamorphoses* | *Metam.* |
| Pausanias, *The Description of Greece* | Paus. |
| Pindar, *The Nemean Odes* | Pind.*Nem.* |
| *The Pythian Odes* | *Pyth.* |
| Caius Plinius Secundus, *The Natural History* | Pliny, *N. H.* |
| Plutarch, *The Lives:* (Life of) Alexander; Caesar; | Plutarch |

Camillus; Cimon; Numa; Pericles; Poplicola;
Pyrrhus; Romulus; Theseus

| | |
|---|---|
| *On Isis and Osiris* | *de Isid. et Os.* |
| *On the Fortunes of the Romans* | *de Sort.Rom.* |
| *Greek Questions* | *G.Q.* |
| *Parallels* | *Par.* |
| *Roman Questions* | *R.Q.* |
| Aristotle, *Politics* | *Pol.* |
| Polybius of Megalopolis, *The History* | Polyb. |
| Quintus Curtius Rufus, *On the Actions of Alexander the Great* | Quint.Curt. |
| Scholia, *Commentary* | Sch. |
| *Ancient Commentary* (on Pindar's poems) | *Vet.* (*in Pind.Car*) |
| *Scriptores Historiae Augustae* | *Scr.Hist.Aug.* |
| L. Annaeus Seneca, *On the Brevity of Life* | Seneca *de Brev. Vitae* |
| *On Clemency to Nero* | *de Clem.* |
| M. Servius Honoratus, *Commentary on Virgil* | Serv. *in Virg.* |
| Gaius Julius Solinus, *Collection of Things Memorable* | Solinus |
| Sophocles, *Oedipus at Colonnus* | Soph.*Oed.Col.* |
| P. Papinius Statius, *The Thebaïs* | Stat.*Theb.* |
| Strabo, *On Geography* | Strabo |
| Cornelius Tacitus, *The Annals* | Tac.*Ann.* |
| *The Histories* | *Hist.* |
| Tertullian, *The Apology* | Tert.*Apol.* |
| Thucydides, *The History of the Peloponnesian War* | Thuc. |
| Valerius Maximus, *The Memorabilia* | Val.Max. |
| M. Terentius Varro, *On the Latin Language* | Varro, *de L.L.* |
| *On Agriculture* | *de R.R.* |
| Velleius Paterculus, *The Roman History* | Vell.Pat. |
| L. Publius Vergilius Maro, *The Aeneid* | Virg.*Aen.* |
| *The Eclogues* | *Ecl.* |
| *The Georgics* | *Geor.* |
| *Culex* (attr.) | *Culex* |
| M. Vitruvius Pollio, *On Architecture* | Vitruv. |

**1. Topography of early Rome.** The heavy line shows the run of the wall known as the Agger of Servius Tullius. The seven hills of the original *Septimontium* were the Palatine, Velia, Cermal, Fagutal, Cispian and Oppian, the Capitol and the Valley of the Suburra. The Fagutal is a prominence between the Oppian and the Velia. Later counts of the Seven hills differ. *After L. Benevolo Corso di Disegno, vol. 2. fig. 226.*

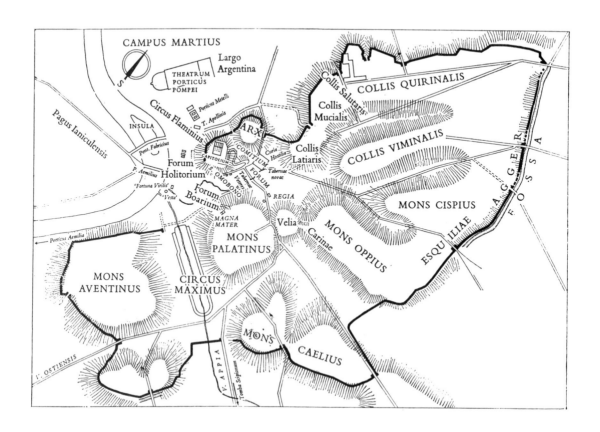

# Preface

We think of the town as a tissue of buildings which grows more or less unpredictably and is traversed by roads, pierced by squares, or else as a mesh of roadways fringed by buildings at the outskirts and webbed by them at the centre. Although we regard them as natural phenomena, governed by an independent, uncontrollable and sometimes unpredictable law of growth or expansion, like that of natural organisms, the truth is that towns do not grow by interior and inscrutable instincts. They are built, piece-meal by individual inhabitants, in larger tracts by speculators or authority. Now and then, particularly when a new town is founded, the authorities. whether local or national, on the advice of their experts treat the public to a display of embarrassment. It appears that civic authorities, or even the planners themselves, are not able to think of the new town as a totality, as a pattern which might carry other meanings that the commonplaces of zoning (industry, habitat, leisure, etc.) or circulation. To consider the town or city a symbolic pattern, as the ancients did, seems utterly alien and pointless. Nowadays if we think of anything as 'symbolic' it is practically always an object or action which can be taken at a single view.

The conceptual poverty of our city discourse is exposed even when we look at the recent past. In the nineteenth century the criteria for establishing its terminology were perhaps still more directly 'positive' than they are now. The distinction between town or city would be made, for instance, in terms of the paving of streets.

Going further back, however, the tone of the discourse changes, as might have been expected. Charles Daviler, a French seventeenth-century theorist, defines a town in his dictionary of architectural terms as 'an ordering of blocks and quarters disposed with symmetry and decorum, of streets and public squares opening in straight lines with a fine and healthy orientation and adequate slopes for the draining of water. . . .'[1] But his description stands at the end of a tradition. 'The city', proposes a recent writer, 'is first of all a physical reality: a more or less sizeable group of buildings, of habitations and public buildings. . . . The city begins only when paths are transformed into roads. . . .'[2] He follows his nineteenth-century predecessors. This definition is a long way from Nicias's rousing words to the Athenian soldiers on the beach at Syracuse: 'You are yourselves the town, wherever you choose to settle . . . it is men that make the city, not the walls and ships without them. . . .'[3]

Traffic in cities has today become so thick and clotted that it is hardly surprising to find this concentration on the road pattern among our contemporaries. Traffic engineering is regarded as having superseded town planning; the street pattern, the railway or underground, are superimposed on each other, and together become that aspect of the city which has the greatest notional and conceptual validity. As traffic congestion and the attendant problems mount, so traffic surgery assumes an increasing importance in the public mind. Nor is this the only aspect of city planning which has turned into a craft of keeping one step only behind current development. Economists have for nearly two hundred years encouraged us to think that the rate of growth of urban population is to be equated with the growth of the gross national product (which they seem to consider good in itself, however it affects the individual). In spite, therefore, of the complaints about crises in traffic or about the shortage of city space, complaints which planners utter ritually whenever these problems are under discussion, when a town fails to expand at an even rate (as has been the case of the Rhine Randstadt), the same planners confess themselves dismayed by such a symptom of economic crisis.

It is commonly assumed, not only by planners, but by public authorities and even by the general public, that future expansion will go on at the present rate, forecasting the future by simple statistical inference. The possibility of new developments is elided from the argument by silence. The conceptual framework within which planners work has been designed to evade the issue of imposing any order of an extra-economic nature on the city. Fear of restriction often appears in the form of a fear of cramping an autonomous growth. That is why town planners, when talking about the way towns live and grow, invoke images drawn from nature when they consider town plans: a tree, a leaf, a piece of skin tissue, a hand and so on, with excursions into pathology when pointing to crises. But the town is not really like a natural phenomenon. It is an artefact—an artefact of a curious kind, compounded of willed and random elements, imperfectly controlled. If it is related to physiology at all, it is more like a dream than anything else.

Although the last half century has accustomed us to regard dreams as objects susceptible of serious, even scientific, study, yet the suggestion of fantasy which the word implies is regarded as offensive in the context of urban planning. This is partly because it is a matter where capital investment is huge, and partly because the well-being of masses, a well-being equated with physical amenity, is at stake.

Here again we are up against the poverty of much urbanistic discourse. The way in which space is occupied is much studied, but exclusively in physical terms of occupation and amenity. The psychological space, the cultural, the juridical, the religious, are not treated as aspects of the ecological space with whose economy the urbanist is concerned. His attention is focused on the more immediate physical problems, the resolution of which seems most urgent. But the solutions proposed, because of their physical presence, impinge on the symbolic world of the citizens; and often the arbitrary forms thrown up by harassed planners and architects are evolved on an irrational residue, motivated by unstated spiritual as well as aesthetic prejudice whose very irrationality contributes further to the instability of the community, and may set up a pattern of interaction between the community and its outward shell which will be disastrous for both.

Such procedures have been criticized by a number of sociologists.[4]

It seems to me that they are right: that some consideration must be given to the model, to the conceptual prototype of the town which its inhabitants construct mentally, and which is often exemplified in their homes. So often the home is felt to be a miniature of the city: not as it is, but as we want it. Patterns of behaviour, even of movement may sometimes be explained as being attempts to reconcile such a conceptual model with the actual, with the physical structure of the city, of which the inhabitants may be aware only in the form of diagrams— as of underground trains or bus routes.

The conceptual model I spoke of is rarely derived from such diagrams. More commonly it is related to views we hold about the space and the time we inhabit. And it is intended to anchor our views to a specific place: a particular home, a particular town.

The very statement of the problem suggests that there is no immediate solution to hand. I therefore propose to examine a closed (because past) situation, which is apparently familiar, and yet full of implications for anyone thinking about the way in which we take possession of our homes. The rectilineal patterns of the Roman towns, which survive in the street patterns and even the country lanes of old imperial lands, from Scotland to Sudan, are often thought to be the by-product of a utilitarian surveying technique. This is not how the Romans themselves saw it: the city was organized according to divine laws. The home was governed by the father of the family as the city was by the magistrates; and the paterfamilias performed in his home the complex rituals of the state religion which the colleges of priests performed for the state. The analogy between city and home, and city and land, was familiar to the Romans as it probably was to the Etruscans before them.

Before the Roman cities assumed the gridiron pattern familiar to us now, the idea of a regular city plan had to be formed in their minds. The rectilineal city was not something at which they arrived by hit-or-miss experimentation, and explained afterwards. On the contrary, it seems to me that such a device would have to have arisen from just such a model as I have mentioned. Its origins are therefore primarily interesting to me because they show the elaborate geometrical and topological structure of the Roman town growing out of and growing round a system of custom and belief which made it a perfect vehicle for a culture and for a way of life.

Over the millennium of Roman imperial rise and decline, the city underwent many changes, interpretations became increasingly elaborate and even conflicting, the rites whose meaning was sometimes forgotten were re-interpreted anachronistically. I will not be concerned with Roman and Etruscan history, except incidentally, as they bear on the development of the model and its transformation in time, which is much slower, much more gradual (as is always the case of ritualized art, ritualized procedure) than the changes in political and sometimes also religious ideas. I have chosen to deal primarily with Roman towns because theirs was an assertively urban civilization, entirely different from the one which we inhabit, and yet very amply, very accessibly documented. But I do not think the Romans' customs and ideas can be understood without comparing them with those of other peoples, usually weaker and sometimes of the most primitive savagery—or so they would have seemed to the Romans. The Romans were not alone among ancient peoples in practising a form of rectilineal planning and orientation. All the great civilizations practise it, all have mythical accounts of its origins, and rituals which guide the planner and the builder. I propose also to consider such parallel accounts to arrive at some estimate of the enormous value which the Romans, and such ancient peoples as have left us records of their beliefs, placed not only on these forms, but also on the procedures by which the forms were drawn. However, always it is the conceptual model and its relation to the place and the plan shape which interest me, rather than the material remains with which the archaeologist must concern himself: definite patterns, definite, assertive configurations of streets and squares, private and public buildings, which will not yield their meaning to the common means of urban analysis.

2. Romulus and Remus.
*Denarius* of L. Papius Celsus
*By courtesy of the*
*Warburg Institute*

## One  Town and Rite: Rome and Romulus

The remains of Roman towns are still visible, are still part of everyday experience in Western Europe and round the Mediterranean: and the more closely they are examined, the more puzzling they appear. In examining them I shall often appeal to associations established by assonance and rhythm, rhyme, alliteration, allusion or simply physical resemblance—all the apparatus of dream analysis, in fact. We have grown so accustomed to one word per meaning, one meaning per word, in any context, that the reader may hesitate to place any reliance on such seemingly vague connections. But in antiquity the idea that everything means itself and something else as well, was general and ingrained: it was taken for granted. In the specific instance of the town plan, its laying-out according to a model was hedged about with elaborate ceremonial, the words and actions of which constituted the conceptual model. The foundation was commemorated in regularly recurring festivals, and permanently enshrined in monuments whose physical presence anchored the ritual to the soil and to the physical shape of the roads and buildings.

*Romulus and Remus*  The most familiar story connected with such a foundation is the account of the death of Remus in Plutarch's 'Life of Romulus'. 'As Romulus was casting up a ditch,' Plutarch says, 'where he designed the foundation of the city wall, [Remus] turned some pieces of work into ridicule, and obstructed others; at last, as he was in contempt leaping over it, some say Romulus himself struck him, others one of his companions. He fell however. . . .'[1]

3. Naked man holding a crooked staff. Possibly **an augur.** Small bronze statuette found under the Lapis Niger in the Roman Forum
*Antiquario Forense Rome*

4. Bronze statuette of man holding a crooked staff, with his head covered. Possibly **an augur.** Etruscan, *c.* 600 A.D.
*After D. Strong 'The Early Etruscans', Evans Bros. London 1968*

There is nothing unusual about the combination of murderer, fratricide and town founder. In scripture, too, the first founder of a town is the archetypal fratricide, Cain.[2] But from the outset there are glaring absurdities in the story: the tiny moat and wall, the gratuitous killing, the hesitant explanation, make one suspect that this is an allusion to a forgotten ritual. The allusion seems reflected in two obscurer legends: firstly Oeneus, the Calydonian wine-god, killed his son Toxeus for jumping over the ditch he had dug round his vineyard,[3] and secondly the hero Poimander aimed a stone at the cynical architect Polycrithos who jumped over the new walls of his fortress. He missed, however, and hit the architect's son Leucippus, killing him instead.[4] Plutarch himself knew that his account of this incident in his 'Life of Romulus' was inadequate. In another book, *Roman Questions*, he says of Romulus and Remus: 'It seemeth that this was the cause why Romulus killed his owne brother Remus for that he presumed to leape over an holy and inviolate place. . . .' Remus then was killed for sacrilege.

This explains the killing, but does not account for the tiny wall, small enough to jump over, nor for its sacred character. In fact, Plutarch is here considering 'for what reason they (the Romans) considered the walls of the city to be sacred and inviolable, but not their gates . . .' and he wonders: 'Is it (as Varro said) because we ought to think the walls so holy that we will die generously in their defence . . . on the other hand it was not possible to consecrate and bless the gates, through which many necessities were transported, and in particular the bodies of the dead . . .'[5] which does not entirely satisfy him. But the *Roman Questions* are not intended to be conclusive, and Plutarch says little more on the subject, but describes the foundation rite to which the incident draws attention: 'and therefore, they who begin to found a citie, environ and compasse first with a plough all that purprise and precinct wherein they mean to build . . .' He refers to this rite in even greater detail in the 'Life of Romulus'. 'The founder', he says, referring to Romulus, 'fitted a brazen ploughshare to the plough, and, yoking together a bull and a cow, drove himself a deep line or furrow round the bounds; while the business of all those that followed after was to see that whatever was thrown up should be turned all inwards towards the city, and not to let any clod lie outside. With this line they described the wall and called it by a contraction *pomoerium*—that is, *postmurum*, after or besides the wall; and where they designed to make a gate, there they took out the share, carried the plough over, and left a space; for which reason they consider the whole wall as holy, except where the gates are . . .' And in *Roman Questions* he ends his more abrupt description with an almost self-evident rider: '. . . because they considered all ploughed land sacred and inviolate . . .' Many other Greek and Latin authors allude to or give some account of this rite, which the Romans were said to have imported from Etruria. It was performed at the foundation or re-foundation of any town which aspired to the title of 'urbs'.[7] The ancients thought it a thing of capital importance for the whole religious and social life of the community; it is difficult for us now to accept their assessment of it. Any account of the ceremony must inevitably begin by setting such ritual formulae against the body of Roman religious literature. The Romans inherited most of their 'scriptures' from the Etruscans. They were apparently written down at an early stage of Latin literacy in archaic Latin. They consisted of tablets, presumably of bone or bronze, and were in the care of the pontifical college. These writings took the form of ritual recipes and formulae, forms of contract with divine powers (many Roman prayers were of this kind), and some hymns. Several instances of a pontiff dictating the form of prayer to the officiating magistrate from a written text are recorded by historians, such as Decius Mus's *devotio* before his suicidal charge at the battle of Veseris.[8] The 'Gubbio tablets' may well be a fragment of the analogous 'ritual books' of the Iguvine people.

*The Ritual Books* The Roman ritual books are usually divided into two portions: the *libri Tagetici*, called after Tages, a dwarf who jumped from under the plough of the augur or *lucumon* Tarchon[9] in the morning, dictated his laws and disappeared in the evening,[10] and the *libri Vegoienses* called after the shadowy nymph Vegoia or Begoia.[11] The Tagetic books deal mostly with the reading of omens in general and the appeasing of the gods (*libri Fatales*), with the dead and the underworld (*libri Acheruntici*), and with the interpretation of sacrificial entrails (*libri Haruspicini*).[12]

The *libri Vegoienses* contained instructions about the interpretation of lightning (*libri Fulgurales*),[13] and the collection of ritual rulings with which I shall be most concerned, the *libri Rituales*.[14] The ancient lexicographer Festus says something about their contents: 'Rituales nominantur Etruscorum libri in quibus praescriptum est quo ritu condantur urbes arae aedes sacrentur, qua sanctitate muri, quo iure

portae quomodo tribus, curiae centuriae distribuantur, exercitus con-
stituant[ur] ordinentur, ceteraque eiusmodi ad bellum ac pacem
pertinentia. . . .' 'Those books of the Etruscans called *rituales* in which
are set out the rules for the rites by which towns are founded, temples
and shrines consecrated, and walls are hallowed, what the laws of the
gates are, how tribes, curiae and centuries are to be distributed, the
army constituted, and how other things pertaining to war and peace
are to be arranged . . .'[15] When compared with Plutarch's or Livy's
account of the doings of Romulus, this summary will appear to be a
fair abstract of his law-giving. So it is hardly surprising that the first
thing mentioned by Festus is the rite by which cities are founded. What
happens before this rite is before recorded history began, and belongs
to hearsay, to legend. Commenting on a similar matter in another context, the great historian Fustel de Coulanges wrote: 'Ancient history
was sacred and local history. It began with the foundation of the city,
because everything prior to that was of no interest—that is why the
ancients have forgotten the origins of their race. Every city has its own
calendar, religion, history.'[16]

The foundation rites of a city provide a key to its history. *Ab urbe
condita* the Romans reckoned theirs.[17] If the annalists' circumstantial
account of the foundation is compared with the vague and cursory
references to the early days of Romulus and Remus and the even vaguer
accounts of their antecedents, it will become evident that for them the
rites of foundation really were the key to the town's history. Moreover,
many of the puzzling features of ancient towns can be explained if they
are related to these rites. Such a confrontation may even provide a
guide to the form of the ancient city, because the performing of the
rites actually fixed the physical shape of the city.

Plutarch's remarks in his *Roman Questions*, and in the 'Life of Romulus'
are only brief allusions to the rite of foundation. And although he has
more to say about it elsewhere, the founding of a Roman or Etruscan
town was much more impressive and ceremonious than he might lead
one to believe. Unfortunately, it is rather difficult to get a clear picture
of what happened on such an occasion. The *libri Rituales* are lost; any
report must be composed from twenty or so fragmentary descriptions.[18]
My account is intended to give some idea of what the ancients thought
and felt about their towns, and how these ideas related to their general
conception of the world, the dead and the immortals.

*The New Community*   New communities were begun in various ways. It seemed to be a
general custom in Italy, for instance, that victors should impose the
surrender of one-third of the vanquished territory, and there found
colonies.[19] The Romans vested power first in the king, probably; later
proceedings would be initiated by a consul or a tribune of the people,
or possibly even by the senate corporately; ultimately it became a
prerogative of the emperor. But there was a custom, to which the wide
diffusion of the Oscan–Umbrian peoples has been attributed,[20] which
is particularly interesting in this connection: the *ver sacrum*.[21] As its
name implies, it was a springtime consecration, and the ritual was, it

seems, originally Italic. All the produce of a given town and its territory during a nominated spring was consecrated to a god in some great national emergency. After a time had passed, the animals and corn were sacrificed and the children born during the specified time expelled from the home town. Livy has recorded the details of the rite when describing the last time it was performed in Rome.[22] On this last occasion no human beings were included in the sacrifice. But ancient writers record the normal presence of human victims.[23] And a number of peoples recorded their origin in a *ver sacrum*, particularly the southern Oscan-Umbrian peoples: the Hirpini,[24] the Samni,[25] the Picentes,[26] the Marsi,[27] the Mamertini[28] and the Sacri.[29] In most of these names the reference to Mars and to the animals sacred to him, the wolf and the woodpecker, are reiterated. March was also the month in which the sacrifice was normally performed, and it still bears the name of the god to which it was particularly sacred among the various people in Italy.

The Greeks had no exactly corresponding custom. The Chalcidians, at one point, vowed every tenth man to Apollo 'for the fertility of the fields', and sent them off to Delphi where the oracle commanded them to found a new town in Bruttium, the modern Calabria; this is the myth of the origin of Reggio.[30] Although Strabo speaks of this as a unique case in Greece, Dionysius of Halicarnassus describes it as most popular among Greeks and barbarians; moreover the sacrifice of a tithe was otherwise closely associated with Apollo.[31]

*Planning Techniques: Rational and Irrational*

Modern writers will always see irrelevant flummery behind what seem to them pedestrian motives: avoidance of overpopulation or economic expansion. They are right of course, nor do I wish to oppose economic to ritual considerations. But the economic and hygienic factors were always seen by the ancients in mythical and ritual terms. Cicero, for instance, lists the various sensible geographic, economic and hygienic reasons which led Romulus to found his new town where he did,[32] but he prefaces this account with the legend about the choice of the site, of which I shall speak later.[33]

The relationship between such common-sense factors as those listed by Cicero and the ritual performance is often dispatched summarily by modern writers. They see the religious duties as a perfunctory introduction to the real business in hand. This could never have been the attitude of the ancients. It is remarkable how thorough and rational, if their premises are accepted imaginatively, their treatment of myth and ritual appear, even in a matter as elaborate in point of ritual as the foundation of a town. On the other hand, their treatment of technological points is very often hesitant and elusive. The order sometimes appears to be topsy-turvy. While myth and ritual are discussed rationally and in detail, all that we would explore systematically nowadays seems to be muddled and insecure. The assumption which lies at the base of this confusion is the relatively modern one of continuity between scientific explanation and technological development.[34] This, however, was never achieved in antiquity: while scientific thought moved in the precise realm of mathematically formulated explanation, technology remained in the baser realm of approximation. In a way, technology was more closely connected with the formulation of ritual, with its interference in the natural order, than with scientific thinking. In any case, even when the two ways of thinking overlapped, their relationship was always articulate. How this was done is demonstrated in an instructive story told by Plutarch in his 'Life of Pericles': my example, therefore, though referring to the classical period in Greece, was written under the Flavian Emperors, even if by a hellenistic intellectual. 'There is a story,' he says, 'that once Pericles had brought to him from a country farm of his a ram's head with one horn, and that Lampon the diviner, on seeing the horn grow strong and solid out of the middle of the forehead, gave it as his judgement that, there being at that time two potent factions . . . in the city, the one of Thucydides and the other of Pericles, the government would come to that one of them in whose ground or estate this token or indication of fate had shown itself, but that Anaxagoras, cleaving the skull in sunder, showed to the bystanders that the brain had not filled its natural place, but, being oblong like an egg, had collected, from all parts of the vessel which contained it, in a point to that place from whence the root of the horn took its rise. And that at that time Anaxagoras was much admired for his explanation by those that were present, and Lampon no less a little while after, when Thucydides was overpowered and the whole affairs of the state and government came into the hands of Pericles.

'And yet, in my opinion, it is no absurdity to say that they were both in the right, both natural philosopher and diviner, one justly detecting the *cause* of this event, by which it was *produced*, the other the *end* for which it was *designed*. For it was the business of the one to find out and give an account of what it was made, and in what manner and by what means it grew as it did, and of the other to foretell to what end and purpose it was so made, and what it might mean or portend. Those who say that to find the cause of a prodigy is in effect to destroy its supposed signification as such, do not take notice that at the same time, together with divine prodigies, they also do away with signs and signals of human art and concert, as for instance the clashing of quoits, fire beacons, and the shadows of sundials, every one of which has its cause, and by that cause and contrivance is a sign of something else. . . .'[35]

Plutarch is taking a defensive position on two fronts: natural science is not blasphemous, while divination is not irrational. The defence would have been unthinkable before the rise of the Eleatic school, or even in the time of Pericles, outside intellectual circles with some scientific interest. The belief in divination is one of the most hardy of the primitive beliefs of humanity, and, although it has been frowned upon for the best part of two millennia by the 'major religions', still continues to be practised by a large proportion of humanity in one form or another.

In a sense, statistical forecasting is a schematized form of divination. Being schematic, it leads to a degree of overconfidence which sometimes proves fatal to the calculators. In antiquity the approach to most matters which we treat with systematic assurance was often extremely insecure. Often it could only be by guesswork or by inherited 'knack'; the erratic forces of nature, above all, could only be understood in terms of personality or be dealt with by some form of address or be conciliated in the form of drama.

*The Choice of Site*     Modern writers always consider the choice of a site for a town in terms of economy, hygiene, traffic problems and facilities. Whenever the founder of an ancient town thought in those terms he could only do so after having translated them into mythical terms. Even when faced with the matter directly, as Archias and Myscellus were, the choice is of one virtue as against the other. The Pythia at Delphi offered the two potential oecists a choice between health and wealth. Archias chose wealth (the obvious choice for a Corinthian) and was sent off to Syracuse, while Myscellus became the founder of Croton, the town where Pythagoras settled and which nurtured a famous school of medicine.[36]

Even if the traditional Delphic pronouncement which Strabo quotes on the authority of Antiochus is a forgery,[37] it is clear that even at a late date the advantages of a particular site were revealed to the colonists as a direct and arbitrary gift of the gods, and not as a calculated gain obtained by the oecist for his colony. Myscellus, according to another tradition, made two further visits to the Delphic oracle, firstly because he could not locate the site which the oracle had 'given' him, and secondly because it looked to him, on reaching it, that the site of Sybaris was altogether preferable. He returned to Delphi, but the oracle snubbed him: 'Myscellus short-in-the-back, hunting for other things besides the gods' command, you are finding lamentations. Praise the gift the gods give.'[38]

In the story of Archias and Myscellus, the oecist chooses outright for the colonists. The oecist was either the leader of a dissident faction in the metropolis, or, if the metropolis was sending out a colony by legislation, was an appointed magistrate. After his death he was usually paid the honours of a hero, including a state banquet at which he was ritually present. The oecist was himself sometimes overshadowed by an eponymous hero or some other founding father drawn from myth: Hercules, or one of the Trojan War heroes whether Trojan or Greek, the *Nostoi*,[39] the Argonauts, or even Cretan figures. The eponymous hero or founder was also worshipped in the metropolis. Indeed, when Cleisthenes reformed the Athenian constitution, he appealed to the Pythia to select ten eponymous heroes from a list of a hundred names which he submitted to the oracle.[40] There was an altar to these heroes in the Athenian *agora*, and statues of them by Phidias, so Pausanias said, were also consecrated at Delphi.[41] Also in the *agora* was an altar to the 'Archegetes', either the eponyms of the twelve tribes into which the Athenians were organized before the Cleisthenian reform, or of the twelve towns which took part in the Thesean *synoikia*. Theseus's tomb and altar were near by.[42] Theseus's body had previously been hidden on Skyros where he died and Cimon had brought the relics to Athens as an ancient oracle required.[43] But there is some doubt about the twelve

5. The sow with thirty piglets.
Antonine marble statue
Vatican Museum, Rome

towns which Theseus united, for the *synoikia* was a destruction, if only nominal, of the separate towns, and was conceived by the Greeks in this way,[44] so that the separate forms did in fact lose their identity. The *apoikia*, the lore of colony and town foundation, would have been much more familiar to us had Aristotle's book on colonies survived, or perhaps the book on city founding by the shadowy Trisimachus.[45] As it is, we can only guess at the exact part which the oracle played in foundations, at the procedure and ceremonial which was followed at the foundation, if indeed there was a 'normal' form of procedure, such as the *ritus Etruscus*, or at the nature of the founder's heroic status from allusions dispersed in literary and epigraphic remains.

*The Founder and the City*    On the founder's relationship to his city we have, for instance, the categoric assertion of an old scholiast on Pindar: '. . . according to custom the founder was buried in the centre of the city. . . .'[46] This was by way of comment on Pindar's description of the monument to Pelops at Olympia: 'Near the ford of Alpheus, by the altar many strangers venerate, stands his much-frequented tomb.'[47] Though Pausanias[48] and the archaeologists[49] have described and located this monument, the practice of burying the hero-founder was not quite as general as the scholiast seems to imply. Like the Romans, the Greeks disapproved of burial within the city walls, even if the Greek prohibitions were never as categoric as those of the Twelve Tables.[50] And yet for heroes the prohibition did not obtain. Indeed, the Delphic oracle on one occasion ordered the building of a bouleterion over the burials of some unspecified heroes.[51] The number of heroes worshipped or buried in the *agorai* of various Greek cities is quite considerable.[52] They were not always city founders, they may have been athletes, particularly winners in one of the national games, or great poets, or just very good looking.[53] But city founding, and the fathering of tribes, as well as the invention of skills and trades are among the 'typical' characteristics of heroes.[54] Heroes are most often thought of as warriors, but this is only an aspect of the heroic life; they have the strongest connection with all matters concerning death, the hunt, games, divination, healing and mystery cults. City founders, therefore, entering on the status of hero, tended to have such matters associated with them. And there is a corollary to be noted: cities which were not known to have been founded by a 'historical' hero may well have devised one from fragments of myth. But historical persons who founded towns were, during their lifetime, given semi-heroic status and honoured as heroes after their death.

It is not a case of arguing causally. The city had to be founded by a hero; only a hero could found a city. In the same way the Pindaric scholiast's assertion implies a polarity: the hero-founder had to be buried at the heart of the city; only the tomb of the hero-founder could guarantee that the city lived. Indeed, the assembly of the primitive *agora*, in the sense in which the word signifies the men and not the place, was often in early literature attracted to a pre-existing tomb.[55] The Greek *agora* continued to have connections with funerary cults as long as the *polis* remained a religious as well as a political force. The founder's commemoration, which I mentioned earlier,[56] is the most striking instance of this side of civic religious life. At Amphipolis the oecist Brasidas was buried in full armour 'at a place facing what is now the *agora*'.[57] Thucydides goes on to describe the monument and the feasts: 'And they enclosed his monument and have ever since made offerings to him as a hero, offering him worship, and instituting games and yearly sacrifices.' Brasidas, the victor of the battle of Amphipolis in 422 B.C., was adopted as patron and *ktistes* of the city as a declaration of defiance by a colony founded by the Athenian Hagnon,[58] whose shrine had been destroyed. Here the ritual act is used to assert political independence. A monument recently discovered at Paestum seems to provide another variant on this feature of the Greek city. Bordering both *agora* and the great *temenos*, a little fenced shrine (18 × 15.6 m), a small independent *temenos*, was discovered just after the Second World War. Off-centre in it was a small building, completely sealed. A short *dromos* led to an entrance which had been blocked up. A double-pitched roof of stone slabs was covered with tiles. Within was a stone bench, supporting six iron rods to which was attached a metal and leather criss-cross of a kind reminiscent of bed-webbing; on top of that there appears to have been laid a linen sheet. By the walls stood eight bronze amphorae of great beauty, and two bronze hydriae, all of which contained honeycombs, still well-preserved, and an Attic black-figured amphora, representing on one side the apotheosis of Hercules and on the other Hermes and Dionysus watching a satyr dance. The vase had had its foot broken and it had been repaired with lead plugs, clearly before the sealing of the shrine. It may therefore be taken to have been considered an object of great value and particular relevance to its placing. It bears an unmistakable reference to hero-cults: Heracles was, after all, the archetypal hero. The honey in the bronze jars again points to the 'buried' shrine as a place connected with the worship of a dead person, a hero,[59] and again the empty bed suggests a cenotaph. The shrine has been interpreted by one scholar at least as the cenotaph of Is, the *ktistes* of Sybaris, the mother-city of Poseidonia; a cenotaph erected when the original tomb was destroyed with Sybaris in 510. This theory at any rate fits with the dating of the deposited objects.[60] It is not absolutely clear whether the whole of the shrine was buried under the pavement of the *temenos*, or the pitched roof protruded above the pavement level. A similar *temenos* existed in the fifth century at Kyrene. It stood on the east side of the *agora*, was enclosed by a low wall, and contained an open stone tomb, covered by pitched slabs. It replaced an earlier tumulus, which had stood a little to the west, and which its excavator dates to the first quarter of the sixth century. The shrine persisted until the Severan period, when it appears to have been buried under a stoa. Its excavators identify it as the tomb of the oecist-king, Battos I, described by Pindar and his scholiasts.[61] At Kyrene there was also a roofless tholos on the west side of the *agora*, which had earlier been identified as the tomb of Battos. At the time of writing, this building has not been re-examined: it appears to have contained a bothros and to have had some connection with an oracular cult.[62]

I mention this particular tholos because Battos of Kyrene is a founder whose doings seem specially interesting. Not so much his various transformations or his peculiar relationship to the Delphic oracle, nor yet the composition of his settlers or of the indigenous population of Libya and the various pre-founders of his city,[63] but the story Pindar tells of Battos's Argonaut ancestor Euphemus and the prophecy of Medea:

> The Omen that shall make
> Thera mother of mighty cities
> Was given where Lake Tritonis flows to the sea,
> To Euphemus once
> a guest, gift from the god in a man's likeness
> A clod: Euphemus, alighting from the bows
> Took it, and father Zeus, son of Kronos
> Well-pleased rang out in thunder . . .
> Eurypylus, son of the undying
> Shaker and Holder of earth
> . . . knew of our hurry: there and then
> Took a clod in his right hand, eager to offer
> What gift he could
> And the hero did not refuse it
> He leaped to the beach, and clasping hand in hand
> Took the piece of wonderful earth—
> But a wave broke
> I hear, and washed it
> Overboard into the sea . . . .
> Into this isle has been thrown
> The undying seed of Libya's wide meadows
> Out of due time.
> For had he come home, and cast it
> Into hell's mouth in the earth

> Had he come to Holy Tainaron—he
> Euphemus . . . .
> With a Danean host, had taken that wide mainland . . . .
> But now he shall lie with foreign women
> And get a chosen race, who shall come to this island . . . .[64]

So Medea goes on to prophesy the consultation of the oracle by Battos of Thera and the foundation of Kyrene. What interests me principally about this epic fragment is Pindar's account of the divine gift, (the hero Eurypylus was really Triton in disguise), and Euphemus' neglected duty to throw it by the mouth of hell at Taenarum, his home.[65]

Pindar's version of the myth is expectedly clipped and allusive: it is repeated more expansively, though less circumstantially, by Apollonius Rhodius,[66] who draws, in all probability, on the same Hesiodic source.[67] The aetiology of this myth may well, as is often the case, go back to ritual. Pindar's telling of it suggests that the story is in any case a familiar matter. If such were the case, it would of course have been recorded not only in action, but in the decoration of the public buildings of the city. The indication of the right hand, in which the clod is taken, and the clasp between the two heroes, and the duty, understood by Euphemus, though neglected by him, to cast the clod into the mouth of hell in his home town, show that the postponement of the foundation followed a breach of ritual practice. The blessing the clod contained is not wholly turned away from Euphemus, however, even though, being miraculously conveyed to Thera, it is associated with another city.

In the Etruscan rite, according to Plutarch,[68] earth from the home town was thrown into a specially prepared ditch, called *mundus*, the world, a homonym for another institution which was the mouth of hell.[69] The mythical event described by Pindar is in a sense a symmetrical transposition of the Plutarchian rite. The clod of earth, given by an aborigine to a visiting hero-founder (even if hero-founder *manqué*), is to be taken to his home town and there thrown into the mouth of hell to mark his possession of the territory to be colonized.

It is difficult to see what weight may be attached to this hypothesis. Whether, for instance, one should suppose that the rite was peculiar to the Theran colonies, or to Kyrene itself, or if it is part of the rites generally connected with any foundation. For lack of corroborative evidence the matter must rest there.

Kyrene, however, provides evidence of another rite, in epigraphic form. This is the so-called 'Stele of the Founders', a somewhat mutilated monument probably carved in the first half of the fourth century.[70] After an invocation of the god (Apollo) and Tyche, and recording the prosperity promised by Apollo to Battos and the Theran founders of Kyrene provided they kept the oaths sworn when the colonizers left Thera on the orders of Apollo Archegetes,[71] the stele records resolutions about the social organization of Thera and Kyrene and the right of Therans who go there, and continues:

> This decree shall be carved on a stele of white marble to be placed

in the ancestral shrine of Pythian Apollo. On this stele shall also be carved the words of the oath which the founders swore when they took to sea to go to Libya with Battos, leaving Thera for Kyrene. The moneys necessary for the marble and the carving shall be levied from those in charge of the accounts of Apollo's revenues.

The Founder's Oath.

Resolved by the Assembly: since Apollo spontaneously prophesied to Battos and the Therans to colonize Kyrene, they resolve to send Battos to Libya as archegetes and king . . . that one son be conscripted from each family; that those who sail be in the prime of life. Of other Therans, every free man who wants to do so may embark. If the colonists succeed in establishing themselves, each one of their compatriots who will go to Libya later will enjoy full civil and political rights, and he shall be assigned by lot a piece of ground which has no owner. If the colonists do not succeed in establishing themselves, and if, the Therans being unable to help them, they are oppressed by necessity for five years, they shall be free to return to their homeland, Thera, without fear, and they shall recover their possessions and their civil rights. Who shall refuse to embark when he has been nominated a colonist by the city shall be liable to the death penalty and the confiscation of all his goods. Whoever has sheltered him, or has helped him to escape, even had it been a father that helped a son or a brother a brother, he shall be punished in the same way.

Both those who stayed and those who were going away to found the colony swore the oath according to the decree, and they proclaimed curses on those who would break the oath and not remain faithful, both among those who were to dwell in Libya and those who were to stay. They made images in wax and burnt them, and pronounced curses in unison; men, women, boys and girls: 'Who shall not remain faithful to these oaths, but will break them, let him melt and liquify as these images, he and his children and his goods. As for those who shall remain faithful to these oaths, both those who depart for Libya and those who stay in Thera, let them experience, they and their children, every prosperity.'

Although this text of the foundation oath of a colony is unique so far, the various elements of which it is made up are familiar enough in the literature of Greek religion: imprecations pronounced in unison against anyone breaking the common oath,[72] for instance, or the use of wax dolls of the kind the oath suggests, are attested in another Kyrenean religious document,[73] as well as in funerary cults of the Greek mainland.[74]

The *Lex Cathartica*, according to its first editor, provides the earliest written ritual formula in the Greek language.[75] Altogether there is something archaic about Kyrene, this hellenic kingdom set down in Libya sometime in the seventh century and governed by kings of its founding dynasty until the second half of the fifth century B.C. No doubt it was this archaic character of the town which appealed to

Pindar. But there is little evidence, certainly at that date, of any radical contamination of Kyrenean religion by African sources;[76] the documents quoted and the myths of the city are part of the common hellenic stock.

*Recording the Foundation*    Unfortunately the other surviving inscriptions referring to foundations deal mostly with constitutional and legal matters, though they also propose punishment for and curses on transgressors. The treaty between Locri and Naupactus is the most explicit and longest of such documents,[77] and the decree concerning the Athenian colony, Brea in Thrace, has interesting implications. 'The adjutants of the oecist', the first complete sentence begins, 'shall make provision for sacrifice in order to obtain favourable omens for the colony, . . . Ten distributors of the land shall be chosen, one from each tribe. . . . Democlides shall establish the colony with full powers to the best of his ability. The sacred precincts that have been set apart shall be left as they are, but no further precinct is to be consecrated. The colony is to offer a cow and panoply to the great Panathenaea and a phallus to the Dionysia. . . . This decree is to be written on a stele and placed on the acropolis. The colonists are to provide the stele at their own cost.'[78]

Of course there was nothing unique or even unusual about these documents. Plato records the use to which such an inscription was put by the kings of Atlantis acting on 'the commands of Poseidon which the law had handed down. These were inscribed by the first kings on a pillar of copper[79] which stood in the middle of the island, at the temple of Poseidon. . . .' The kings gather and judge; but before they utter judgement, they perform a sacrifice as a pledge, in which one of the free-ranging bulls of the temple is captured with staves and a noose, without use of weapons, 'and the bull which they had caught they led up to that pillar and cut its throat on the top of it so that the blood fell upon the sacred inscription. Now on the pillar, beside the laws, was inscribed an oath invoking mighty curses upon the disobedient.' The judgement and the oath are then described in detail: the only feature I wish to cite here is that swearing the laws inscribed on the pillar by the sacrifice performed before it (a common enough practice in Greece) and giving judgement was to take place by the light of the sacrificial fire only, at night.[80]

The judgement by the light of the fire only points to another foundation custom, that of transferring fire from the city hearth of the mother country to that of the new colony. Of the Ionian league of twelve cities, or dodecapolis, Herodotus says that those Ionians considered themselves most noble who left 'from the Prytaneum of the Athenians', the place of the sacred hearth;[81] implying what the old scholiast on Pindar's Eleventh Nemean ode says explicitly, that the colonists took fire with them from the mother city to light the fire on their own sacred hearth.[82]

The picture I have been able to piece together here is very fragmentary. But, even from the fragments I have quoted, it is clear that the Greeks had established customs in the matter of the founding of towns. These customs are alluded to by poets and historians.[83] According to the 'ancient custom' Thucydides says, the Heraclid Phalias, a Corinthian, was summoned from Corinth, the mother city of Corcyra, when they decided to found Epidamnus on the mainland.[84] The elements of the ceremonial appear fragmentarily. There may have been various customs for various nations, the Asian Ionians may have had a different ritual from the mainland Greeks.[85] But even non-Greek nations are recognized by Greek historians to have behaved as the Greeks did. Herodotus records that when Cambyses wanted to attack Carthage, the Phoenicians in the mother country of the colony refused to sail on the expedition, because 'they said that they were bound to the Carthaginians by great oaths, and would commit an impiety in waging war on their own children.'[86]

What we have to gather, from scattered fragments of literary and epigraphic evidence, was clear to the inhabitant of every Greek city who, in the *agora*, could see, inscribed on marble or bronze stele, the decrees and oaths which bound his city to its colonies, or, if it was itself a colony, to the mother town, and described in detail the part which they undertook to play in each other's political and economic life, which was symbolized in the community of the religious life.

## Two

**City and Site**

The Kyrenean oath I described earlier[1] seems a reflection, an analogue of the great oaths and laws inscribed on the copper column which stood at the centre of Plato's Atlantis. It is an index of an aspect of the problem which modern commentators have, on the whole, preferred to ignore.

Plato and Aristotle are usually quoted in support of a 'commonsense' view of ancient planning. In the *Politics*, for instance, Aristotle makes quite explicit recommendations for a site: 'The land upon which a city is to be sited should be sloping, that we must just hope to find, but we should keep four considerations in mind. First and most essential, the situation must be a healthy one. A slope facing east, with winds blowing from the direction of sunrise, gives a healthy site, rather better than the lee side of north, though this gives good weather. Next it should be well situated for carrying out all its civil and military activities . . .'[2] and so on; this passage is echoed by Vitruvius, who also seems familiar with Aristotle's authority, Hippocrates;[3] though Vitruvius is more circumstantial than the former and less than the latter. 'The choice of a healthy site must come first,' he says; 'such a site will be high, neither misty nor frosty, the climate neither too hot nor too cold, but temperate. Further, there should be no marshes in the neighbourhood. . . . Again, if the town is on the coast and exposed either to the south or the west it will not be healthy. . . . In founding towns, in short, beware of districts where hot winds can blow on the inhabitants . . .'[4] and so on.

*How to Choose the Site*
*(i) The Theorists*

Although such common sense notions were current enough in Vitruvius's time, they were not often applied in practice. In the fifth century B.C., when Hippocrates formulated them, they must have seemed eccentric as well as revolutionary: they seemed to go right against the Pythia's advice to incipient colonists over the past four centuries. Agrigentum (Ἀκραγας) for instance, a town founded about 580 B.C. by colonists from Gela, faced directly south-west on to the Mediterranean and was protected by a rocky escarpment, the Athenean rock, along all its northern limit. Some time in antiquity a breach was made through the escarpment to admit the north wind. Popular tradition has it that it was carried out on the advice of Empedocles, about a century and a half after the foundation of the town, which had, however, been founded on a site which would not have satisfied the Hippocratean conditions at all. The same is true of many towns on the southern coast of Sicily, the Tyrrhenian seaboard of Italy, and so on. Rome itself was founded on the Palatine hill, it is true, but overlooking the notorious malarial marsh in the valley of the Forum. On the point of orientation even the theorists are not altogether consistent. Aristotle had himself (in another book) found a site facing only south acceptable,[5] and Xenophon,

quoting Socrates, actually recommends it.[6] While there seems, therefore, to have been general agreement about how important it was 'that
the greatest care should be taken to select a very temperate climate for
the site of the city, since healthiness is the first requisite',[7] yet there
seemed to be a great deal of disagreement among authorities as to the
right way to achieve this. Consider another matter, the relation of
street layout to the direction of the winds. Vitruvius, again following
his Greek preceptors, warns planners that 'if the streets run straight in
the direction of the winds then their constant blasts rush in and . . .
sweep the streets with great violence. The lines of houses must therefore
be directed away from the quarters from which the winds blow, so that
they may strike against the angles of the blocks and their force be broken
up and dispersed.'[8] To the planner, Vitruvius described a sixteen-rayed-
tablet arrangement for orientating the main streets at an oblique angle
to the strongest winds. Writing 300 years after Vitruvius, Oribasius, the
editor and reviewer of Galen, recommends the exact opposite:

> 'When streets are parallel in a town, some in length and some in
> breadth, the first running from east to west, the others from south to
> north, so that they pierce the town through length and breadth
> without any obstacles, and none of the winds meets any building
> which might obstruct its course . . . [the town will be] well aired
> and sunlit, healthy and clear. For all the winds, Boreas and Notus,
> Eurus and Zephyrus, which are the dominant and most regular
> winds, sweep through the streets without meeting obstacles and pass
> freely without causing any disturbance. . . . This kind of plan also
> makes the town a good suntrap because at sunrise and sunset the sun
> lights up the streets which run east-west, and at midday those that
> run north-south. . . .'[9]

Such snatches of medical opinion as we have, therefore, contradict
each other directly; clearly there is not enough material to allow any
generalized account of town-planning theory in this respect. Nor does
archaeology provide the evidence on which theory might be related to
practice. There are, in the matter of orientation, plenty of orthogonal
plans of all periods, and in all geographical locations, which seem to
conform to the Hippocratean rule: Miletus, for instance, Naples,
Pompeii, Selinus or Aosta. There are even late imperial foundations of
this kind, such as Trier, Avranches, Turin, Zara (Zadar), Carnutum.
On the other hand, there seems to be an equal number of orthogonal
plans which might accord with Oribasius's formula, some very ancient:
Marzabotto, Capua, Laodicea, Priene, Paestum; and, again imperial
ones: Cologne, Silchester, parts of Constantinople, Lucca.

It is impossible to conclude, on the basis of what is known at present,
whether any systematic relationship was established by the Greeks (or
the Romans) between town-orientation and the principal winds, and
similar factors. There is no record of any device for doing this. It may
well be that if all the material available were adequately tabulated,
some indication of a system, or several conflicting systems, would
emerge. But on the information available I must conclude that the

advice of theorists about the choice of site is a pious gloss without any very radical undertones.

Of course an ideal site would have to be fine and healthy, as Vitruvius says. But the choice, when explicable in rational terms, was often made for quite different reasons than hygiene; for commercial and military reasons, for instance. The injunctions of the theorists do not seem to have been followed. In the legend of Archias and Myscellus we actually have the account of an oecist preferring wealth to health; the theories read more like *post-facto* rationalizations than direct precept.

Modern writers on town planning who look for the progressive development of a sensible planning method in antiquity, tend to emphasize out of proportion the very little evidence which is available— which is mostly in the form of incidental remarks. They tend to neglect, however, the obscure magical and religious rituals which, with most of our contemporaries, they find unattractive and unedifying as well as irrelevant. Roland Martin, for instance, in the first chapter of his fine book on Greek towns,[10] quotes this passage about the ideal city from the *Laws* of Plato: 'Some places are subject to strange and fatal influences by reason of diverse winds and violent heat; some by reason of waters; or again from the character of that subsistence which the earth supplies them, which not only affects the bodies of men for good or evil, but produces similar results in them.'[11] There Martin cuts short his quotation, but Plato, who is considering the moral and psychological influence of physical environment, goes on to say: 'In all such qualities those places excel in which there is a divine inspiration, and in which the gods have their appointed lots, and are propitious to the dwellers in them.'[12] It is the good will of the divine powers which is transmitted in the favourable physical conditions. Its assurance might have been more easily obtained, if the recent readings of Platonic urbanism are taken correctly, by establishing harmony between the city and the structure of the created universe rather than by any other means.[13] Even in historical times, the founder of a town would therefore prefer to trust himself blindly to the unpredictable, if approachable, divine powers and follow their dark hints. We have no notice of a founder who sought a site by working out the theoretical advantages of various choices as they are set out by theorists. Herodotus reports an exceptional case. The Spartan Dorieus[14] thought that he could found a town on a site he fancied without worrying about divine sanction or performing the usual rites, though apparently even he had consulted some private diviner. Two years after its foundation his town was wrecked by an alliance of Libyans and Carthaginians, although it had been 'the best site in all Africa'. For his second attempt, although again fortified by private revelation, Dorieus preferred to consult the oracle. The prophecy was 'fulfilled' again in a failure, the death of Dorieus and the dispersal of his second colony, founded this time in western Sicily.[15]

The second failure is not really disconcerting: the myth also recalled, in any case, the premature fulfilment of the prophecy in an incidental victory Dorieus won on his way, so that his ultimate failure was attributable to his not having obeyed the oracle to the letter. Had the second foundation, however, been an unqualified success, there would not have been a more or less relevant conclusion to draw. But I am not here concerned with how successful the Pythia had been in forecasting the exact future of a colony. On the contrary, what interests me is why the sanction of the oracle was required by a founder, how it related to his own status with his fellow citizens, and how this fitted into the general pattern of town foundation. What the city founder thought he was doing and its mythical 'rightness', or what his followers saw him do is more interesting in this context than his historical success or failure. It is the *idea* of the town which concerns me here: ostensible motives are as valid—or more valid—for this consideration as any arguments that would nowadays be thought convincing by a new town finance committee.

## (ii) The Rites Observed

'The choice of the site', says Fustel de Coulanges, 'a serious matter on which the whole fate of the people depended . . . was always left to the decision of the gods.'[16] The historical part which the Delphic oracle played in the foundation of the colonies has been set out in detail by the two authorities I have already cited frequently.[17] Nor does it seem as if the innumerable myths about the intervention of divinity in town foundations, through the agency of a sacrificial animal, for instance, can be reduced to simple aetiological mystification. This intervention was clearly an integral part of the foundation proceedings, and was always incorporated into the notional apparatus of the inhabitants about their home. The animal may have been a common sacrificial animal such as a goat,[18] a cow,[19] a bird, such as a falcon[20] or a crow,[21] or yet again a creature appertaining to the earth, such as a snake,[22] or a swarm of bees;[23] or even an aquatic beast, such as a dolphin,[24] might play this role. In later times even more complex methods of divination were employed, as when animals were sacrificed and pieces of the sacrificial meat were exposed for birds of prey; the site was fixed where the first bird dropped its find.[25] Pius Aeneas himself followed a pregnant sow to a place where it farrowed, and founded Alba Longa on that spot—which would have been quite unacceptable on health grounds.[26]

## Romulus Again

In founding Rome, Romulus also followed this practice. 'Had Romulus been a Greek,' says Fustel de Coulanges, 'he would have consulted the Delphic oracle; had he been a Samnite, he might have followed some sacred animal like the wolf or the woodpecker. Being a Latin, a neighbour of the Etruscans and an initiate in the science of augury, he asked the gods to reveal their will through the flight of birds. . . .'[27]

On the other hand, two of the authors who tell the story add a further detail, with Italiot overtones: they say that Romulus and Remus agreed to found the city near the place where they had been picked up by the she-wolf. The exact spot where this occurred was said to have been the site of the Lupercal shrine.[28] Here the two brothers separated, and each went on a hilltop to watch for the auspicious birds. This was the *inauguratio*.[29] The inauguratio was a complex rite. It consisted of a prayer,[30] a naming of signs, and a description of the augur's field of view. The augur watched for the signs and when they appeared, he determined their exact significance. The specific terms for the culminating acts were *conregio*, *conspicio* and *cortumio*.[31] This is how the augur carried out his duties. For the *conregio* the augur drew a diagram on the ground with his curved wand, his *lituus*.[32] Livy gives an account of this part of the rite in his description of the inauguration of Numa as king of Rome: 'The augur, with his head veiled, took a seat on his (Numa's) left, holding in his hand a crooked and knotless staff called *lituus*. . . . He prayed to the gods (*deos precatus*) and fixed the regions from east to west, saying that the southern parts were to the right, and the northern to the left.'[33] This fixing of the regions, and the naming of landmarks, such as trees, which bounded them, while he pointed to them with his staff, constituted the *conregio*. The *conspicio* seems to have been parallel to the *conregio*. The direction of the augur's eyes followed his gesture, and by taking in the whole view, town, and country beyond, he contemplated it, and united the four different *templa* into one great *templum* by sight and gesture. As Livy puts it: 'He fixed the guiding mark in his mind[34] as far as his eyes could see before him.'[35] Marks he determined, though in some cases they were probably traditional, after he had drawn his diagram. And then he spoke the covenant, the *legem dixit*,[36] that is, he announced the matter about which he was to decide and what incidents were to be taken as portents. Livy continues: 'Having passed his staff (from right hand to the left) the augur put his right hand on Numa's head and prayed: 'Father Jupiter, if it is right (*fas*) that this Numa Pompilius, whose head I touch, should be king of Rome, then let your signs be clear and unmistakable between the boundaries I have made.' He then announced what kind of signs he wished to obtain.[37] These were sent, Numa duly proclaimed king and all went down from the high place where the auspices were taken.

*Templum*     The contest between Romulus and Remus was decided by the appearance of flying vultures. Romulus won because he saw more of them,[38] though tradition is not unanimous on this point. In any case, when the portentous animals appeared, the augur had to assess the event by the rules of his science: this was *cortumio*,[39] and with it, the whole ceremony of *contemplatio* was finished.[40] *Contemplatio* was so called after the diagram the augur drew, his *templum*; a solemn word, Norden says, and a contentious one for scholars. So let me turn first to an ancient author who has already proved very helpful—Varro. In discussing words denoting place, he begins with *templum*, and quotes a line of Ennius about Romulus: 'There will be one whom you shall raise to the bright temples of the sky.' He goes on to say: '*Templum* is used in three ways: with reference to nature, to divination, and to resemblance, with reference to nature, in the sky; to divination, on the ground; and to resemblance underground.'[41] He derives the word from *tueri*, to look, gaze, stare, observe. But modern etymologists tend to think of *templum* in connection with the Greek word τέμενος (temenos), a sacred enclosure, in turn derived from τέμνω (temno), I cut, hew, wound. The evidence has been taken to suggest that the word even implies a fixed hut, of sawn, cut wooden planks for the taking of augury.[42] But this would take me away from the argument, and in any case there clearly is an analogy here. *Temenos* is a piece of land defined by boundaries and devoted to a particular purpose, a shrine. And Varro tells us, when he comes to discuss the terrestrial *templum*, that it was a 'place set out according to certain definite forms of words for the taking of auspices or for augury.'[43] But as Varro implies later in the same passage, the word had wider and more general applications. A *templum* could be any space set apart for definite functions of state and religion. So for instance a *senatusconsultum* was not valid unless it had been passed inside a *templum*, and between sunrise and sunset.[44] As the general's tent in a Roman camp was called *auguraculum*, after the augur's tent, which he set up on the *templum* sometimes, so the camp itself could be regarded as a *templum*. It was certainly, as was any properly consecrated town and even certain rural tracts, *liberatum et effatum*: freed of evil influence and consecrated.[45] The normal *templum*, as Varro says, 'ought to have a continuous fence and not more than one entrance'.[46] Now the town, the *urbs*, had three entrances ritually, but it was certainly an *ager effatus*, a 'place that had been consecrated',[47] and shared many characteristics with the *templum*. Without wishing to give the matter too much weight, it is worth emphasizing the importance of this 'cutting off'. 'This insistence', says Kurt Latte, 'on a purifying enclosure of lands is in any case characteristic of Roman religious thought.'[48] But the town shared other characteristics with the *templum*, besides that of being ritually enclosed. The most important of these was the *conrectio*, the division into four parts, like those of the diagram the augur drew, and the bringing of the four divisions together again by formula and gesture. In a place which had an unobstructed view of the neighbourhood[49] the augur drew a shape divided into four parts, forward and backward, left and right, divided by lines drawn from east to west, from north to south.[50] I have deliberately kept the description rather clumsy, instead of saying that the circle was divided into four by lines running north–south, east–west, because in the context of divination, the words left and right, forward and backward are technical terms. Which leads to another problem: what shape exactly was it the augur drew and divided? It certainly had an outline, all the directions agree on that. Varro provides the essential clue by implication: he considered the heavenly *templum* first.[50a] This was circular and quartered. Many ancient peoples, including the Romans of course, believed that the earth was circular, and that the sky formed a vault or dome over it;[51] so much has been written about the matter that I need say no more about it here.

The association of the heavenly *templum* and its dividing lines raises yet another unresolved problem: that of the association between the dividing lines of the templum and the main orientations. This has never been adequately examined. Varro firmly sets the augur at the 'north' point of his diagram, facing 'south'[51a]. Frontinus, when applying the same terminology to surveying, and claiming to use the system of the *haruspices*, turns Varro's scheme at 90°, so that the surveyor, and the *haruspex*, faced west. While they agree on the terminology for the lines of augury and surveying (*cardo* and *decumanus*) they therefore applied the terms for the quarters (left and right, hither and beyond) quite differently.[51b] Unfortunately, the system sets even more complex problems, as is shown by Livy's circumstantial account of the inauguration of King Numa. Explicitly following Romulus' example at the city founding, Numa ordered that the bird-omens be consulted about him: 'An augur, whose service on this occasion was afterwards recognized by the grant of a permanent state priesthood, escorted Numa to the citadel (i.e. on the Capitol, presumably where the *auguraculum* was later situated) where he took his seat on a stone with his face to the south. And so Livy goes on to describe the ceremony which I analyzed earlier.[51b(i)] I refer to it again here, as a 'type' of augural procedure, which—in spite of the analysis—remains as hermetic, as the science of the augurs, which was secret.[51c] But something has come to light about the nature of the auguraculum: those of certain Roman cities have been examined: like Roman towns, so these auguracula did not have a fixed orientation.[51d] Indeed it seems as if the dividing lines of the Augurs' *templum* were, like those of the surveyors' guide-lines later, rather haphazardly related to the cardinal points. And yet it would seem that—certainly by imperial times—the terms left–right, forward–backward had passed into ordinary speech, as synonymous with the cardinal points.[51e]

How the augur drew the diagram, what position he occupied in relation to it, is not made absolutely explicit by the texts. Sometimes he drew it by gesturing with his staff in the air: Servius explicitly says that it was forbidden to Augurs to do this with the hand alone, but had to be done with the *lituus*;[52] at other times he certainly seems to have drawn it on the ground.[53] It may well be that both operations were essential. Its relation to the cardinal points was essential—notionally at least—to the surveyors at any rate, if not to the augurs. The frontispiece of one of the oldest surveying treatises makes this quite clear. It is a starry circle representing the sky which is quartered as the augur quartered his diagrammatic circle.[54] The size of the diagram did not have any relation to its power, since its working was analogical. It worked *ex parvo in magnum*, the divisions and limits of the sky being transferred from the little diagram which he had drawn onto the landscape the augur saw in his *conspicio*. I take it that the various formulae, such as that of Varro and that of the Iguvine tables, are a record, almost a prompt copy, of what the augur *said* and cannot be used as evidence about what sort of diagram the augur *drew*, as some scholars have wanted to use them. The landmarks which the various formulae named are sometimes wide apart. To maintain that each time the augural operation was repeated (and it was daily) it involved the augur in drawing lines several hundred yards long with his stave does not make sense. The purpose of drawing the diagram was to set the general order of the sky in a particular place, with the augur at the heart of it. This was accomplished when the great temple of the sky was first condensed into the ideal form of the augur's diagram, and then projected on to the tract of land before him by the ritual formula. That is why we are never

told what shape the earthly *templum* was to take; though Varro does describe it as 'a place set aside for augury or the taking of auspices, limited by an incantation, which was not the same for every place', and in this context records the particular one used in the Capitoline *auguraculum*.[55] Elsewhere he reports[56] that every *templum* should have an enclosure broken only at one point. When the *templum* was fixed in this permanent way with a fence or wall, it was called a *templum minus*,[57] and this last term came to be applied in an exclusive way (without the *minus* qualification) to what we now call temples. But the augural *templum* could be set down anywhere, and did not necessarily need physical enclosure. It might, in certain places, have had visible and permanent physical bounds, but its real boundaries were not fixed by them. The *templum* was bounded by the words of incantation, by *verba concepta* which drew a magical net round the landmarks the augur named. It is this naming, and not any drawing on the ground with a staff, which actually fixed the boundaries of the *templum*. These ceremonies and ordinances were not used for special purposes only, but were the common Roman way of dealing with matters of location. The military camp for instance was related to the augural *templum*. It also had permanent boundaries, and was carefully orientated, so Polybius explained,[58] from a white flagpole which stood in the centre of the *praetorium*, the camp's staff headquarters. Near the flagpole was the *auguraculum*, the general's tent, from its door the general read the omens, and to the left stood the tribune from which he addressed his soldiers after he had ascertained the will of the gods.

Pliny records a primitive method of orientation.[59] Writing about orientation (not for divining, but for the rural common-sense kind of forecasting) he recommends that you should cast your own shadow at the sixth hour (i.e. at midday) facing south, then turn to face north, so as to see the shadow: 'through the centre of it make a furrow with a hoe,

7. **Bronze cross**, inscribed 'Antiqua/Postiqua'. Found attached to a stone block at the Temple of Aesculapius at Lambesis in North Africa
*After Paul Monceaux, 'Note sur une Croix de Bronze trouvée à Lambèse' in 'Comptes-Rendus de l'Académie des Inscriptions et Belles-Lettres', Paris, 1920, pp. 179 ff.*

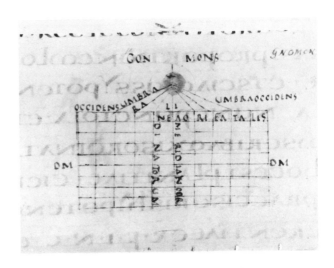

8. **The surveyor's gnomon (marked 'con mons') in relation to a centuriated area.** This confusing diagram shows the surveyor's instrument set in a circle where it has been cut by seven shadows. It illustrates a passage in Hyg. Grom., and the lines of the shadows are misleadingly joined to the regular divisions of the land. The word on the far right should read *oriens* for *occidens*. The meridian line is the line joining the centre of the circle and the bisected chord, and the other *cardines* are parallel to it, while the *decumani* (only the principal one is marked here 'DM') are simply cut at right angles. The *umbra* are impressions and are not intended to coincide with the diagrammatic *cardines*. *Codex Arcerianus 53 r.*

or strew a line twenty foot long, say, with ash. Half-way along it, that is at the tenth foot, draw a little circle, which is called the navel (*umbilicus*). The direction of the apex of the shadow will be that of the north wind. . . . Through the middle of it draw another (line) which will run from the direction of the equinoctial sunrise to that of equinoctial sunset. A boundary cutting the field in this direction is called *decumanus* . . . two further oblique lines must be drawn through this intersection (*decussis*) . . . all running through this same navel, all equal, and with equal distances between them.' Pliny finds it necessary to apologize for this method as being fit only for technical simpletons, and suggests that more expert people might have this diagram, essential for determining wind directions, registered permanently on some kind of tablet.

Vitruvius describes the construction of such a 'wind-rose' in great detail.[60] Vitruvius's rose is more detailed than Pliny's, having sixteen divisions instead of eight. These sixteen compartments of the winds relate, of course, to the sixteen divisions of the sky in Etruscan divination;[61] further analogies (such as that to the sixteen names of Osiris) would involve me in too elaborate a speculation.[62]

*The Surveyors*

Pliny's method of orientation was country wisdom. Even Vitruvius describes a much more accurate way, which was used by surveyors and planners;[63] and his near-contemporary, the surveyor Hyginus (Gromaticus), condemns Pliny's primitive method as misleading, and recommends the standard surveyor's way as the only one ensuring accuracy, which it does.[64]

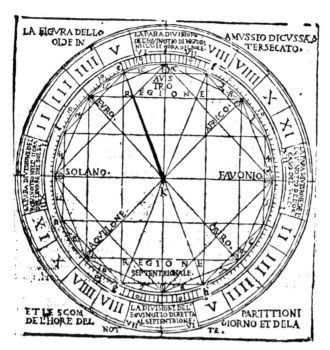

10. Fragment of a Roman 'rose of the winds' of late Imperial date. The names of the winds are given in Greek and Latin; the numbers of the inner ring refer to the regions of the sky in the Etruscan discipline
*After 'Philologus', Vol. LXXXVI, section a, Leipzig, 1931, p. 200*
*University Museum, Prague*

9. *La figura dello amussio dicussato oice (cioe?) intersecato et le scompartitioni del'hore del giorno et de la notte.* The face of the sundial divided up, that is intersected, and the divisions of the hours of day and night. *L'amussio collocato a la libella* (the dial set by level). Illustrations of the 'rose of the winds' according to Vitruvius
*Engravings from Giambattista Caporali's 1536 edition (Perugia)*

This is how Roman surveyors worked: a *sciotherum*, an upright bronze rod, was set in the centre of a circle, probably on a marble tablet. The shadow of the rod was then observed, and the two points at which its tip touched the circumference of the circle before and after midday were marked and joined; the chord was bisected, and the line joining the centre point of the chord to the rod was the *cardo*, while the chord itself was the *decumanus*.[65] Having established the main axes, or else accepted the orientation of some notable feature of the place, such as a main road like the Via Emilia, running through the site, the surveyor operated with an instrument called *groma* or *gnomon* (the *sciotherum* was also called *gnomon*, and this has led to some confusion). This was a composite instrument: a sheet-metal cross (*stella*) with plumb-lines on each arm of the cross was set horizontally and eccentrically on a wooden frame (*ferramentum*) so that the cross could be sited directly over a tablet with a cross drawn on it (*decussis*), one of the main lines of which was made to coincide with the line (*cardo* or *decumanus*) previously selected by the surveyor. The lines were then established by inspection.[66] The *stella* on its *gnomon* was to the surveyor what the *templum* was for the augur: an 'essence' of his method. In fact a *stella* of bronze appears to have been fixed to the thresholds of *templa minora*,[67] and it may even be that the augural *lituus* also had a small *stella* fixed to it.[68]

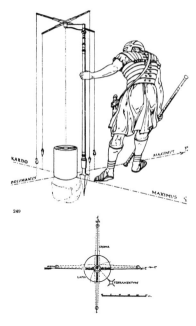

249

11. **The Roman agrimensor at work.**
Reconstruction drawing by P. Frigerio
*After Frigerio, 'Antichi Istrumenti Technici',*
*Como, 1933*

12. The Roman surveyor's instruments. **The**
**stele of the agrimensor Lucius Aebutius**
**Faustus,** Ivrea, North Italy. The relief shows a
dismantled *groma* and Aebutius's symbols of
authority
*From H. Schone in 'Jahrbuch des kais.*
*deutsch. archäol. Inst. 16', 1901; O. A. W.*
*Dilke, 'The Roman Land Surveyors', David and*
*Charles, Newton Abbot, 1971*

*Haruspication*  The auspices were taken. Either that day and on that site, or, if the gods were not agreeable, on another, better site and more favourable day, a sacrifice was offered.[69] The entrails, particularly the liver and perhaps the intestines, of the animal sacrificed were then opened and inspected for further omens. This was done by a special kind of diviner, the *haruspex*, or liver-diviner. Like the reading of auspices, haruspication was traditionally an Etruscan skill, and remained so well into the Christian era. Inspecting sacrificial entrails for omens was a universal practice.[70] The specific method of divining by the liver seems to have originated in Sumer, and spread to the Hittites and beyond.[71] In the context of primitive religion, this form of divining appears obvious. The liver is a large and delicate organ which at any time contains a sixth of the stuff of life, the body's blood.[72] So the liver was thought of as the seat of life, and it followed that in any animal consecrated to the gods, and whose every smallest movement was anxiously observed, the liver, as the focus of its being, would in a particular way become a mirror of the world at the moment of sacrifice.[73] It is worth noting that sheep in Mesopotamia (they were the most common sacrificial animal there)

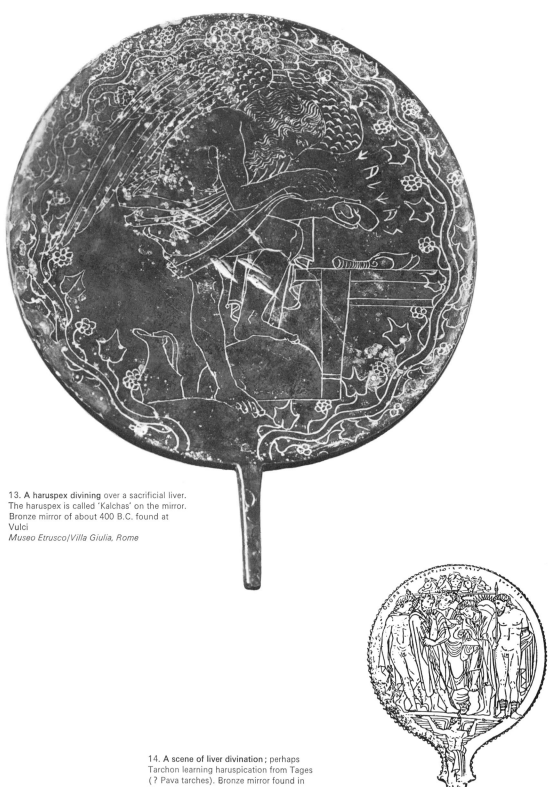

13. **A haruspex divining** over a sacrificial liver.
The haruspex is called 'Kalchas' on the mirror.
Bronze mirror of about 400 B.C. found at
Vulci
*Museo Etrusco/Villa Giulia, Rome*

14. **A scene of liver divination**; perhaps
Tarchon learning haruspication from Tages
(? Pava tarches). Bronze mirror found in
Tuscania
*Museo Archeologico, Florence*

15. Reclining figure holding **a divinatory liver,** or a model of such a liver: the resemblance to the miniature Piacenza liver is evident. Presumably the portrait is of a haruspex. (Lid of an alabaster cinerary urn, with some fragments of colour adhering. Known as 'La Tomba dell' aruspice'. Early third century B.C.) *Museo Guarnacci, Volterra*

were prone to a disease which resulted in strong marking of the liver, and the suggestion has been advanced that a system of 'correspondences' was developed between the markings and external events. At some stage the lore was codified, giving the practice all the semblance of a 'trade' with schools and licensed diviners, case histories and disputes about interpretation. There was nothing 'inspirational' about it at all.

Although several documents relating to it have survived,[74] we know very little of the actual rules and procedure of Mesopotamian liver divination, and even less of the Etruscan system. The most important of the Etruscan documents to survive is the bronze model of a liver, now in the museum at Piacenza. Most scholars have thought that this model was used for instruction in a divining school, some others that it was only an amulet. Whatever purpose the object served, round the edge of its more 'populated' surface are sixteen compartments containing names which correspond fairly closely to the names of the sixteen Etruscan gods of the divinatory sky recorded by Martianus Capella.[75] The augur's divisions of the sky correspond to the haruspex's divisions of the liver, both referring to an 'idea', a 'model' of the world, so that it is not surprising to find a haruspex doubling duties as thunder diviner.[76]

Besides the liver, another internal organ was important in augury: the intestines. In augury the intestines were called 'palace of the intestines' or just 'great palace' (the Akkadian *ekkalu,* like the Hebrew היכל (*heichal*) means both 'palace' and 'temple').[77] 'Palace of the

16. **The examination of entrails and the council of diviners.** Probably auspices taken before Trajan's war against the Dacians. Partly restored bas-relief from Trajan's Forum, late first century A.D. *Louvre, Paris*

intestines' was also the name of the underworld in Mesopotamia, of the region of the demon Humbaba, the intestine-man. Together, the intestines and the liver seem to represent the universe in Mesopotamian divination. What is more, the terms of Mesopotamian divination, 'mountain', 'river', 'station', 'passage', 'fort', 'main gate', and so on, add up to something like the description of a landscape. There seems to have been some sort of direct link between details of a landscape, such as the surroundings of a besieged town, and parts of the sacrificial victim's entrails.[78] In Italy entrail divination in general, though practised, was much less important than it had been in Mesopotamia. The great Etruscan skill concentrated on liver divination.

The founder of the town had already consulted the flight of birds, the movement of stray animals, thunder perhaps, the motion of the clouds, to find out if the site and day were propitious. Why then was divination by the liver so important? It remained an essential part of many ceremonies when auguration had fallen into desuetude. Vitruvius is most insistent that the examination of livers should not be neglected: 'Our ancestors,' he says, 'when they built a town or a military post, sacrificed some of the cattle that fed on the site and examined their livers; if the livers of the first victims were dark or abnormal, they sacrificed others to see whether the peculiarities were due to disease or to their food. They never began building walls in a given place, until they had made several such examinations.'[79]

Even without corroborating evidence, Vitruvius's 'rationalist' statement would have been sufficient to establish the practice of haruspication at the foundations of towns, though his reasons for it may not have appealed to earlier founders or their diviners. The divinatory procedure was lengthy and tedious. Unfavourable omens could be cancelled by a

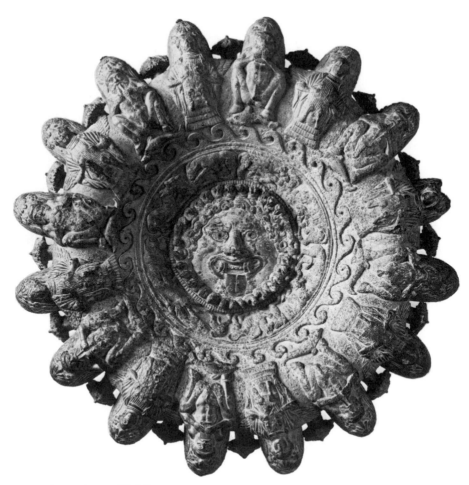

17. The underside of **a bronze hanging lamp**, *c.* 450 B.C., perhaps from Vulci. There are sixteen lights, each a human figure (eight male, all playing pipes, and eight female). At the centre is a gorgon-head, surrounded by waves and animals. *Museo Accademia Etrusca, Cortona*

18. Face of **the entrail-demon Humbaba**. Pottery. Babylonian, 700–500 B.C. *British Museum, London*

19. Terracotta model of divining liver showing markings in their 'houses'. Babylonian
*British Museum, London*

21. The upper face of the Piacenza liver transcribed

20. Etruscan model of liver, inscribed with diviner's divisions or 'houses', which are filled with the names of Etruscan deities. The use of this small object is unknown. It was made in the third century B.C., when the locality in which it was found was already in Roman, not Etruscan, occupation
*Piacenza, Museo Civico*

more favourable configuration of entrails or markings of the liver. Sometimes the entrails were 'dumb' and the sacrifice had to be repeated because of that alone. In any case they could occupy several days. And their results were not taken simply as being the gods' yes or no answer to a specific question, but could give precise indication of action. The presence of these sacrifices in the ritual of town-founding is not in itself significant, since they were one of the most certain ways of assuring the participants of an action that the gods sanctioned what they were doing. But the topographical nature of the divinatory language seems to indicate that the nature of the inquiry regarded the site before them. I do not think that I am stretching the evidence when I suggest that this form of divination may have been practised to determine some of the features of the layout on the site: the terminology of haruspication might have suggested the line of the wall, and the actual layout of some of the principal public buildings of the town.

We have no guide to tell us how the ancients laid out the public buildings and temples in relation to the plan of the town. In the case of a Roman military camp, we know at least that a more or less level site was always selected. But even here, where a strict specification was

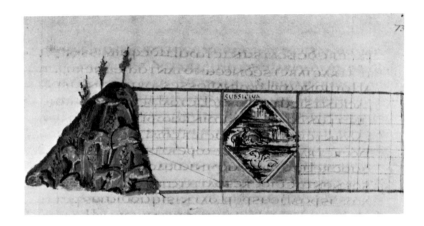

22. Ager **Subsicivus** resulting from irregularities of the water line *Codex Arcerianus, 70r.*

given for the layout, this was more a topological indication than an actual layout, even in the form in which it survives in late imperial writings. In a town there were, as a rule, many irregularities of the ground and changes of level to be taken into account, and such irregularities were very difficult for Roman surveyors to chart.[80] Even the largest-scale maps which survive from antiquity, like the *Forma Urbis Romae*, do not register changes of level.[81] It seems possible, therefore, that when an irregular site had to be laid out this was not done in accordance with a previously established drawing, but carried out on the actual ground, and may have been related in some systematic way to the reading of the victim's entrails.

There is no direct evidence to support my suggestion. But in other circumstances divination was directly applied to the lie of the land. The Roman augur Actius Navius, for instance, first showed his skill when looking for an extra large cluster of vines in his vineyard to sacrifice to Jupiter. He stood facing south and divided his vineyard into four parts: by observing birds he rejected three of the quarters, and located his offering in the fourth.[82] This is the only clear instance of the augural *templum* being used for divination referring to exact siting. In the various accounts of Constantine's foundation of Constantinople, there are stories of his divinely inspired enlargement of the city boundary which had been fixed previously.[83] It is not unnatural, therefore, to assume that divination was applied topographically. But there is little hope of ever discovering in what measure the details of an urban foundation were worked out in consultation with diviners.

*Mundus*  The time had now come to prepare the auspicated site for new occupants. According to one writer,[84] the first step was to light brushwood fires at various points of the site for all the future citizens of the new town to leap over so as to clear themselves of all faults and impurities. It may be that this account merely reflected the custom of leaping over brushwood fires on the feast of Pales, the birthday of Rome.[85] Next a hole, a round hole according to some,[86] was dug in virgin soil (or the solid rock) and into it were cast first fruit,[87] or unspecified and enigmatic 'good things',[88] and/or earth from the settlers' home country.[89] This hole was called *mundus*; like *templum* it is a contentious word. In the context of ritual it seems to have signified a hole in the ground leading to a (vaulted?) chamber,[90] or two such chambers[91] one above the other,[92] and was consecrated to infernal gods. It crops up in different guises in Roman religious practice. One appears to have been dug at the foundation of Rome. But even about this the ancient authors disagree. Some say that Romulus's *mundus* was on the Palatine,[93] others on the Comitium in the Forum.[94] We know that in some way *mundus* was a shrine of the *manes*, the propitiated souls of the dead. It was opened three times a year, and the days on which it was opened were dangerous and all sorts of public business, including the joining of battle, were forbidden.[95] On those days the spirits of the dead came among the living. There was also a *mundus* devoted to Ceres, goddess of the crops, which even had a special priesthood.[96] The cult of the dead, the infernal powers and the deities of vegetation are closely connected of course, and I take it that in general the *mundus* was, among other things, the mouth of the underworld. That is why attempts to locate the *mundus* of Rome and to discount the evidence of one group of ancient writers must fail. 'The soil of Rome', as one scholar has remarked, 'was riddled with hell-mouths.'[97]

Though we may never know where Romulus actually dug his hole, it is worth noting that it seems to have been connected in some way with the *decussis* of the *cardo et decumanus maximi*.[98] Whether it was dug at the actual crossing of the lines, or to the north or west of them cannot be determined. After whatever was to be deposited was put in, it was covered by a stone, and an altar was set upon or beside it, and a fire lit on the altar, perhaps by rubbing firesticks;[99] this fire was the 'focus' of the town. At this point the city may also have received its name. The only ancient writer who describes the naming ceremony as part of the foundation is the Byzantine historian John Lydus, who says: 'Taking the priestly trumpet (which the Romans call *lituus*[100] in their language, after the word λίτη (*lite*, prayer), he (Romulus) pronounced the name of the town. . . . A town had three names: one secret, one priestly and one public. The secret is Amor. . . ; the priestly Flor or Florens (and that is also why this day was commemorated by the feast of Floralia); the public is Roma.'[101] Although Lydus is often suspect, there can be little doubt of the fact that Rome had a secret name, for Pliny records the execution of a magistrate who had revealed it.[102] Although many scholars and grammarians have speculated about it, and in spite of the fatal indiscretion of Valerius Soranus, the name remains secret: Lydus's information is isolated. The assumption has, however, been made recently that it was the name of an androgynous deity.[103] So far Lydus appears to have been correct, and this deity, who may have appeared openly in the religious life of the town in other guises, also acted as fortune and as genius of the town which it protected.

*Orthogonal Planning and the Surveyors*

At this stage in the ceremonies, the town may be said to have been born. The gods had demonstrated their benevolence towards the community, the site had been purified and marked out, and the augur had taken supernatural stock of it. The community had taken possession of the ground by the mixing of the earth from the site with that from the settlers' homes. Perhaps it was at this point that the surveyors took over the site and marked out the streets, and the building plots. It may be, however, that they were working while other parts of the ritual were going on, or they may have started only when the last part of the ritual had finished. Their intrusion here raises the whole vexed issue of the origins of orthogonal planning, which would have been impossible without recourse to some form of surveying technique.[104] Although it is not at all evident whether surveyors operated within or outside the foundation ritual, yet their discipline, (as Roman writers on surveying claimed,[105]) had its origin in the divine mysteries, as did the Etruscan rite. In any case, when Roman surveyors appeared on the fresh site with their elaborate and mysterious-looking rig of marble and bronze, they must have looked as solemn and impressive as the augurs. Their method of operation, even if it were performed without any ritual, prayers, sacrifices, etc. (which is very unlikely), must have had something of the character of a mystery. Even nowadays surveyors at their business look as if they were performing a ceremony. And of course, like modern surveyors, the ancient ones also had to start from some form of datum. This, apparently, was the *decussis* of the *cardo maximus* and of the *decumanus maximus*: the *umbilicus*[106] of the place. There the surveyors' principal instrument, the *groma*, was auspiciously set.[107] The surveyors' terminology alone would have been enough to connect their operations with the Etruscan rite.

They also appealed to another authority worth mentioning: Mago the Phoenician. Mago was a common Phoenician name; but this particular Mago seems to be the same one as the author of a treatise on agriculture, whom Varro and Columella mention as their most important predecessor.[107a] In the Corpus Agrimensorum, however, he appears as a shadowy figure, sharing an opinion on the sanctity of boundaries with Begoia. He seems to re-appear, in that curious document, the Phoenician History of Philo of Byblos, as the co-founder of settlements and of agriculture.[107b] These rather scarce fragments do not really help to determine the Roman debt to Carthage in the matter of surveying. But they suggest that some such debt existed. Perhaps when some clearer idea is gained of Phoenician—and Carthaginian— planning and surveying, this debt might be established, and the place of the Etruscans in this connection re-examined.

When the surveyors had finished their work, the land which they had measured out was distributed by the drawing of lots.[107c] The exact procedure is uncertain, but it is clear that the surveyor 'handed over' the land to the settler by leading him to it. The ownership of the land lots was recorded by the surveyors on bronze maps, one of which was kept by the community, and another deposited in the Tabularium in Rome. While this procedure seems to have been standard in imperial times, it had solid republican precedent, and must have gone back to a pre-Gracchan antiquity at least.

The maps of the surveyors, the bronze *formae* which were the

23. A fragment of the Severan Forma Urbis
Romae, the great marble plan of Rome displayed
in the portico of the Temple of Peace. It shows the
portico of Octavia, with the Temples of Jupiter
Stator and Juno Moneta. Adjoining the Portico
is the Temple of Hercules and the Muses

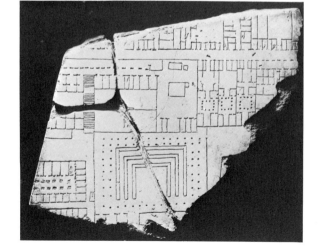

24. A fragment showing a public building of
unknown character, and houses on what seems a
steep slope. A wide stairway is indicated. The small
triangular shapes in some of the rooms probably
indicate staircases
*Palazzo Conservatori, Rome*

ultimate authority in all disputes about land, show that the *agrimensores* were concerned with the laws of land tenure as with surveying proper. It has therefore been suggested that the references to the Etruscan rite in the writings of the *agrimensores* are a later imposition of rather fancy cosmic notions on a pedestrian, though useful, bit of technology.[108] This would be entirely contrary to all we know about Roman thinking. I would suggest that the rather modest allusion to the cosmic implications of surveying in the *agrimensores* are a 'rationalized' and weakened survival of the Romano-Etruscan belief in the sacredness of land titles and boundaries. This is very heavily underlined for us by the terrible penalties primitive Roman law imposed on boundary-breakers[109] as well as the cult of the god Terminus with its repeated blood-sacrifices.[110] Perhaps a further point is worth noting. No other civilization, (and most civilizations have very strict regulations about the inviolability of boundaries), had practised, as the Romans did during the late republic and the empire, the imposition of a constant, uniform pattern on the towns, on the countryside, and also on their military establishments, with almost obsessional persistence.

There is about this complex of the laws of property and the techniques of surveying, with its rather indistinct religious echoes, something rigid and inexorable, something unimaginative: as if it were atrophied after a long development. It does not suggest to me a cosmic 'graft' on a pre-existing technique, but on the contrary a move away

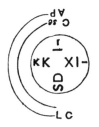

25. The inscriptions on the top surfaces of Gracchan Cippi:

1. (left) Atina in Lucania (now in the Museo Nazionale, Naples)
2. St. Angelo in Formis (now in the Museo Nazionale, Naples)
3 and 4. Rocca San Felice (whereabouts unknown)
*After 'C.I.L.', 639, 640, 643, 644, vol. I pt. 2*

26. The Templum of the earth.
*Codex Arcerianus, p. 41 v.*

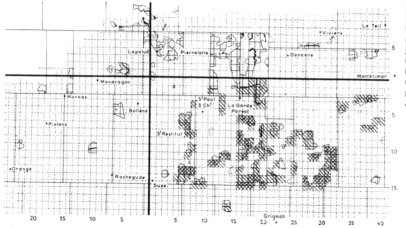

27. **The countryside between Montélimar and Orange**, centuriated according to the marble map. The dotted lines (continuous joints in the marble plaques) indicate centuries. The thick lines indicate the Cardo and Decumanus Maximus. Only the shaded portions of the map survive
*After A. Piganiol*

28. Fragments of the marble map of the district between Pierrelatte and Donzère, through which the Cardo Maximus runs. The centuriae ran between Citra Cardinem III to Ultra Cardinem VI and between Dextra Decumani XVI to XX
*After A. Piganiol*

29. Marble fragment of the **Map of Orange**, section B, frs. nos. 193–5
*After A. Piganiol*

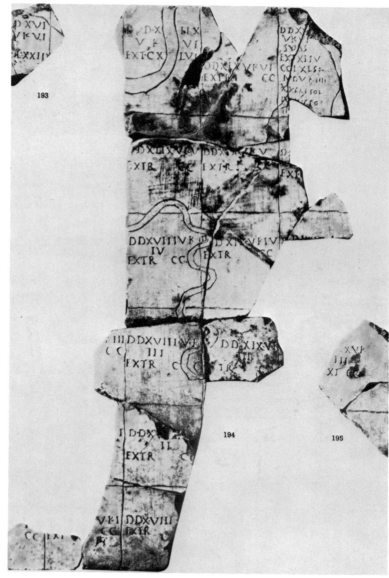

31, 32. **A ritual ploughing scene,** with ithyphallic figures and ornaments. Objects made up of Villanovan or primitive Etruscan fragments by an eighteenth century Italian antiquarian or forger
*British Museum London*

BY GOLLY SALLY I GESS
YER HIT SOMETHIN"

HARDTIMES ON THE FARM

30. **Hard Times on the Farm.** American cartoon (?)
*After 'L'Angelus de Millet' by S. Dali*

from a complex of religious, scientific and technical opinions and practices.

It was this kind of process, in other scientific disciplines, that Simone Weil noted when she wrote: 'Only such a mystical conception of geometry as that of Pythagoras could have generated the degree of attention necessary in the first days of that science. Anyone will agree that astronomy came from astrology and chemistry from alchemy. But this succession is interpreted as a progress, although it involves a lowering in the degree of attention. Astrology and alchemy, which are transcendent, are the contemplation of eternal truth through the symbols provided by the movement of the stars and the combination of substances. Astronomy and chemistry are degraded forms of these sciences. Astrology and alchemy, become magic, are even lower degradations. There is no perfect attention except religious attention.'[111]

This may be too grandiloquent a statement for my present subject of surveying. The converse, however, is put more succinctly and more acceptably by Claude Lévi-Strauss in another context. Discussing the 'uselessness' of many of the animals or plants which may be found as 'totems' in primitive societies, he points out that they were chosen 'not because they were good to eat, but because they were good to think'.[112] Astrology, alchemy, a totemic system—all these may be an explanation of the world's working, as may be the amalgam of divination and orientation which performed this most important part for the Etruscans and the Romans.

*The First Furrow*   There is here, too, a direct link to a notion which exercised the Romans powerfully: 'The striving to delimit boundaries sharply', I quote Kurt Latte again,[113] 'is in any case characteristic of Roman religious thought.' And the most important part of the whole founding ceremony, to which I now come, was the cutting of the *sulcus primigenius*, the initial furrow. This was performed by the founder with a bronze plough[114] to which (Cato reports according to Servius[115]), a white ox and cow were yoked, the ox on the outside of the boundary, the cow on the inside. If therefore the various accounts of Romulus's route may be believed, then the procession must have gone anti-clockwise, starting on the south-western corner of the site.[116] The founder then gathered with his followers at the agreed spot. Having set his plough aslant,[117] so that all the earth would fall inside the furrow, his head covered by the edge of his toga which was wound tightly round him,[118] he ploughed round the site of the city. If any earth happened to fall outside the furrow, the founder's followers would pick it up and throw it inside the city boundary. When he came to the places on the boundary where the gates were to go—there were three of these according to the Etruscan rite[119]—he took the plough out of the ground and carried it over the span of the gate. According to ancient writers it is this carrying (*portare*) which provides the root of *porta*, a gate.[120] Also, the walls which followed the line of clods cut by the founder's plough were sacred, while the gates were subject to civil jurisdiction.[121] The new town was now fully constituted. The new inhabitants had taken possession of the site and expelled such

33. The founder of the town performing the cutting of the sulcus. Obverse of a coin of Berytus (Beirut) in the reign of Claudius. This type of coin was cast by many colonies throughout the empire, not only to commemorate the foundation of the town, but apparently also at other times
*British Museum*

previous ghostly inhabitants as were unfriendly. They had given it a name and invoked a protecting deity, lit the fire on its hearth and set out the boundaries. All this was done publicly. If any of the ceremony was secret, it was the deliberately 'mysterious' element, such as the deliberations of the augur in his tent or the uttering of the town's secret name. From the first moment of drawing the *templum*, the future inhabitants took part in the rite, if only as witnesses:

> Was the city to be called Roma or Remora?
> All were agog to know which of the two
> Shall rule. They watched: as when the consul
> Raises his hand to start the race
> The crowd's eager eyes fix on the mouth of the trap
> Through whose showy door the chariot will rush,
> So the people waited and wondered in fear;
> Whose shall be the victory and the great reign.[122]

This is how Ennius records the inauguration in his annals, and how it was probably carried out in his day. The city was constituted publicly, its order was accepted and acted out by the whole people in the rites of foundation, and reiterated for them through festivals and the accounts of annalists. It could be inspected daily on those monuments of the town which recalled a legendary past, so that citizens never forgot the

34. **Coin of Berytus** (Beirut). *Obverse:* cutting of sulcus. *Reverse:* Claudius
*British Museum*

35. **Coin of Celsa** (Spain), late republican period. *Obverse:* founder cutting the sulcus. *Reverse:* coining official
*British Museum*

36. **Coin of Caesarea Augusta** (Saragossa). *Obverse:* founder cutting the sulcus. *Reverse:* Claudius
*British Museum*

37. **Coin of Caesarea Augusta** (Saragossa). *Obverse:* founder cutting the sulcus. *Reverse:* Caligula
*British Museum*

connection between the topography of their city and the rite by which its order had first been established.

*Castrum*    Much of what I have said is in conflict with the conventional account of Roman towns and their planning. The convention is that the Roman town was a more formal version of the military camp. It is quite common to read of the Roman surveyors laying out the military camp orthogonally, and measuring out the land in rectangular fields from the axes of the camp. To some extent this is due to the excellent account of Roman surveying given by Polybius in his account of Roman military organization. There is also the impression created by the word *castrum* (anglicized as 'chester'), 'a camp', which has insinuated itself into modern place-names: Chester, Cirencester, Winchester, Manchester, Silchester, and so on.

But the convention inverts the truth. The Roman town was not a formalized and enlarged camp. On the contrary, the Roman military camp was a diagrammatic evocation of the city of Rome, an *anamnesis* of *imperium*. The Romans did not treat the setting up of the camp as a makeshift for a night's sleep: it was part of the daily military routine that no army was permitted to settle down for the night without setting up camp ceremonially.[123] The first act was to plant the general's *vexillum* at a chosen spot. It was from the *vexillum* that the *praetorium* was paced out. On the border of the *praetorium* and the principal road a *groma* stood to ensure that the streets were laid out at right angles.[124] The line between the *vexillum* and the *groma* gave the surveyor the main axis of the camp; the *groma* in the camp, as on the site of a new town, was auspiciously placed.[125] It gave the direction of the *cardo maximus* of the camp, and led to the *Porta Praetoria*, the principal of the four camp gates. According to one author, this gate always faced the enemy,[126] while according to Polybius and the surveyors it was orientated according to the cardinal directions.[127] Perhaps both practices were followed. To the right of the *praetorium* was the *auguraculum*, the place where the commander sacrificed and omens were read, so the essential decisions about the future of the campaign were taken according to the will of the gods. Opposite, on the left side, stood the tribune from which the commander addressed his troops after the decisions had been made and the augurs consulted.

The whole of the *praetorium* came to be called *auguraculum* in fact. And this setting of what seems to us a trivial and irrelevant piece of nonsense at the centre of military discipline and decisions on high strategy does re-emphasize the absolutely essential character of divination in Roman life. The senator Appius Claudius Crassus, as quoted by Livy,[128] puts it in a sentence: 'It is by auspices, in peace as in war, within as abroad, that all things are governed: everyone knows this.' Consequently the struggle of the plebeians for power, and for military power in particular, focused on the right of the plebeian magistrates to divinatory skills and powers.

In all probability the rites for setting up camp were considerably younger than those for founding cities. The rules Polybius sets out are

38. **Carrying a plough.** Detail of the bronze bucket/situla found at Certosa, Bologna.
Etruscan, sixth to fifth century B.C. *Museo Civico, Bologna*

already elaborate, but cut-and-dried. They were practised well into the imperial period, allowing for changes due to growth and development of organization, changes in the structure of command and so on.[129] The origin of the camp layout is obscure. Frontinus writes that it was devised by Pyrrhus of Epirus, and that the Romans were so impressed by the camp he abandoned outside Beneventum (then still called Maleventum) in 275 B.C., that they adapted it to their use.[130] Plutarch, on the other hand, tells of Pyrrhus admiring 'the order, the appointment of the watches, their method and the general form of their encampment'[131] as he inspects the Roman camp across the river Siris (now Sinno) before the battle of Heraclea (the Pyrrhic victory) in 280 B.C. Livy repeats the same story, but about the camp of Sulpicius Galba on the Athacus, during the Macedonian campaign of 200 B.C. against Philip V.[132]

Polybius, the earliest and most explicit of the ancient writers on the subject, says nothing about the Greek origins of the Roman camp. Livy, who so often follows him, may be suggesting the very opposite in the passage which I quoted. Inevitably, archaeological material bearing on the matter is rather meagre; however, round the ruins of Numantia, the Celto-Iberian town in Castille, there were found extensive remains of the seven camps Scipio Aemilianus erected round the town for the blockade.[133] For all their irregularities, they conform to the description of Polybius, who himself witnessed the siege. It may well be, therefore, that even at the time of Pyrrhus's Tarentine campaign, there were already Roman camps to be admired, as Plutarch suggests. The close correspondence of town and camp foundation inclines me against Frontinus's account.

In any case, during the Early Iron Age in Italy, when Rome was founded, the Roman army probably had little call to set up camp: its enemies were within a day's reach. The declaration of war was made for the Roman state by a special priest charged with certain official and legal declarations, the *Pater patratus*, who proclaimed the grievances of the Roman people and declared a war by throwing a spear of dogwood hardened in the fire (or an iron-tipped lance) into the enemy territory. When the lines had moved beyond the daily reach of the Romans, a field by the temple of Bellona near the Circus Flaminius, was nominated a token territory, *campus hostilis*, for the purpose of this ceremony.[134]

*Destruction Rites*     As the town was constituted ritually, it had a more than physical existence; not only in the obvious sense to which the defeated Athenian general Nicias appealed, encouraging his soldiers before Syracuse: with the ringing phrase about the transcendence of Athens, which I quoted at the opening of this book.[135] The town had a hardy and devious quality of existence, as ancient custom recognized, in that a victorious war-leader was usually not satisfied with burning a town or otherwise razing it, he also had to unmake the town ritually, to disestablish it. Servius mentions 'the custom of the ancients [which decreed] that as a new town was founded by the use of a plough, so it should also be destroyed by the same rite by which it was founded.'[136]

Little is known of the over- or undertones of the greatest destruction of classical legend, that of Troy, as the *Odyssey* and the *Aeneid* do not deal with this particular episode, although the Trojan horse has disturbing symbolic connotations.[137] There is, too, a curious allusion in the *Culex* to Achilles dragging the body of Hector after his chariot three times round the city walls: 'and with Hector's body the victor purified (*lustravit*) Troy.'[138] Much more is recorded about the destruction of Carthage, the historical antitype of the fall of Troy. Scipio followed the general Roman custom in assuring his victory; during the siege he 'vowed' his army and the town, summoning its tutelary gods and goddesses ('If there is a god, if there is a goddess . . .'[139]) by an incantation (*carmen*) to pass over to the side of the Roman people and receive their worship. The augur had to make sure through haruspication that the summons had been heard before the final assault could take place.[140] After the town had been taken and destroyed, its site had to be ploughed, or rather 'unploughed'. Perhaps the plough was drawn clockwise over the ruins, while the founder's plough had been drawn anti-clockwise round the city site.[141] The legal implication of such a ceremony was evidently that: 'if revenue was due to a city, and the city had been ploughed over, this city had no further legal existence. So Carthage ceased to exist and its revenues were treated as those of some-one dead.'[142] The ceremony was, of course, not limited to the Roman world. Abimelech, for instance, when he captured Shechem, 'slew the people that was therein, and beat down the city, and sowed it with salt',[143] much as Scipio had cursed Carthage with sterility. Mantinea is a curious example from the Greek world: when the town was captured by the Spartans in 418 B.C., it was not destroyed, but disoicized (opposite of synoicized) into four constituent villages, as she had been 'in the old days'.[144]

Returning to the Roman world, the ceremony was familiar enough to make a commonplace poetic reference.[145] Horace went so far as to allude to it casually when disposing of a cross young woman: 'Rage', he says, 'has been the cause for which high cities were blotted out and an insolent army drew a plough over the place where the walls had stood.'[146]

There could have been few towns founded in Italy or the Roman empire in prehistoric and classical times without the performance of some rites of the kind I have described. Their order may well have changed, some ceremonies were no doubt omitted, others added or varied. As I have been very eclectic in my use of sources—from the Iguvine tables to John Lydus—my account reads as if there had been no change or development of religious ideas between these terminal documents; but, of course, many changes did take place, and the rite must have been continuously coloured by them. The underlying patterns of the rite seem, however, to be much older than any of the sources I have quoted: long before they were codified most of these ceremonies must have formed an important part of the religious life of Italy, antedating perhaps even the beginnings of urban settlement in the ninth and eighth centuries B.C. As for the origins of the rite, I am not at all sure that anything so complex and at the same time so hoary and vigorous can be traced back to two or three clearly identifiable sources. It is surely a syncretic phenomenon, made up of bits which originated in different parts of the world, which are varied, sometimes unrecognizably transmuted. The whole complex grew and fused over centuries, altering in flavour perhaps and in emphasis as the context of religious ideas changed or developed. Nevertheless, the structure of the rite: divination, limitation, relic-burial, orientation and quartering, are more primitive than the written history of any Italian people. The Romans ascribe its institution to the Etruscans. No evidence is available to date for a different ascription, though it is true that Roman writers had a rather confusing way of referring to all the ancient Italians as 'Etruscans'. But this *monitum* has little force against this fixed, traditional appellation.

*The Etruscans*   By raising the problem, I allude, however distantly, to another and far greater one: the origin of the Etruscan nation,[1] and consequently—if indirectly—to the source of that religion by which the Etruscans were reckoned, even in the context of antique piety, to be obsessed.[2] Fortunately, a discussion of that vexed and complex issue is out of place here. But another, connected problem, more general and equally involved, does touch on my argument more directly: that of the origin of orthogonal planning in Italy.

Orthogonal planning, chequerboard planning of a town or site, is not immediately dependent on the Etruscan or any related rite, so it is a pity that the two problems have become so intimately involved. Orthogonal planning has appeared everywhere, in South America, China, India, Egypt, Mesopotamia, wherever elementary forms of surveying were developed, and in the wake of any system of land tenure. In Italy it appears to have been practised with great sophistication and assurance by the end of the sixth century B.C.[3] The implication therefore is that the technique had been developed over a period of time and had already become perfectly familiar. How long the period of time had been is impossible to assess in the present state of knowledge.

*Terramare*   It was supposed some eighty years ago that the practice, together with the Etruscan rite, had been brought to Italy by the people of a culture called *Terramare*[4] early in the Bronze Age, or even towards the end of the Neolithic period. Rather fanciful attempts were even made to find monumental remains of the practice of the Etruscan rite in its fully mature form among the rather friable remains of various *Terramare* settlements. Even more questionable now seems the attempt to identify the *Terramaricoli* with the ancestors of the Latins.[5] Subsequent scholars have re-examined the evidence offered by the excavators between 1860 and 1910, when the material was more or less exhausted, rather than carry out any field research themselves. As against the over-confident assertions of the earlier archaeologists, the most exacting modern scholar in the field, Gösta Säflund, has been over-stringent.[6] His rather sceptical attitude to the material evidence is valuable, but his more general conclusions seem to me questionable in view of his rather rigid, (and unstated), anthropological presuppositions, which appear in comments such as these: 'The *raison d'être* of the pile structures (the piles sometimes being as long as 6 m) should not be sought in presupposed religious or traditional conceptions, but only in the hydrographic conditions, which made it essential to raise the level of habitations.'[7] Curiously enough, a few paragraphs later, in discussing the absolute chronology of the culture, Säflund gives its terminal date, 700 B.C., not in relation to hydrography, since about this time hydrographic conditions would have been almost at their worst on his showing, but by reference to the beginning of the Celtic invasions. He suggests, therefore, that the *Terramare* were part of a whole cultural pattern which disappears at the time of the Celtic invasions, and not simply as a result of the hydrographic problem.[8] There is no reason to assume that the inhabitants of these highly organized and technically rather advanced settlements were radically different from the rest of the ancient world or even from their less technologically advanced neighbours in having no rituals of foundation or religious and traditional conceptions related to the forms of their dwellings. While it was foolish of Pigorini and Chierici to see a *mundus* where they were perhaps simply dealing with a ditch of peculiar shape, the evidence of the roughly rectangular shape of the villages cannot be altogether dismissed. Moreover there is no doubt that in many cases there is evidence of a definite delimiting earthwork, whether dike or defence. And in one definite case, the large settlement at Castione, the wall was either reinforced by or constituted of large square coffers, about 4.6 m square, and built of roughly worked logs morticed together and packed with clay and rubble.[9] Now Säflund makes much of the uniqueness of this construction,[10] though it had become a commonplace in Later Urnfield and even Celtic Europe, and had plenty of forebears further east. 'The timber-framed wall-rampart',

39. **Pigorini's restoration of Castellazzo di Fontanellato,** based on his sketchy excavations. *Key*: (A, B, C) fossa; (D) wall; (m, p) insulae; (E) pomoerium; (H) forum; (G) mundus; (F) pons; (L, M) cemeteries

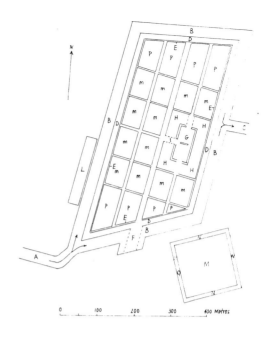

40. Pigorini's reconstruction of the timber Caissons of the rampart at Castione

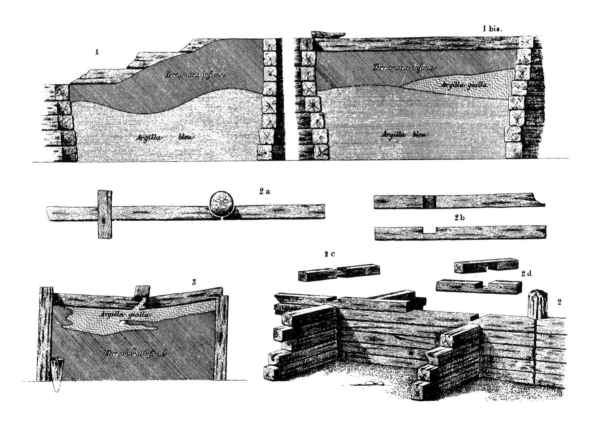

41, 42. Pigorini's **excavations at Castellazzo di Fontanellato** in 1877

43. Barakau village, about twenty miles east of Port Moresby, Papua, New Guinea
*By courtesy of the American Museum of Natural History*

says Stuart Piggott[11] 'could of course be an indigenous invention of Barbarian Europe, but it must also be remembered that such walls have a very long history . . . in the Near East and in the Aegean.' Säflund argues the originality of these ramparts from the absence of similar remains, though such ramparts may well have existed among the many villages destroyed for manuring. This is a curious method of argument that is prepared to infer a whole primitive inhumating phase of this culture in spite of the total absence of any burials from it. On the contrary, I would assume that such an extensive and highly developed piece of construction could not be isolated, and that there must have been other villages with similar coffered earthworks. The presence of square-coffered earthworks, even of rectangular houses within them, is no proof of the rectangular plan of the whole settlement of course: evidence the oval village or town at Biskupin in Poland, which shows this form of construction in its most highly developed form.[12]

If the *Terramaricoli* cannot be credited with the introduction of both the Etruscan rite and of orthogonal planning, the fact remains that their settlements had approximately trapezoidal outlines, and that the methods of construction they used favoured a rough regularity of plan analogous to that of modern pile-dwellings in South-East Asia. Though the *Terramaricoli* almost certainly practised some form of foundation rite, it may well have had no direct connection with the *Ritus Etruscus* (though this *a priori* supposition is not more reasonable than the opposite one). Yet it is also possible that the irregular, roughly circular villages of their Emilian neighbours in the Bronze Age may have been founded by some such form of rite as the one I have described, and may well have been *quadrata* in the sense in which I used the word, without the least trace of it showing in the remains of such villages as have been excavated in our times.

The introduction of the orthogonal plan into Italy is often ascribed to Greek influence,[13] but evidence is not entirely conclusive about this. Recent excavations at Megara Hyblaea, for instance, one of the earliest Greek settlements in Sicily, have shown some archaic dwellings, which seem roughly orientated, and roughly correspond to the traditional date of the founding of the town, in the last quarter of the eighth century. They are very dispersed, however, and their orthogonality

44. **Scene, probably showing the construction of a hut** . From the Bedolina rock
*After E. Anati, 'Camonica Valley', Jonathan Cape Ltd., London, 1965*

45. **House with stairs.** From the Naquane rock
*After E. Anati, 'Camonica Valley', Jonathan Cape Ltd., London, 1965*

46. **Sections (Area I, A–C, 11–7) of the Great Naquane rock.** This shows a number of houses raised on pile foundations (nos. 175, 207, 255) as well as the great maze (no. 270)
*After E. Anati, 'Camonica Valley', Jonathan Cape Ltd., London, 1965*

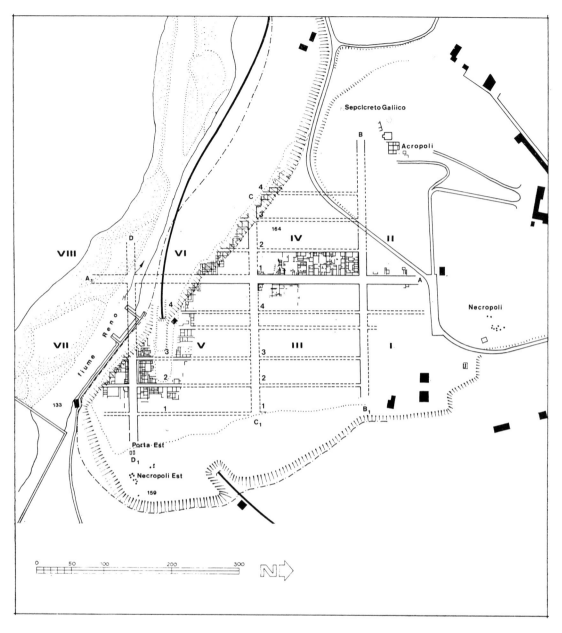

Sepolcreto Gallico

Acropoli

164

Necropoli

Necropoli Est

47. Marzabotto. Present state of excavations. *By courtesy of G. A. Mansuelli*

may be apparent.[13a] The first truly orthogonal layout in mainland
Italy at any rate, and one which seems also to be fairly accurately
oriented is the small necropolis in the Contrada Gaudo about 1 km
north of Paestum. It was discovered accidentally during the building
of an American airport in 1943, and is still only partially excavated;
moreover no trace has as yet been found of the settlement which it
served. 'What strikes one about it' writes the archeologist who con-
ducted the main excavation, 'is the layout which can only be called
"urbanistic".'[14]

48. Marzabotto. Aerial photograph of the site. The acropolis is among the cypresses in the right foreground

The area of the cemetery which has been explored so far is about 60 × 40 m, and covers about twenty tombs containing up to twenty-five skeletons, mostly in the 'womb' position. The tombs are of a shape known as 'a forno' and enclose usually two, sometimes three, chambers divided by heavy partitions. They contain a good deal of pottery of an unusual type for Italy, and stone implements. There is also a little bronze. The tombs are cut in soft rock and are aligned on straight lanes, 40–60 cm wide, also excavated in the rock. These tombs some-times are connected with the outside by a channel, which may be a libation opening. A mass of stones in the centre of the excavated area has been interpreted as a primitive altar. The lanes are orientated north–south within 5 degrees, and appear to be cut by wider lanes running east–west. Again, according to the excavators, the type of pottery found in the tombs is unique in Italy.[15] The character of this pottery and the physical type of the buried individuals suggests that the necropolis was used by a community of immigrants from the Aegean, perhaps more precisely from Anatolia, who reached Italy sometime before 2000 B.C.

*Marzabotto*  The salient piece of evidence on the Etruscan practice of orthogonal planning is the remains of an Etruscan town near the village of Marzabotto, in the province of Bologna. This was clearly a sizable settlement, and was almost entirely destroyed early in the fourth century B.C. by the Gauls. It had been laid, if the evidence of Greek ceramic remains may be taken as conclusive, no earlier than the beginning of the sixth century, perhaps the very end of the sixth.[16] It was laid out over a slightly earlier settlement, probably not orthogonally planned; to this the excavators ascribe the small temple over a spring which is the earliest monumental stone building in the north of Italy.[17] Marzabotto was first excavated in the 1830s and has been studied ever since. In 1961 a similarly orientated, if much smaller, settlement was discovered not far away at Casalecchio di Reno, a village at the Apennine foothills, some 10 km out of Bologna.[18] Like Marzabotto, it was destroyed by the Gauls, who seem to have done a fairly thorough wrecking job. The river Reno has eroded Marzabotto, the railway has caused minor damage; the museum was wrecked by the Germans in 1944, when Marzabotto tragically re-entered history.

After the Gauls destroyed it, Marzabotto, and probably the smaller settlement, were not re-occupied by the Etruscans or the Romans later, and remained completely unknown.

The main outlines of the plan are becoming clear: one main *cardo* survives, running north–south, and is crossed at right angles by three *decumani*, all the main streets being about 15 m broad. The lots between are divided into sections 130–60 m long, of irregular width on average 6 m, taking either a single row or two lines of back-to-back houses, which front alleys 5 m wide parallel to the *cardo*. The houses were of an impluviate type; in the middle of the house, there is an open court with a well, sometimes also a cistern, sunk in the floor. The living-rooms cluster round the court, while the rooms facing the street are ware-houses, shops and workshops. The probable outer bounds of the town are suggested by two necropolises outside the city gates: foundations of one eastern gate, leading to its necropolis have been found. On the hill overlooking the town from the north (or rather NNW) stands a small group of buildings which have a clearly sacral character, the acropolis or *sedes deorum*. Most of these buildings are again accurately orientated. The low hill, the apparent lack of any fortification there or in con-junction with the gates, suggest that the town was never a fortress. A curious feature, not so far found elsewhere are *cippi*, buried at cross-roads, in the centre of each crossing. The *cippus* found at the crossing of the *cardo* and the *decumanus* labelled 'C' by the excavators was scored with a cross, unlike the other *cippi*. There seems to have been no sort of sacrificial deposit associated with these *cippi*: which suggests that they refer to the surveyors' rather than the diviner's proceeding; and it may well be that the scored *cippus*, at the presumed centre of the town, was where the *groma* was originally 'auspiciously set'.[19] The *cippi* were not, as they would have been in a later Roman town, indicators or markers: the hilly site meant that it would have been difficult, if not impossible to vise with their help. They remained therefore only as buried wit-nesses to the surveyors' passage: the evidence of a ritual or at least quasi-ritual procedure is clear enough.[20]

This evidence of probable ceremonial practices at the laying-out of Marzabotto is still isolated. In Greece surveying does not seem to have been accompanied by any such practice. Marzabotto was laid out at the end of the 'orientalizing' phase of Etruscan culture, soon after 500 B.C., if the evidence of Greek pottery fragments is to be relied on. More important perhaps, the house plans are quite unlike contemporary Greek house-types.[21] The layout in long *insulae*, though common in later Greek cities in Magna Graecia, is found commonly elsewhere on

49. **Marzabotto. Acropolis**, building 'd'. This was probably an open altar

50. **Marzabotto. Acropolis**, building 'd'

51. **The Acropolis of Marzabotto.** Building 'b'

52. **The town from the Acropolis.** In the foreground, building 'd'

53. **Spina.** Remains of the
**north embankment piling** and of
the pile foundations, probably of a
house, near Paganella
**from the N.W.**
*Courtesy of Soprintendenza alle
Antichità, Emilia e Romagna*

the Mediterranean seaboard. But there is nothing Greek about the
mouldings or indeed the general forms of the sacral buildings on the
Acropolis: they seem typically Etruscan. The contemporary Greek
pottery found over the site in fair quantities is not in itself conclusive
evidence of Greek 'presence'.

The orthogonal and precise character of the plan contrasts with the
rather ramshackle nature of the building. The houses were built of sun-
dried brick over pebble and rubble foundations, the rubble roughly
mortared with mud. The technique is a common Mediterranean one.
But the fictile revetments (most of the early ones unfortunately now
destroyed), the fictile drains and the character of the stone mouldings
of the more permanent buildings on the acropolis do not suggest
obvious Greek analogies.

*Spina*   More puzzling evidence is offered by the recent excavations of Spina:
unlike Marzabotto, about which ancient writers were practically
silent, Spina was an object of much curiosity to ancient historians and
geographers; and much more recently its name was obscure in the local
nomenclature.[22]

But unlike Marzabotto, whose remains have been known since the
middle of the sixteenth century, and which has been explored more or
less systematically since the 1830s, the remains of Spina were unknown,
and its siting misjudged,[23] until the first tombs of the cemetery in the
Valle Trebba were struck when an irrigation canal was dug through
the necropolis in 1922. By 1953, some 1,200 tombs had been found there;
another cemetery, in the Valle Perga near by, was found in 1954 and

54. Aerial photograph of
the harbour quarter of
Spina. *After Arias*
1. The Ancient Harbour
2. Canals of the ancient
city
3. The occupied 'insulae'
5. Modern irrigation canals

had yielded another 2,400 burials by 1960.[24] In 1956, aerial photographs revealed the existence of an ancient, silted-up canal system in the Valle Perga.[25]

This canal system is now recognized as the harbour and city of Spina, which seems to have been laid out as a group of associated settlements, grouped in the two valleys in a lagoon situation, behind the lido which is now part of the inland sand-dunes. It may well have lain at a point where the Lido was broken. A main canal ran from the Pado Vetus (a branch of the Po delta, whose dry-bed is now called Pavero), first sharply north, and then turned eastward and seems to have led into the sea. Opening off it, two systems of canals have been found, about $1\frac{1}{2}$ km apart, which were probably the harbour zones. These and the rest of the settlement seem to have occupied the vast area of 740 ha, and have been said to have accommodated as many as 500,000 inhabitants at the height of the town's prosperity, towards the end of the fifth century B.C.[26]

The grave goods are very splendid in the richer burials. Most spectacular are the Attic vases, ranging from the late sixth to the early third century B.C. There was also Etruscan pottery and Etruscan bronzes as well as Tarentine jewellery. Clearly the written and the archaeological evidence concur: Spina was one of the main harbours in the ancient world, and the chief centre for the importation of Greek wares into Etruscan lands—over the Bologna/Florence route on which Marzabotto stood—and beyond, to the Celts of the Po valley and even beyond the Alps. The ancient geographers mention the three-day road from Spina to Pisa as a familiar one.[27]

The position of Spina, like that of Ravenna later, and Venice until more recently, seemed to guarantee its security. At any rate, weapons are very rare among the grave goods found so far.

It is difficult to conjecture why Spina fell: it may have been, as at Marzabotto, due to a Celtic attack or siege. More likely, such an attack was combined with the continuous silting of the lagoon and canals, and the slow sinking of the land below sea-level, which still continues. The Celtic attacks were contemporary with the eclipse of northern Etruscan power. The decline of piracy and of Phoenician power in the Mediterranean also contributed to the decline of Adriatic trade.[28]

Spina and Adria to its north were the main Adriatic harbours, until Ravenna and Aquilea took over; for two or three centuries, they were the most prosperous harbours in all Italy. By the time Strabo wrote, however, the village which he considered the heir of Spina was 16 km upstream from the coast; though, in fact, even now, the site is only about 10 km inland. But silting and bradyseism have resulted in the large marshy tract, sunk below sea-level, called the Valle di Comacchio: excavation in this water-logged terrain is very awkward. The cemeteries in the old dunes, with their harvest of Greek vases, have yielded clearly datable material. The excavations of the town, begun much later and in equally trying terrain, have not so far shown a clear picture of the occupation of the site. What has so far been uncovered shows a grouping of orthogonal sandy *insulae*, caissoned with pile-reinforced timber structures, and with timber superstructures. It is clear that unlike Marzabotto (or any other Etruscan town), Spina was a town built of timber.[29] The pile and caisson construction was, of course, familiar in the Po valley, as well as further north. It was the common construction of the *Terramare* settlements, which approached the limits of Spina both in time and in distance. Whenever Spina may have been founded, whether about 550 B.C. as the earliest archeological material found so far suggests, or much earlier, as legend has it, there were probably occupied *Terramare* settlements not too far away when the site of Spina welcomed its first dwellers.

Ethnic distribution is difficult to establish. No firm agreement exists as to the language spoken by the *Terramaricoli*.[30] Spina itself, as the graffiti on vases show, was inhabited by both Etruscan and Greek speakers.[31] Greek historians, though clear about the Etruscan allegiance of Spina, maintained that it was a pre-Etruscan foundation. Dionysius of Halicarnassus, following Hellanicus of Lesbos, suggests that it was a Pelasgian settlement.[32] Justin thought that it was founded by Thessalians.[33] Pliny the Elder gives the name of the Greek oecist as Diomede —one of the *Nostoi*.[34] Although this last tradition is not mentioned by any Greek author, Spina was treated as a quasi-Greek town, had its treasury at Delphi and was even admitted into the Delphic Amphictyony.[35]

The physical aspect of Spina is still extremely difficult to reconstruct. It was unlike any Etruscan or any Greek town, and bigger than most of them. Its buildings and those of the nearby Adria must have had a very definite character: Varro indeed derives the word *atrium*, that characteristic Etruscan and then Roman impluviate hall, from the name Adria, the Etruscan foundation which also gave its name to the Adriatic sea.[36]

It is very probable that its aspect, as well as much of its function passed—when the changing hydrographic conditions deprived it of its harbour—to Ravenna, and later to Aquilea further north, beyond the Venetian lagoon. Strabo visited Ravenna, and described it. A harbour town, it was 'built entirely of timber, laid out on canals, the traffic being served by bridges and ferries'.[37]

Such towns existed further up on the unstable marshy coast of the Po delta, between the Venetian Lido and Ravenna. As the harbours of Ravenna and of Aquilea silted up and the dunes advanced inexorably into the sea, the island villages of the Venetian lagoon bound themselves into that powerful unit which gave us the city of Venice.

To return to Spina: no positive evidence can yet be gathered from its remains. Clearly enough, it was not a typical Etruscan town;[38] the supposition that there may have been some link, in terms of material culture, even if not *ethnē*, between the *Terramaricoli*, whoever they were and the founders of Spina, seems at any rate plausible.[39] At Spina, the Etruscan skill in harbour-building, as well as in surveying, made the town one of the richest harbours of the ancient world; further excavation may show more of the nature of Spina's trade and structure: an independent urban unit, not just a convenient market place for Greek fancy goods.

*Spina and Orthogonal Planning*

A reconsideration of the evidence at Marzabotto raises a radical matter. If Greek imports to the town are in the form of luxury products, such as Attic red-figure ware, and the occasional piece of sculpture, then how did the recondite Greek thinking on town planning (or rather its practice) take such strong root among the Etruscans? The evidence about orientated orthogonal plans of early Hellenic cities has proved somewhat thin. Among the older towns, Smyrna provides the only well-attested example. At the other end of Anatolia, however, on the northern shores of Lake Van, the Urartian kings built a wholly orthogonal town, now known as Zernaki Tepe.[39a] The ruins have never been built over; the town has no obvious limits or walls. It lies on an undulating hill-top overlooking a valley in which lies the modern town of Ercis. It covers about a kilometre square. The layout is regular, the blocks almost uniform squares, about 35 m. to a side; each block consisting of two pairs of semi-detached houses, back-to-back, and separated by a passage or alley. The houses may well have been intended to have a second story. The site is clearly quartered by two wider streets at right angles which cross each other about the centre of the settlement. Zernaki may well never have been completed or inhabited, perhaps because of the difficulties of water-supply, but more likely because its construction was overtaken by the destruction of the Urartian kingdom by the Medes about 590 B.C.

There are no analogous plans, Urartian or other of a similar date. The Urartians were of course practised in orthogonal planning on even quite a large scale, but this settlement is remarkably ambitious.

Perhaps, like Marzabotto, and like the orthogonal towns of the Greeks in Italy and Sicily, it was a new settlement in which old rites and old cosmogonies had become incorporated in the practice of surveyors and geometers. It may be worth reiterating that the founding of Marzabotto, like the layout of Zernaki, has all the marks of an organized, even 'traditional' procedure which suggests that we are dealing with a matter of some antiquity. Allowing a century or so, we retreat into the beginnings of the 'orientalizing' period of Etruscan art. Greece had not much to offer in terms of technological know-how at that time. It was the time of the first colonies. Are we to assume that nevertheless the technique of surveying was taught to the unwary Etruscans by some itinerant Greek γεωμέτρης (*geōmetrēs*). Or that the Etruscans sent surveyors to Greece for training? Or that some Etruscans were so impressed by the sight of a Greek colony as to adopt their methods of layout, without attempting to copy the other features of the city?

Orthogonal layout is not, after all, a technique which may become isolated from its social religious context to percolate over decades, through trade exchanges. It is hardly analogous to the adaptation of pottery forms, for instance, or the profiles of mouldings. On the contrary, it is the product of a tight discipline and its adoption by a people like the Etruscans was not in the least likely to have occurred as a simple matter of convenience. The orthogonal plan and the matter of orientation was too important in the life of a people to have been taken over arbitrarily as one good idea among others. It must in fact have had a context in the general world picture of the Etruscans into which it might fit, or else have modified that world picture in such a way as to leave definite traces of the upheaval. But there is little evidence for the second supposition, unless the myth of Tages[40] were improbably used to justify it. The fully orientated plan at Marzabotto, moreover, implies the use of a quite developed *groma* of the kind I described earlier, and not the rough working out Pliny the Elder considered approximate.[41] Nor can the resorting either to orientation or to orthogonality be justified by the argument that the obvious way to divide the site into equal plots is to lay it out on an orthogonal grid, because the parcels of land, as well as the *insulae*, are all unequal. Orthogonal planning is closely associated with Hippodamus of Miletus, who cuts such an ambiguous figure in Aristotle's *Politics*.[42] Although some authors merely credit him with having stated the rationally self-evident,[43] from a more sophisticated view his theories are given a definite cosmological content.

Hippodamus, the ancient authors insist, was a planner. Yes, but also a political theorist, and μετρόλογος (*metrologos*), a student of celestial phenomena. The Hippodamian city is not different from others just because it is orthogonal, (note that there is no suggestion to the contrary) but because it is zoned according to the class of the inhabitants, (warriors, farmers, artisans) and the form of land tenure, (sacred, public or private). Hippodamus's land-tenure zoning corresponds to the sort of tripartite division which Dumézil considers fundamental to all Indo-European societies. In their excessive concern for the matter of orthogonal planning, the use of the 'rational' right angle, many modern writers have failed to give Hippodamus his full due. In particular, the cosmological context of his speculations has been neglected. A French scholar, J.-P. Vernant, has pointed out recently how much the Hippodamian city is dependent on the view of the world order expressed by another Ionian, Anaximander. 'As a philosopher whose aim is to explain nature, Hippodamus nevertheless does not neglect civic life. He is evidently integrated within the universe of the city. His thought does not separate out physical space, political space, urban space; but unifies them in one speculative exertion.'[44] Yet even if Hippodamus had been the inventor of Greek orthogonal planning, which he was not, this device is insignificant without the context of his constitutional reform and cosmological speculation. Interestingly enough, the only other Greek urbanist known from Greek sources is Meton of Kolonos, who like Hippodamus was a 'metrologist'. He is most familiar through the caricature of him by Aristophanes in *The Birds*.[45] Whether Meton had actually planned a circular Athens with radiating streets, and Aristophanes (finding the notion ridiculous) lampooned him for the airy-fairy figure he seemed,[46] or whether Aristophanes was hitting out much more generally at fanciful town-planning schemes,[47] is matter outside my competence. But the notion of the town plan, even in this joke version, is given a cosmological setting.

Although Hippodamus was undoubtedly important both as a theorist of town planning and as a practical 'urbanist', and although he undoubtedly made orthogonal plans,[48] it would be foolish to attribute its invention to him. Orthogonal planning was found (as I have already pointed out) all over the known world, and so were orientated towns, in which, as far as the ancient writers are concerned, the Greeks showed no interest until Plato. Indeed the difficulty about the particular case of Marzabotto is that the nearest contemporary orthogonal (though unorientated) layout which survives is the vast palace platform at Persepolis, which had no equal in scale and richness anywhere in the Greek world.

But orientation was a familiar matter in the old river civilizations. The first strictly orientated building found to date is the *mastaba* of the fourth Pharaoh of the First Dynasty, Uadji, at Sakkara, built well over two-and-a-half millennia before Marzabotto.

Herodotus describes the parcelling out of Egypt by Sesostris[49] for taxation purposes and adds: 'Perhaps this was the way in which geometry was invented, and passed afterwards into Greece; for knowledge of the sundial and the *gnomon* and the twelve divisions of the day came into Greece from Babylon.'[50] Herodotus is not easy to contradict on this point. There is no corresponding tradition of the hellenic origin of surveying among Roman authors, although it was common enough to make such acknowledgements to the Greeks. The very word *groma*, which some lexicographers have derived from the Greek γνώμων (*gnōmōn*), has now been given an independent ancestry.[51] It may well be that the Etruscans were the superiors of the Greeks in surveying techniques; we know little or nothing, too, of the surveying skills of the

Phoenicians. Recent aerial photography and subsequent excavation have produced new evidence of Greek skill in this matter, though at the time of writing results have not been fully sifted. At any rate, Megara Hyblaea, the first Dorian colony in Sicily, may have been given an orthogonal plan at the time of its foundation about 725 B.C.;[51a] Selinus, founded about a century later, may also have had an orthogonal plan at its foundation; a century later again, an orthogonal plan, and orthogonally divided fields appear at Paestum. But further photography and excavation may yet reveal even earlier Greek, as well as Etruscan remains than have been found so far. But this will not affect the drift of the argument: that, as ancient authors suggested, orthogonal planning was the product of grafting a law of land tenure on to some form of quasi-astronomical surveying, which gave landed property divine, and in particular celestial, sanction. But the form which orthogonal planning took in Etruria and later in Rome was conditioned by the *Ritus Etruscus*, which absorbed it. The rite was of course completely independent of anything as conscious, as explicit, as a planning theory. The origin of this kind of rite cannot ever be found in speculation, whether 'rational' or 'mythical'. Its origin will always be in a *dromenon*, in an action, and such origins are always lost. The search for the 'pure' and original form of the rite would be entirely fruitless.

*Myth and Rite*    Without setting out a tabulated analysis of the elements of the rite, it is fair to say that further inspection will show it as operating and vital until well into the Christian era. As long as a myth is '*aperçu*' as a myth, says Claude Lévi-Strauss (of the myth of Oedipus) it remains a myth. Freud's record of it, he goes on to say, has as much relevance to consideration of the whole myth as the version given by Sophocles.[52] What is true of the myth is even more true of the rite. As long as it survives, marking even late medieval and Renaissance ceremonial, it retains its hold over the imaginations and the ways of thinking of the people who witness or practise it. In this context, therefore, a 'misunderstanding' of the rite is impossible, or at any rate, the statement has no real meaning. The rite is 'truly' understood as long as it is practised. And it was practised as long as it was needed. It is foolish to consider a rite of such fundamental importance to the social life of communities during a millennium as something 'fancy', something arbitrary, or external to the true life of those peoples, and contrary perhaps to their real interests. The nature of urban life in the Roman world cannot be understood without reference to their rites. The communities who went through them were both actors and witnesses of the *dromenon*, and they appear to have required its periodic re-enactment. The rite performed a function in the life of the community: it answered a need which could not be assuaged by its single performance at the foundation of the town.

So much has already been said about these ceremonies, which are even today carried out by practically all primitive communities, as well as some which are not primitive at all, that there is little to add here by way of comment. For the Romans, at any rate, it was an essential part of daily business. 'Almost nothing of any importance,' says Cicero ruefully lamenting the decline of his augural dignity, 'not even on a private business, used ever to be done without auspices being taken.'[53]

Of course the testimony of ancient writers is not unanimously solemn and pious. Cato the Elder warns his bailiff against charlatan fortune-tellers,[54] for instance. Yet, when talking about divination nowadays we tend to forget that the petitioners and the diviner are not in the first place forecasting, but finding out the will of the gods: it is on the gods' consent that success will depend. When the diviners have been proved wrong, this is attributed either to a fault in performing the sacrifices, which are consequently rendered invalid and therefore misleading, or to a mistake by the diviner.

But a vast amount of lore about correct divining survives. The frequency of consultation, the passionate interest in its intricacies, the absolute dependence of vast state enterprises on its outcome, have to some scholars the appearance of a collective neurosis. And yet 'the huge machine of information which Rome had set up in the face of the un-seen'[55] left the Roman, paradoxically, greater freedom of manoeuvre than a public authority would have against 'expert advice'. The Roman had a number of subterfuges at his disposal. He could, for instance, simply refuse to observe the omens which appeared;[56] or he could con-sult two or three times to get a different opinion;[57] or he could, by means of a formula or a sacrifice, turn away the bad force of an omen, especially of one which he had not 'provoked'.[58] It was even possible to cheat at omens, as Romulus did. However, at the town foundation the goodwill and sanction of the gods, *pax deorum*, was essential. The new city amounted, after all, to the foundation of a new religion. There was, even here, some room for manipulation, but not very much, and only within strictly pre-established limits.

Having been given the first sign propitious to the site,[59] the founders proceeded to a complementary rite: inauguration. This second divi-natory procedure was quite distinct: the augur determined in his inauguration whether the persons involved, and the time, were accept-able to the gods, and he operated by turning the hilltop on which he performed the rite into the centre of the universe. The augur's act in drawing his diagram on the ground changed the earth he touched from anywhere to this unique and only place. Consider the language of augural incantation: '*Ollaber arbos quirquir est quam me sentio dixisse* . . .' ('This tree, wherever it may be, which I name to myself exactly, let it mark the boundary of my *templum* and *tescum* to the left; that tree, wherever it may be, which I name to myself exactly, let it mark the boundary of my *templum* to the right . . .').[60] With this formula, according to Varro, the Capitoline augur began his watch. The idea is more clearly set out perhaps in the legend of Olenus Calenus. Pliny tells it like this:[61]

> Olenus Calenus was an augur in the Etruscan city of Veii. Having heard that a skull had been found during the digging of the founda-tions for the new temple of Jupiter on the Roman Capitol, he wished to transfer the force of this fortunate omen from Rome to his own

city. When Roman envoys came to consult him, as the most famous
of all Etruscan augurs, about the meaning of this omen, he drew a
*templum* on the ground with his augural staff, and gesturing with it
asked: 'Is this what you are telling me, you Romans, *here* will be the
temple of Jove Optimus Maximus, *here* we found the skull?' According to Livy, the annals insist that the good fortune which the omen
portended for Rome would have passed to the city of Veii had the
Roman envoys agreed; but they had a premonition (according to
Pliny they were warned of Olenus's intention) and so contradicted
him, saying: 'No, not *here*; what we say is that the head was found
in Rome.'

The power of such words is impossible for us, now, to appreciate.
They are the language of incantation, *verba concepta*, a language which is
achieved in the words: 'This is My body, this is My blood.' The function of such incantations is to interrupt the ordinary passage of time,
and by repeating the archetypal gesture of some mythical ancestor or
hero, to renew his powerful action; to take the given place at which it is
applied out of the normal influences acting on it, and insert the great
time of revelation into the passage of time at *this* given moment. That
also is why it was necessary for Roman augurs to recall the actions of
Romulus, and again, it explains the great power and importance
attributed to Romulus's staff.

The rite of the founding of a town touches on one of the great
commonplaces of religious experience.[62] The construction of any human
dwelling or communal building is in some sense always an *anamnesis*,
the recalling of a divine 'instituting' of a centre of the world. That is
why the place on which it is built cannot arbitrarily or even 'rationally'
be chosen by the builders, it must be 'discovered' through the revelation
of some divine agency.[63] And once it has been discovered, the per-
manence of revelation in that place must be assured. The mythical hero
or deity attains the centre of the universe or the top of the cosmic
mountain by overcoming epic obstacles. The ordinary mortal may find
this place anagogically through the agency of ritual. In the case I am
considering, through the ritual of orientation.

It is therefore hardly surprising that Roman augurs, impelled by
ritual necessity, divided their *templum* into four quarters by *cardo* and
*decumanus*, or that the founders of the town used the same divisions on
the town site, and that Roman surveyors based their seemingly trivial
operation of parcelling up the land on the same basic diagram, using
the same terminology. The three procedures were three modalities of
the same ordering of the experience of space. Writers who wish to give
the last of these three 'modes' a logical, and therefore a temporal,
priority, often do so without stating their emotional preference for a
'functionalist' solution, and ignore the unity of experience in such a
society as that of the primitive Romans, nor do they recognize the inevitably arbitrary nature of their own discipline.[64]

However, Roman writers on surveying were not plagued by such
problems. 'The origin [of the setting up of boundaries]', writes Hyginus

Gromaticus at the beginning of his treatise,[65] 'is heavenly, and its practice invariable. . . . Boundaries are never drawn without reference to the order of the universe, for the *decumani* are set in line with the course of the sun, while the *cardines* follow the axis of the sky.' The meaning of the second of these terms is obvious enough, even from this text alone, *cardo* is 'axis', 'axle', 'hinge' or 'pole', the line round which the sun runs its course, and therefore the axle of the universe. The other term, *decumanus*, the ancients found much more difficult to explain. By the time Hyginus wrote, antiquarians as well as technical writers had produced some rather fanciful explanations.[66] The *decumanus* was drawn as a chord of the *templum* circle, while the *cardo* was drawn at right angles to it by bisection. Pliny suggests that it owed its name to the resemblance the two lines had to the number X, whose primitive form was $+$.[68] Hyginus Gromaticus thought that *decumanus* was a contraction of *duodecimanus*, meaning either the line of the twelve hours between the rising and the setting of the sun, or some reference to the twelfth hour, the hour of sunset.[69] Festus had already described the *decumanus* as the line which runs from the rising to the setting of the sun.[70] In the passage quoted earlier, Pliny describes the *decumanus* as the line of the equinox.[71] If this is taken in conjunction with another remark of Hyginus's, repeated by Frontinus,[72] that *duodecimanus* was so called because it divided the world into two parts, the cosmological association of surveying terminology is inescapable. 'Surveying is derived in the first place', Varro had said, 'from the Etruscan Discipline.'[73] Hyginus and Frontinus both agreed with this. By the simple act of drawing his cross within the circle, the augur, standing on his hilltop scrying the southern horizon for significant birds, had put himself at the hub of the sacred universe. From that first act of divination, and until their destiny was accomplished, all the inhabitants of his given site would move within the order which his *templum* had 'prophesied'. Inevitably it is from these two lines that the two main streets of the town had to be drawn.

I suggested earlier how this relationship might have been worked out,[74] and how augural discipline was alluded to, darkly, in liver divination. Everything about the ritual of *limitatio*, which followed next, suggests that by the time it was begun the future boundaries of the city had already been determined. This is certainly clear from the example which is most explicit, the legendary account of Romulus's *limitatio* of the Palatine Rome. The various accounts of the route which Romulus followed do not, expectedly, entirely agree.[75]

*The Boundary of the First Rome*

The oldest, and most detailed account is that given by Solinus, which he derived from a lost work of Varro's. He is not explicitly concerned with the *pomoerium* but with that confusing entity, *Roma quadrata*.[76] If he means the *pomoerium* by it, then according to him Romulus started 'in the grove in the enclosure of Apollo'[77] and ended very near, by the top steps of the stairs of Cacus. This location, just over the Lupercal, and 'near where the hut of Faustulus had stood', is heavily impregnated with memories of the founding legend. The Lupercal was the place where the she-wolf had found the twins, and Faustulus was their foster-

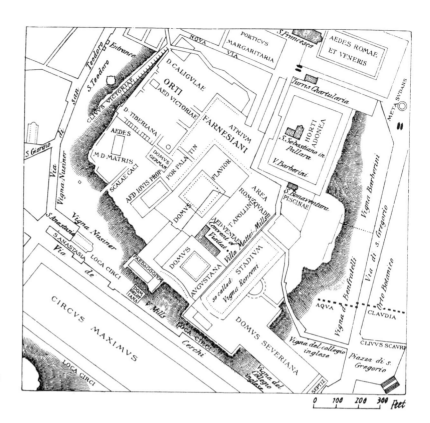

55. Map of the Palatine Hill and its surroundings, showing the rough divisions of the Imperial Palaces and other ancient buildings, and the modern street plan. The Lupercal was about the *Scalae Caci* and the Temple of the Magna Mater. *After Lanciani*

father.[78] Cacus himself, though an unsavoury character, was only semi-human, being the son of Vulcan, and therefore able to breathe fire. He is also said to have been offered a cult in the form of fire, like Vesta's tended by virgins.[79]

Unfortunately, Solinus does not give any notion of the area his *Roma quadrata* covered. Dionysius of Halicarnassus also says rather vaguely that Romulus 'drew a square about the Palatine' round which he ploughed. In another place he suggests that the temple of Vesta was left outside this boundary, but he gives no more precise reference to other boundary marks.[80] Tacitus, in a more explicit description, says that its boundary started in the Forum Boarium (just below the Lupercal), where, he remarks rather oddly, you may see a bronze figure of a bull, the animal which is yoked to the plough. The furrow so begun was extended to include the great altar of Hercules, then following the boundary stones set at regular intervals it ran along the foot of the Palatine to the altar of Consus, thence to the Curiae Veteres, and finally to the shrine of the *Lares* in the Forum Romanum.[81] As Lugli points out,[82] Tacitus refers to the ritual boundary of the city, not to the defensive walls of primitive Rome, which seemed to be in Varro's mind. Tacitus's account is obliquely reinforced by a note of Aulus Gellius[83] that Romulus's original (*antiquissimum*) *pomoerium* went round the foot of the Palatine mount, while another late author[84] talks of a statue at the edge (*pes*) of the Romulean hill, between the temples of Antoninus and Faustina and that of Vesta at the Fornix Fabianus.

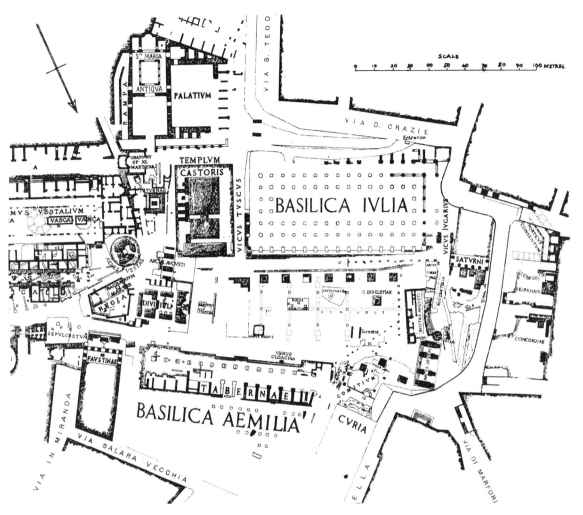

56. The **Forum Romanum**, from the House of the Vestal Virgins to the foot of the Capitol. The North point corresponds to that of the Domus Caligulae in fig. 55. *After Murray*

Varro, however, does suggest that he was aware of the larger *pomoerium* when he says that the month of February was called that after the purification day, *dies februatus*, because then the people are purified, that is, the old Palatine hill girt with flocks of people is lustrated by the naked *Luperci*.[85]

*Luperci and Lupercal*    The *Luperci* purified the city. Practically all ancient writers (about the matter) agree on this. The city was also purified in other ways and at other times throughout the religious year, but the *Luperci* are specially interesting since the shrine which they served and the route they followed were particularly connected to the foundation of the city, and the aetiological myth of the ritual again tied it back to the foundation myth.[86]

The festival took place on 15 February.[87] February was the last month of the Roman religious year in the ancient calendars, and the *Lupercalia* its most important function.[88] The very name of the month was derived from *februum*, which Varro gives as the Sabine translation of *purgamentum*,[89] while Ovid lists several other 'purifying' agents which carry that name.[90] It is applied particularly to the strips of newly cut goathide with which the running *Luperci* struck any women in their way.[91]

But though the race[92] of the *Luperci* was the most prominent part of the festival and, thanks to Shakespeare, the most familiar to the modern reader, the festival had other features. It started at the *Lupercal* with rites about which we are not entirely certain. We do know that there was first the sacrifice of some goats and a dog,[93] as well as the final portion of the cakes of *mola salsa* which had been prepared the day before by the Vestals.[94] The goats were immediately flayed, the dog perhaps buried. In the course of the sacrifices 'two young noblemen's sons being brought forward, some are to stain their foreheads with the bloody knife, others presently to wipe it off with wool dipped in milk; the boys must laugh after their foreheads are wiped. . . .' Either before or immediately after the sacrifice there seems to have been a feast at which more was drunk than eaten. There were many runners: St. Augustine, who must, judging from this description, have watched them from the Forum Romanum says: 'The going up and down of the *Luperci* is also interpreted in such a way as showing men who seek the mountain tops because of the flood waters rising, and then come down to the foothills when the waters retreat.'[95] Augustine produces this remark in the course of a discussion of the flood in pagan custom, and it echoes, too, the Roman legend that the basket containing Romulus and Remus was deposited at the *Lupercal* by the flooding Tiber.[96]

Back at the *Lupercal* the winners in the race received their prize, in the form of entrails (*exta*) of the sacrificed goats, half-cooked on willow spits.[97] There is at least one obvious 'initiatory' element in the rite, the 'blooding' of the two youths at the beginning. It is never made clear whether this was a form of admission into the brotherhood, or merely an ancillary rite. Plutarch considers why the *Flamen Dialis* is forbidden to touch or even name dogs and goats; and wonders whether it is because of the contempt in which both animals, and particularly the goat, were held, as being subject to many illnesses: '. . . there seems to be no animal in existence so prone to epilepsy as the goat, nor does any animal infect quicker those that either eat its flesh or even touch it . . . It is said that the reason for this is the narrowness of the passages by which its spirit passes . . . and this is argued from the thinness of its voice . . .'[98] All of which underlies the 'low' character of the wolf/dog—goat priesthood, their apparently trivial actions, such as the boys' laughter. Now laughter, in ritual, was an expulsion of spirits, a wolflike and brave defiance of the blood; though it is characteristic enough of the jolly and even ribald characteristics of the feast.[99]

Jane Harrison produced some remarkable comparative material in considering a Kikuyu custom of initiating a boy at about the age of ten. There are several similar elements: a goat is flayed and disembowelled, the boy wears strips of goatskin, while the gut is wound round the mother, the boy sits on her knees, the gut is cut (simulating severing the umbilical cord), the mother groans, the boy cries like a baby, etc.[100] Unfortunately Jane Harrison had not the occasion to give further attention to the rite. But her intuition is related to an earlier and rather different interpretation. The German philologist H. Jordan[101] contests a functional interpretation of the festival as protecting flocks against wolves (*lupus* and *arcere*)[102] and suggests that the priests assumed wolf-nature: *lupercus* from *lupus* like *noverca* (stepmother) from *novus*.[103] The suggestive rhyme *lupercus-novercus* recalls the other *lupa* in aetiological myth, Acca Laurentia, the wife of Faustulus, and like the she-wolf, stepmother to Romulus and Remus.[104] The myth of the she-wolf is euphemistically explained by reference to the dubious habits of Acca Laurentia, *lupa*, a whore,[105] and even a female deity, *Luperca*, is mentioned.[106] But the patron of the festival and of the brotherhood was without a doubt Faunus, the goat-legged shepherds' god, whom the Greeks assimilated to Pan.[107] The brotherhood had just that implication of a disorderly life. Cicero, defending a client, rejects the implication that the young man's membership of the priesthood was circumstantial evidence. It is 'a wild fellowship, obviously pastoral and rustic, of the brothers *Luperci*, whose woodland meetings were established before civilization or law.'[108]

But Faunus not only presides over this return to a pre-civil condition, a moment of misrule before the institution of the new year, he is also a civilizing king of the ancient Latins, and in this aspect a confirmer of the institutions. His feast comes not only plumb in the middle of February, but also in the middle of the days consecrated to the dead (*Dei Parentales*). To separate the wolf from the goat in the ritual as coming from two different ethnic sources is as misleading here,[109] as is the attempt to assimilate the switches of goathide to the apotropaic, noisy, 'beating the bounds' of the Salii.[110] The truth is that the *Luperci* show little apotropaic intention, nor do the ancient writers say much in this context about guarding against evil or averting it. On the other hand the implications of fertility, of easy birth, are made abundantly clear, as are the notions of purifying, by dissolving the community and reconstituting it. Inevitably, therefore, there are implications about kingship, on which Ovid touches.[111] In a minor key, there is the clear indication of an initiation into a priestly fellowship which, however, officiated on 15 February only.

The *Lupercal* aetiological myth recalls the adoption of the founding brothers of the city, saved miraculously from the flooding river-water, their adoption and the contest between them, which was commemorated in the two groups of *Luperci*.[112] The foundation of the city is not mentioned in it. The runners were not concerned, though they ran around the old boundary, to purify the city territory: they purified the people who stood round the foothills of the city hill like flocks. They may have stood on either side of the boundary, or even outside it altogether. It was the people, not the territory, that were concerned. The whole festival suggests a celebration of pre-legal virulence which the myth implied, and the passage to a civilized, an agricultural state through adoption into the order of the hero-king.[113]

Another procession, a much more formal, and also a longer one, lustrated the city on two occasions at least during the year: the dance of the Salian brothers. The Salii were a much more important college—from the point of view of the state and the city's religious life during the republic and the early empire—than the barbarous *Luperci*.[114] Their prestige as well as their ritual were related to their treasure, the *ancile*, a shield which had fallen from heaven—or so their legend had it—one 1st of March in the reign of Numa,[115] while other traditions consider Morrius, King of Veii their founder, and generally find them an Etruscan institution;[116] or connect them with Dardanus and the Samothracian Penates;[117] or find an eponymous hero, the Arcadian Salius, a friend of Evander, who taught the sacred dance to Aeneas's Trojans, the mediate founder.

The *ancile* which fell from heaven was one of the three guarantees of the Roman state—with the fire of Vesta and the Temple of Jupiter Optimus Maximus. It had been copied for the use of the brethren by the mythical victim-smith Mamurius Veturius; and the shields suffered various vicissitudes.[118]

The brothers, of whom there were several companies, danced with their shields, perhaps to open and to close the war season. Unlike the Arval brothers (who performed their dance in secret round an altar in a shrine outside the city, at the fifth milestone from the Porta Portense down the river) or the Sodales Titii of whom practically nothing is known, the Salii appear to have this at least in common with the Luperci: as far as their ritual is concerned they both passed round—or through—the city festively and protected its venerable boundaries.

57, 58. The Salians moving the
ancilia, both third to second
century B.C.
*After the sardonyx of Attius and a
cornelian in the Louvre, Paris*

## Four

**Guardians of Centre, Guardians of Boundaries**

*Roma Quadrata*     I now return to the place from which the *Luperci* had started out, or just above it on the hill, the edge of *Roma quadrata*. The term had two meanings: the larger one, of the city 'in the form of a square' which Romulus had founded on the Palatine hill acording to the Etruscan rite,[1] and the subsidiary one, of the ritual monument to which I have already referred and which I will discuss in greater detail later.[2]

Following Dionysius of Halicarnassus many modern scholars have taken *quadrata* here to mean 'square', and the interpretation has given rise to a great deal of trouble. Apart from Dionysius, no one suggested in antiquity that Romulus ploughed to a square outline, and there is no archaeological evidence suggesting that there were Etruscan or Roman square towns. Some of the ancients, Varro for instance, seem to imply that the route which Romulus had taken was more or less round, while Plutarch talks outright of a circular plan. At least one modern writer has taken the evidence to mean that Romulus was supposed to have made two foundations, of a square town on the Palatine, and a circular district, centred on the *mundus* in the Comitium, so disposing of the difficulties in Plutarch's account.[3] It is a clumsy expedient, however, and creates a host of other problems, the most important being the absence of any historical or archaeological record of a circular foundation of a town or other unit in the Roman sphere of influence. Circular towns, in spite of utopian writers, are extremely rare anywhere. And there seems to have been no town in the ancient world even approximating to a circle with radiating streets, even if that is the plan described by Meton in the *Birds*.[4] Like the Median city Ecbatana, founded by Deoces and described by Herodotus,[5] they would suggest a divine ruler seated at the centre of a web under the dome of his palace, or at the top of some heaven-scaling tower.[6] The only truly circular town which does survive, the late Hittite Sam'al (Zinçirli), has an irregular acropolis at the centre, three gates, not disposed regularly, even though one of them is orientated due south. No indication has so far been given of what the internal plan of the settlement may have been. Another puzzling site, where a circular wall with eight regularly spaced gates surrounded a circular fortress, is Darab (Darabjerd), founded by Darius perhaps. The evidence about the plan of Kadeš, in spite of the relief in the Thebes Ramesseum, is not quite conclusive.[7] In Greece there seem to have been no circular towns, though it is true that Mantinea is nearly elliptical. Plato developed a circular plan for the ideal city of the *Laws*[8] and Xenophon says that Lycurgus recommended circular camps to the Spartans, but this amounts to little: there seems to have been neither a diffused theory, nor sufficiently common practice anywhere to construct any consistent account of circular towns. It remains a puzzle that the circular form, which would be easier to establish than a rectangle, should never have provided the model for town settlements, even among peoples who built circular dwellings, and even if their conception of space was dominated, as it was among the Romans, by the circle.[9] This is true despite the fact that there are many surviving Stone Age circular constructions of a sacral nature. The whole idea of a circular town was completely alien to Roman practice. Even the later, wilder, Roman emperors, such as Commodus and Heliogabalus, never went so far as to make a circular town foundation.[10]

To return again to *Roma quadrata*. For various reasons the explanation that *quadrata* simply means 'rectangular' seems too abstract for a ritual term. The only translation of *quadrata* which might fit this context is 'quadripartite'; or 'squared' in the sense that the four angles at the centre are right angles.[11] It would mean that all Varro and Ennius tell us about the topography of the Palatine city when they describe it as *quadrata* is that its *cardo* and *decumanus* crossed at right angles. This was done, as all the evidence quoted confirms, so that the town could be 'square', immovable in and at harmony with the universe at whose centre it was placed; *quod ad equilibrium foret posita*.[12] '*Quadrata*', then, is no guide to the shape of the primitive outline of the Palatine city, and offers no explanation, as a ritual term, of the way the *pomoerium* was drawn. But *Roma quadrata* had a secondary meaning; it was the enclosure in front of the temple of Apollo 'where the things of good omen used for the foundation of the town were kept, and the entrance of which was covered by a square stone.'[13] This description has led some scholars to identify it with a feature of the ancient rites and of the ancient city called *mundus*[14] of which I shall speak later; the identification was reinforced by the situation of *Roma quadrata* in that nexus of ancient monuments at the west corner of the Palatine which were connected with the mythical origins of the town. But this part of the hill has been so much dug and built over that its location will remain as enigmatic as the axial divisions of the 'regal' village which I postulate. Enigmatic, too, is the run of the earliest fortifications: Palatine, Esquiline and Capitol were enclosed by walls, in part at least, perhaps for defensive, sometimes for retaining purposes:[15] their date is in dispute. But the traditional chronology finds some acceptance by scholars, in the manner of the earliest settlement.[16]

As to the earliest walled hill-settlements, there is no evidence yet when these walls were linked by an enclosure: certainly not until the construction of the *agger* sometime between the end of the sixth and the beginning of the fifth centuries B.C., on the latest estimate.[17] This encloses a Rome which was *quadrata* in another sense: the city was divided into four tribes by Servius Tullius, named after the four sections of the city: Suburran, Esquiline, Colline and Palatine. This division is connected with another piacular festival, the rite of the Argei: a puzzling ceremony, in which straw bundles made up to look like manikins, tied hand and foot, were thrown off the Pons Sublicius into the Tiber by the Vestal Virgins in the presence of the priesthood and the magistrates.[18] No satisfactory explanation of this rite has yet been given; I only mention it here as an archaic witness to the fourfold territorial—against the earlier tripartite—division of the city.

But at its centre Rome was *quadrata* in another sense. Its main public space, the Forum which lay between the Capitol and the Palatine and was crossed and drained by the Cloaca Maxima, of legendary Royal construction[19] though it has been effective ever since, also had two clearly orientated complexes of buildings at either end. The Atrium Vestae with its temple and the Regia, still belonged to the Palatine city. At the other end was the Comitium, which we know to have been a *templum*—we are even told that the augur took auspices standing on the rostrum which overlooked it[20]—and which was the place where Romulus and Titus Tatius met after the Forum battle: hence its name. It was the meeting, until 145 B.C., of the Comitia Curiata, while the Plebeian assemblies took place on the Forum itself.[21] Throughout the later republican period (as well as under the empire) it was diminished in extent and in dignity. It is impossible at present to decide how much of the different pieces of orientated construction—such as the tract of wall under the equestrian statue of Domitian[22] may not have been related to it. Certainly the two building complexes influenced the layout of the rest of the Forum. Fragments of orientated paving of various dates have been found at scattered points in the Forum, and at different levels under the present Neronian and post-Neronian flagstones.

Until the end of the republic therefore, the city would have been said to be *quadrata* in two ways: its urban territory was divided into four districts, and its central—in constitutional, not geometric terms—areas of assembly were certainly consecrated and perhaps even geometrically regular.

What the Romans of the earlier republican times, let alone the period of the kings, might have called these divisions is not known. Recent scholars have tended to be sceptical about the use of the terms of *cardo* and *decumanus* for the streets of a Roman town in antiquity.[22a] Even if evidence is too scanty to allow of the drawing of conclusions, I would suggest that the analogies between augury, from which the term *cardo* is almost certainly drawn in the first place, and surveying (as well as the augural *templum* and the town) imply that the analogy between the dividing lines of Templum, centuriated fields, and regularly laid-out city (and before it, the 'inaugurated' town or village) had some force from the earliest towns.

*Vesta*   Like the augural *templum*, the city was quartered, though there was no correspondence between their outlines. The *templum* was always circular, the Roman city never was. On the other hand, when the abstract, notional *templum*, or at most the *templum* drawn on the ground, became incarnate in a building (as it did for countless Roman civic/religious purposes) this *templum minus* was never circular. On the contrary, the circular temple of Vesta, the most notable of all the circular temples in Rome, was not a *templum* at all in the ritual sense,[23] in spite of the fact that the adjoining house of the vestal virgins was,[24] apparently because the religion of the hearth was not concerned with the authority of the sky.

Vesta ruled both the household fire of the individual family and the civic hearth of the city. Hers was the fire which warmed and nourished,

59, 60, 61. **Three Villanovan bi-conic cinerary urns;** the outer ones covered with different types of helmet, the central one with a cup
*Villa Giulia, Rome*

a benign and fertilizing power. But Vesta was an earth-bound power, who tied the household to the house, the people of a city to its soil.[25] The *templum* belongs to the *di superi*.[26] That this identification was quite explicit is clear from the double prohibition reported by Aulus Gellius: that the decrees of the senate were not valid if they were passed before sunrise or after sunset, and equally invalid if they were passed outside the bounds of a *templum* properly *effatum*.[27] This rule implies that the sunlit day is the equivalent in time to the space of the *templum*. Transferring this to the present theme, the *conrectio* of the town, the division into four regions presumably placed it under the tutelage of the law-guaranteeing sky.

The temple of Vesta was certainly circular, chthonian and not a *templum*, but this does not imply that there was a direct relationship between a female-chthonian-circular complex on the one hand and a male-ouranian-square on the other. The notions I am considering here are too complex and rich to be reducible to such elementary antitheses. Modern writers, particularly those given to occult speculation, have a tendency to conceive hieroglyphs of this kind. In antiquity this would have been impossible: the evidence in current religious belief and practice would have been too confusing to have been so tidied. The temple of Vesta may have been circular, but so was the augural *templum*. The *templum minus* was rectangular, but the Pythagoreans, for instance, claimed Egyptian precedent for associating the square with Vesta herself, as well as with Rhea, Ceres, Venus and Juno,[28] and consequently with the earth. In the very centre of the *Aedes Vestae* there seems to have been a regularly formed trapezoidal (nearly square) sinking which went down to virgin soil.[29] The lowest level of its walls is

62. Villanovan bi-conic cinerary urn covered with a model roof *Villa Giulia, Rome*

63. House urn and bi-conic cinerary urn covered with a model roof *Villa Giulia, Rome*

64. Villanovan bi-conic cinerary urn; detail of lid

already built of rubble in grey-bluish *pozzolana* concrete of the kind usual in late republican times, so there is no archaeological information on an earlier temple. A great deal of speculation, not always entirely sensible, has been devoted to the possible functions of this opening.[30] However, like so many Roman cults, that of Vesta was partially secret,[31] and it is therefore difficult to draw much inference from evidence available about what actually went on in the little sanctuary. The Vestals were not only the guardians of the sacred flame, although that was their most conspicuous role. In their treasury or store, the *penus Vestae*, they guarded certain sacred objects associated with the city's origins,[32] as well as (inter alia) the *Fascinus Populi Romani*,[33] the phallus which was attached to the axle of the triumphing general's chariot. Vesta was, of course, present in the fire on every Roman hearth, and worshipped there. But the fire which burnt on the hearth of the circular temple on the edge of the Palatine represented the unique *Vesta Populi Romani Quiritum*.[34] When, for instance, the Vestal virgins were escaping the approaching Gauls, they carried this sacred fire with them in a vessel.[35] And ultimately it is this fire which descends from the one which the city's founder kindled at the foundation.[36] Ovid, who records the first thatched Vestal sanctuary built of osiers, suggests that it was originally part of the king's palace (he specifies the unshaven Numa), therefore implying that the public Vesta is the glorified Vesta of the royal hearth. However, the *Rex sacrorum* had no part to play in her worship. The male priest who presided over it, and was the only man allowed inside the *penus Vestae*, was the *Pontifex Maximus*.[37] Moreover, though it was separated from the shrine of Vesta only by a narrow street closed to traffic,[38] the Regia had its own splendid hearth, which was used in such

65. **House urn**
*Villa Giulia, Rome*

sacrifices as the October Horse, a ritual which had no direct connection with the cult of Vesta. On the other hand, there is no doubt that the hearth of the Regia was regarded as very holy and that it was very ancient, for the stones of which it was made had been relaid over the same place since early republican, times.[39]

The temple of Vesta was allegedly also very ancient. Ovid had spoken of that first thatched hut of osiers.[40] Two later temples were burnt, one by the Gauls of Brennus,[41] and again when, according to Livy, L. Caecilius Metellus rescued the *sacra* (the Trojan Palladium, to be precise) from the burning shrine.[42] It is generally assumed that both these temples were at least partially of wood, and from that time on of stone. Indeed, the existing ruin preserves a fairly accurate record from the first stone temple onwards.[43]

Although Ovid says that the cult was founded by Numa and the temple built by him,[44] other writers believed the religion of Vesta to have been founded by Romulus himself when he lit the fire on the first altar at the foundation of the city.[45] If not certainly the first, Vesta's was probably the last pagan temple at which public worship was offered in Rome. It was closed by order of Theodosius in A.D. 394.[46] Throughout its existence it was regarded by the Romans as one of the three guarantees, with the shrine of Jupiter Optimus Maximus on the Capitol and the shields of the Salii, of the identity and the survival of the city.[47] The hearth of any city had a claim to being considered its primary

66. **House urn** *from the Villa Coraletti Tomb, Grotaferrata Museo Pigorini*

67. A, B. **House urn**
*Museo Pigorini*

68. **Rome, Forum, Sepolcretto, Tomb GG.** Section
*By courtesy of Soprintendenza del Foro Romano e Palatino*

69. A reconstruction of a Palatine hut
*Model in the Antiquario Forense, Rome*

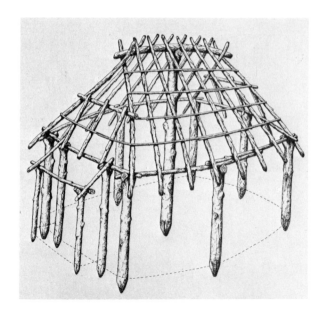

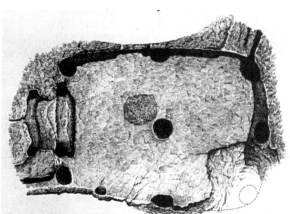

70. **Rome, Palatine. The rectangular hut belonging to the earlier** settlement. Survey of site and reconstruction of the structure
71. **A rectangular hut on the Palatine**
*Hypothetical reconstruction by A. Davico*

altar, the birthplace of its identity and the spring of its religious life. This view was shared by both Greeks and Romans. Hestia, the Greek goddess of the hearth, had much in common with Roman Vesta, and during imperial times there was even an Athenian priesthood which worshipped the Roman goddess as Ἑστία Ῥωμαίων (*Hestia Romaiōn*).[48] The names of both goddesses derived probably from some common Indo-European root. Perhaps it was *wes-*, to live in, to occupy, but more probably *əeu*, to burn.[49] Both names had the archaic ending *-ta*, *tia*.

Hestia was not a popular mythological figure: yet she had her other attributes, of course. The omphalos at Delphi was called her throne,[50] for as Hestia *koiné*, the Hestia of the community, she had an altar known as the *umbilicus*, the omphalos of the town. Hestia was often associated with Hermes,[51] who was known to be her friend, when the two deities

72. **The Palatine village** *Part of a reconstruction in the Antiquario Forense, Rome*

would be worshipped together in town centres, Hermes having a square shrine beside a round one of Hestia. The essential shrine of Hermes, the herm, was itself rectangular.[52] But in the context of the city religion, Hestia was more particularly the 'focus' of the internal space of the city, which the Greeks saw as feminine. Hestia was the 'home you start from', while Hermes was the protector of travellers and patron of the roads, concerned therefore primarily with external, masculine space.[53] Although Hestia's personality remained shadowy, she was a proper member of the Olympian family. The youngest sister of Zeus, she was the last of Kronos's children to be swallowed and the last to be disgorged: the youngest twice over, therefore.[54] Like Vesta, she remained a virgin, though wooed by Poseidon and Apollo and assaulted (comically, unsuccessfully) by Priapus.[55]

Vesta was even less defined as a person. There are no myths about her, only myths about her priestesses. Romulus and Remus, for instance, were sons of the Alban Vestal Ilia or Rhea; the founder of Praeneste, Caeculus, is born of the hearth.[56] The second founder of Rome, Servius Tullius, has a similar genealogy.[57] It has been inferred from all this that there was a structure of the 'vestal' myth in which the city founder was engendered by some anonymous divine begetter on a virgin priestess mother.[58] Although by historical times the two goddesses were worshipped in rather different religions, Hestia at the hearth of the *prytaneum* of most Greek cities (by male priests or widows or women who had renounced sexual relations) and Vesta by a college of virgin priestesses in a circular *aedes*, yet both goddesses had explicit earth connections.[59] In the narrow context of the *pomoerium* corner or bend as in the Roman Forum, moreover, the temple of Vesta seems in place. Tacitus starts the *pomoerium* at the *Ara Maxima Herculi*, draws it to the *Ara Consi* in the *Circus Maximus*, then turns it to the *Meta Sudans* (by the Colosseum), thence to the *sacrarium* of the *Lares Publici* on the *Forum*

*Romanum*, and, having presumably taken in the temple of Vesta, back to the bronze bull on the *Forum Boarium*.[60] It may, of course, be accidental if Tacitus, who had none of Livy's archaizing interests, chose to name in this list only shrines with chthonian and attendant phallic associations. The sense of the passage is altogether too casual, too accidental, to allow of such a definite interpretation. In any case, while the corner shrines were chthonian, Tacitus also records that round the primitive *pomoerium* still stood some of the terminal *cippi* which had been placed there at the foundation of the city.

*Boundary and Terminus*     The *cippi* are an utterly different kind of object from the shrines mentioned by Tacitus. They are also altars: they are also phallic. But they are not of the earth, not chthonian. On the contrary, they would seem to be in the province of the sky. The possession of land in general was in the particular province of sky-gods as far as both the Etruscans and the Romans were concerned.

According to the words of the nymph Vegoia, as they had been taken down by her amanuensis, the haruspex Arruntus (Aruns) Veltymno, 'Jupiter, knowing the avarice of men, ordered, when taking over the land of Etruria, that camps and fields should be set out with visible boundary stones and publicly acknowledged'.[61] The

73. **The Temple of Vesta on the Forum.** Survey of existing remains *According to Boni, 'Sacrario di Vesta', Rome, 1900*

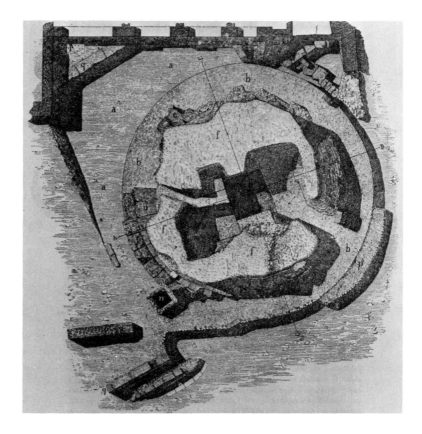

boundary stone has an evident relation to Jupiter, the *deus fidus*, the guardian of oaths and lord of the all-seeing sky. In fact the great temple of Jupiter Optimus Maximus on the Capitol contained a shrine of Terminus, the god of boundaries, who was offered public worship by the state, while private individuals worshipped him at the boundary stones of their fields.[62] Terminus, the grammarians claimed, had been there before Jupiter himself, but that is a matter outside my concerns here.[63] The hierophantic character of boundary stones, however, is not. Jupiter Terminus is worshipped in the form of a stone; the god Terminus himself resides in any boundary stone. In Greece there is no exactly parallel cult. Two forms of worship were, however, closely enough related to be equated with it in antiquity. The most obvious is that of Ζεῦς ὁροῖος (*Zeus horoios*), Zeus of the boundaries, who guarded the boundaries not only of privately owned land, but those between states as well.[64] All over Greece ὅροι (*horoi*) bounded public and private land. One of the early surviving boundary marks, found fairly recently on the Athenian *agora*, did not proclaim: 'This is the boundary of the *agora*' but '*I* am the boundary of the *agora*', ὅρος εἰμι τῆς ἀγόρας. (*horos eimi tes*

74. **The Atrium Vestae, the Aedes Vestae, the Regia and the Sanctuary of Juturna,** flooded, *c.* 1880, showing the outlines of the walls
*By courtesy of Soprintendenza del Foro Romano e Palatino*

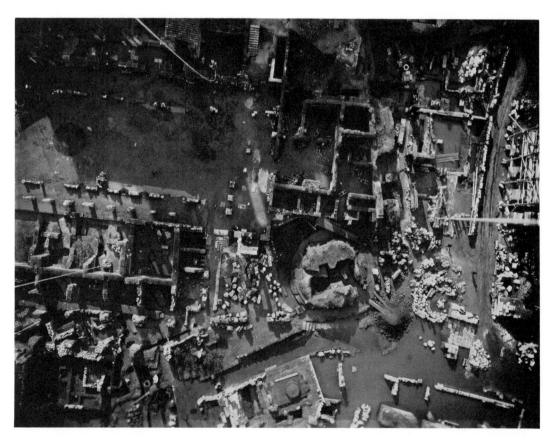

75. Reconstruction of the 'original'
Aedes Vestae and Regia
*After H. Müller-Karpe*

76. **Hut-urn from the Sepolcretto on the Forum in Rome.**
Terracotta, seventh century B.C.
*Antiquario Forense, Rome*

77. The Temple of Vesta, and the
image of the Emperor on **a denarius
of Vespasian.** *British Museum, London*

78. **The Temple of Vesta** in the Roman Forum. This relief, in marble, of the first century A.D., is usually taken to represent the temple after its restoration by Augustus. The oak tree may represent the Lucus Vestae, where Aius Locutius was heard. *Uffizi Gallery, Florence*

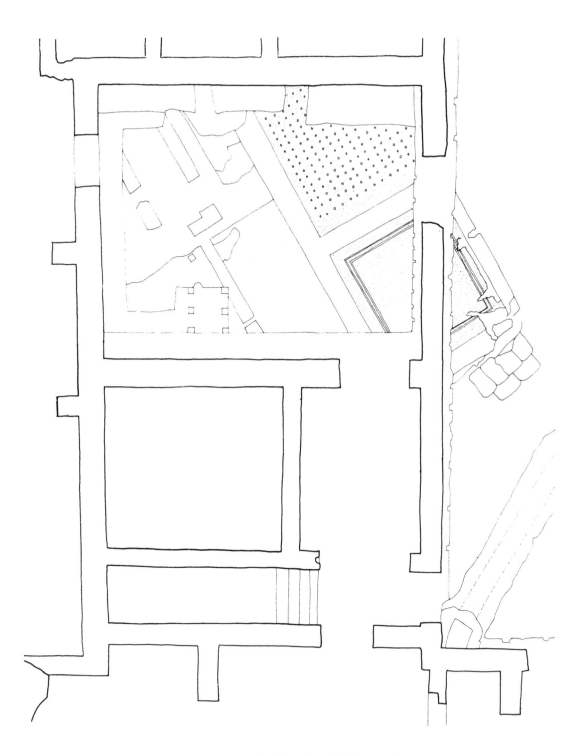

79. The north-west angle of the Atrium Vestae. Pavements of earlier, orientated buildings may be seen running at an angle and at a lower level than the wall of the Neronian Atrium

80, 81. **The Atrium Vestae**, north-west angle. Pavements of earlier, orientated buildings running at an angle under the walls of the Neronian Atrium

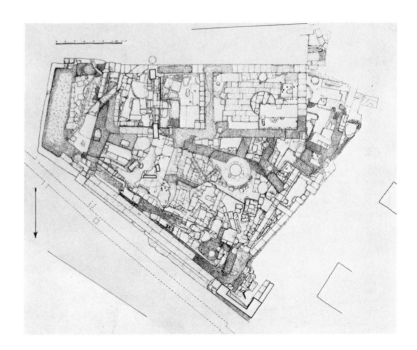

82. **The Regia.** The excavation survey as it was in November 1965. Only the most recent excavations, not fully surveyed at the time of writing, will modify the general picture revealed by this plan

*agorās*).[65] Though not unusual, this use of the first person relates the horos to another, more familiar form of sacred boundary keeper, the herm: a square stone, sometimes garnished with a head or male pudenda, or both. The male member was often erect: it was the destruction of several phalli on herms in the streets of Athens that put Alcibiades under suspicion of impiety endangering the state.[66]

The image goes back to an archaic period. Martin Nilsson remarks on the archaic character of the hairdressing which herms retain into the hellenistic period.[67] But the name of the god he derives, with K. O. Müller and Preller, from ἕρμαξ, ἑρμαῖον, ἑρμαῖος λόφος (*hermax, hermaion, hermaios lophos*), a heap of stones, with one stone erect in the middle or on top. Such heaps could be landmarks, boundary marks or tombs, and herms remained a familiar form of tombstone.[68]

The punishment for the unauthorized moving of boundary stones was most severe. 'Numa Pompilius decreed that whoever ploughed up a boundary stone would be/outlawed/cursed/, he and his oxen.'[69] Nor should this be understood simply as a protection of private property, since public as well as private property could be protected by terminal stones. Numa's decree, moreover, does not indicate whether the punished individual acted in his own or in some other (private) interest. It was, as most of the *leges sacratae*, a punishment for the infringement of the divinely ordered compact between sky, earth and man, the breech of which threatened the whole community. Again, the cosmic order of the division of land is echoed by the law protecting boundary stones, which tradition attributes to the remotest antiquity. Boundary stones are of course vulnerable, because boundaries are. Hence the dreadful curses which protect them, and which inevitably

83. **Aerial view of the Regia and the Aedes Vestae.** The circular hearth of the Regia is visible about the centre of the picture. Behind it is the Temple of Julius Caesar; in the background the Temple of Castor and Pollux and the Basilica Julia

get more severe as the general political and social guarantees decline. A great many inscribed boundary stones survive from the Kassite period in Babylonia, on which the actual land donation was recorded. In most cases the formula of donation or other transaction ended with a curse:

> Whenever in future times . . . one shall rise up . . . and . . . shall bring an action, or make a claim or cause a claim to be made, or shall send/another/and cause him to take or lay claim to, or seize it or shall say 'This field was not granted' or the boundary-stone of that field, through any wickedness shall cause a fool or a deaf man or one who does not understand, to destroy or shall change it, or break it up, or shall cause/someone/to burn it . . . or to throw it into water or in the dust or shall cause someone to hide it, may Anu, Enlil and Ea, the great gods in the anger of their hearts look upon him. . . . May all the gods, whose names are mentioned on this boundary stone destroy his name, and may they bring him to naught. . . .'[70]

This is only a fragment of a fulsome execration in which many deities

84. **Altar to an unknown god.** Rome, Palatine. Late republican. Inscribed: *Sei deo sei deivae sac(rum) C. Sestius. C. F. Calvinus pr(aetor) de senati sententia restituit*
The archaic nature of the shrine is indicated by the *restituit* of the inscription. Nibby, who first described it, and Mommsen in *C.I.L.* (I, 2, 801) following him, suggest that it is a shrine of Aius Locutius, the mysterious voice which announced the invasion of the Gauls; others have related it to the Lupercal, or even considered it one of the terms of the Romulan *pomoerium*
*Palatine Museum, Rome*

85. ꟿꟿꟿꟿ (munthuch) with another goddess attendant on a third personage. Detail of an Etruscan bronze mirror, third century B.C.

86. Hermaphrodite, boy with pan-pipe and term. Late antique bronze
*Louvre, Paris*

87. Hermaphrodite as term, second century A.D., marble
*National Museum, Stockholm*

were implored to strike the transgressor with their particular displeasure. The formula against the unwitting accessories to the removal or destruction of the stone is standard enough, although the terms of damnation vary a little from stone to stone. In practically all of them the top of the stone is carved with animals and emblems of clear ouranian denotation. Some commentators have attempted to read the complete zodiacal cycle from the *kudurru* images, but while many of the animals clearly represent constellations, these images do not state a system of such identifications, even if they may take it for granted.

There is not much to be deduced here from the Indo-European origin of the Kassite rulers or of the Semitic origin of their subjects.[71] The later Semitic rulers of Babylon continued to sanction *kudurru*, and the fact that no pre-Kassite boundary stone survived does not necessarily mean that there was no way of marking boundaries in pre-Kassite Babylon, or that this way had no divine sanction. Kassite rulers tended to emulate their non-Kassite predecessors in the matter of custom, rather than depart from precedent, and there is a great deal of evidence from the ancient world, as well as from various primitive societies, that the boundary stone was a cult-object. Boundary markers belong to a larger class of divinized stones whose peculiar character had a double

88. The Comitium during the
excavations of 1900. The *Lapis
Niger* is at the centre of the picture
*By courtesy of the Soprintendenza
del Foro Romano e Palatino*

implication. The placing of sacrificial remains beneath the stone (Sicculus Flaccus regrets the passing of this custom, but reports finds under older displaced *cippi*)[72] would seem, like their phallic character and their association with tombs, to indicate a chthonic implication which is echoed by the fact that the violator of boundaries is 'damned' to the infernal gods. On the other hand the alliance of Terminus with Jupiter and the association of the *cippus* with a *templum* often cut on it, would seem to imply an ouranian connotation. The truth is that the terminal *cippus*, like so many baetylic deities, belonged to both regions of the supernatural, and indeed formed a passage between them.[73] Hence the association of the chthonian and phallic shrines with terminal *cippi* is not as inapposite or as contrary as it might have seemed.

Sicculus Flaccus, the surveyor, describes in detail the neglected rite at the setting up of a terminus:

> The ancients (*antiquos*) when they were to draw up boundaries, would set the same stones upright on the solid ground near that place where a ditch had been made for the stone to be set up permanently/: and they would anoint it and crown it with bands

and wreaths. In the ditch then in which they were going to place it, they sacrificed, and when the victim had been set fire to with a torch, they poured blood into the ditch and threw incense and fruit into it, as well as beans and some wine which it is the custom to offer to Terminus. When the fire had consumed all the sacrifices they placed the stone over the still hot (*calentes*) relics and made it sure with the greatest care, reinforcing it roundabout with broken stones that it may stand more securely.[74]

Sicculus Flaccus's elaborate terminal sacrifice relates closely to another custom, the making of the *mundus*, described by Ovid:

> A ditch was dug down to the firm clay
> Fruits were thrown to the bottom,
> And earth from the neighbouring fields.
> The ditch was filled again and an altar put on it.
> And the new hearth
> Was decked with kindled fire.[75]

*Boundary and Centre:*
*Mundus and Terminus*

The digging of the ditch, the fruit, the earth, the double sacrifice, and the fire altar (no doubt in the form of a stone) over the ditch are the elements of the making of the *mundus* in this account, which is the most circumstantial. These elements suggest that the rituals of the making of a *mundus* at the town foundation were analogous to those of setting up a boundary stone. The analogy, and perhaps the tension, between centre and periphery is something to be considered later, after having examined in greater detail the ceremony in the middle.

The digging of the *mundus* was an essential part of the Etruscan rite.[76] In late antiquity Servius[77] suggested that every shrine to the chthonian deities is properly called *mundus*. This opinion is not given enough weight nowadays. Nevertheless it is true that *mundus* was applied to several different types of shrine much earlier, in particular, exclusive claims have been advanced for *Roma quadrata*, the enigmatic shrine which Festus described.[78] In another place, however, Festus describes a *mundus*, a shrine, of Ceres, without making any connection between the two holy places.[79] *Roma quadrata* has not been identified by archaeologists, though a search for it is more warrantable than the one for the generalized *mundus*, and, moreover, it was known to have existed as late as the third century A.D.[80] Its contents, to which Festus elusively and infuriatingly refers, have been variously assumed to be the staff of Romulus, *primitia*, or the bronze plough and the yoke used by Romulus in the original rite of foundation.[81] Whatever the shape, contents and meaning of this particular monument, it certainly appears to have had some connection with the rites of foundation, and to have stood somewhere near the edge of the Romulean city. Although *Roma quadrata* eludes the archaeologist, a shrine which corresponds sufficiently strikingly to its description by ancient writers was found on the *arx* of a Roman colony at Cosa (near Ansedonia), called *Cosa quadrata* by its excavators.[82] It consisted of two features. Firstly there is a levelled site about 12.5 m square, approximately orientated to within 12 degrees

89. The little sixteenth century **church of St. Joseph of the Carpenters** with its vault, and underneath them the two superimposed chambers of the carcer Tullianum, now dedicated to SS. Peter and Paul in memory of their imprisonment there

*The upper room* was an execution chamber for the prisoners who had been made to walk after a general's triumph along the Sacra Via. Jugurtha and Vercingetorix died there

*The lower chamber* is vaulted by corbelling blocks, and not as shown here. It contained a spring (*tullius*) after which the prison is named, and was once the well of the Capitoline enclosure

*The lowest chamber* is archaic and of uncertain date; *the upper chamber* is late republican. The Tullianum is another candidate for the title of *mundus*

*After Ch. Hülsen*

off true, and, secondly, just under 3.5 m inside the edge of the square, and on its axis, is a natural crevasse, about 1.8 m × 1.4 m and about 2–2.5 m deep. This crevasse was also found to be centred under the axis of the tricellar principal temple of Cosa, (which the excavators called Temple 'D') whose axis does not, however, correspond to that of the two shrines. The spot was, clearly, particularly venerable. 'The meagre evidence yielded by the crevasse', say the excavators, 'suggests that it was, at least upon one occasion, the receptacle of a mass of vegetable matter, which carbonized as it rotted. Given the religious context, it is to be presumed that this vegetable matter consisted of offerings deposited as part of a ritual act.'[83]

The nature of the square and its levelling in the rock imply that it never carried any substantial foundation. The excavators suggest a dry-wall platform, perhaps surrounded by a low wall. The curious orientation, related neither to the principal points of the compass, nor to the street plan, nor even to the later layout of the capitol, the excavators suggest was 'a function of a field of vision delimited by significant natural features of the immediate horizon.'[84] In view of all that I have already said about the Capitoline *auguraculum*, this interpretation would naturally seem the most obvious one, and, being less cautious than the scientific excavators, I would suggest further that the crevasse, which was to seem such a sacred spot to the later inhabitants of the town, was

90. **Aerial view of the Comitium** and the arch of Septimus Severus before excavation, *To the right,* the church of St. Hadrian, now restored as the Curia, and, *to the left,* St. Joseph of the Carpenters. The façade of St. Joseph's is correctly orientated, on the foundations of the outer wall of the Carcer Mamertinus. *By courtesy of Soprintendenza del Foro Romano e Palatino*

91. **The 'Lapis Niger'**, known as 'Tomb of Romulus', during excavation. Beyond, the Arch of Septimus Severus, and the basement of the Rostra. In the middle foreground, the base of the Decennals of the Tetrarchs

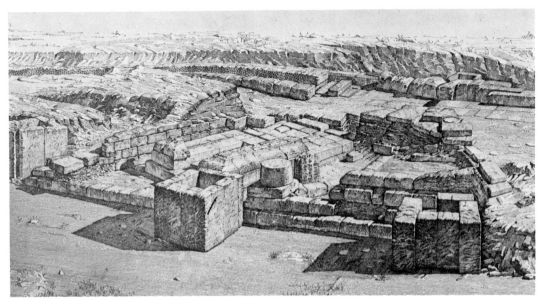

92. **The monuments under the 'Lapis Niger'**, as excavated in 1900
*Drawing by G. Cirilli*
*By courtesy of the Soprintendenza del Foro Romano e Palatino*

probably on or near the very place which the gods had indicated as the foundation spot of the town, equivalent to the place where Aeneas's pregnant sow had farrowed, or perhaps to the point on the Palatine from which Romulus had seen the vultures, or perhaps to both.

In any case, *Cosa quadrata*, and by analogy *Roma quadrata*, must have had some connection with the foundation rite. But interpreting the specific meaning of this particular antiquity is not so germane as the significance of the *mundus* in the context of the foundation rite. I have already pointed out that there were echoes of the *mundus* rite in the religion of Terminus.[85] The elements of the terminal rite have an extra element, a bloody sacrifice, which is lacking in the rite of the *mundus*, and which in turn is replaced by a sacrifice of earth, of which there is no mention in connection with Terminus. It is not a straightforward substitution. The Terminus offering, for instance, involved specifically wine and beans (the food of the dead), while the *mundus* sacrifice is more generically one of *fruges*. The sacrifice of earth is worth considering here, however. In antiquity it usually involved not just a handful of soil, but the turf on it.[86] It was the traditional offering of submission to a victor, even animals made it, according to Pliny.[87] Maybe the *fruges*, the fruit which Ovid mentions, is no more than the grass growing on the offered clod of earth. Even if this inference is unwarranted, the term *fruges* is too generic to be interpreted as 'first fruit'. There could not

93. **The 'Lapis Niger':**
(a) *The lower level*, showing the disposition of pre-republican monuments: (H) a bustrophedon *cippus*—the inscription has not been satisfactorily deciphered; (G) a circular *cippus* of unknown significance, of *c*. 500 B.C.; (A, B, D) a 'U' shaped base with a moulding, perhaps forming the wings of an altar; (C) a tufa block
   The whole appears to have been truncated at some date and covered with a Greek black marble pavement which appears in (b), *the upper level*, some time in the second–first century B.C. The earth between the ancient fragments and the pavement was filled with bones of sacrificial animals and votive figurines, suggesting a sacrifice expiating the desecration involved in the truncation of the older monument. The reorientation of the upper level of the monument made its sides parallel to those of the Curia Hostilia, where the Senate usually met
*After Ch. Hülsen*

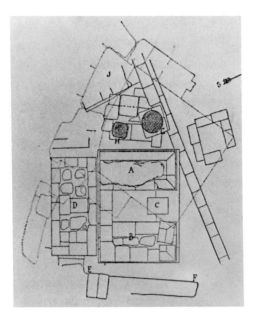
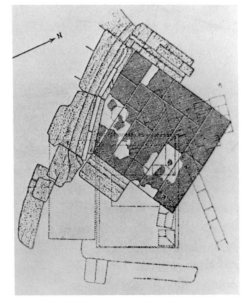

94. **Cosa. The Capitol,** with the Temple of Jupiter from the Via Sacra in Period I, 4

95. **Cosa, sections of the Capitol** during period I, 4.
A, through the axis of the minor temple, showing the façade of the temple of Jupiter
B. Through the axis of the temple of Jupiter, showing the impluvium between the porch and the cella.

96. **The Templum of the Earth**
*Codex Arcerianus, p. 41v.*

97. **Cosa. The crevasse in the rock** under the centre of the cella of the temple of Jupiter

98, **Cosa.** Ruins of the **Temple of Jupiter** on the Acropolis

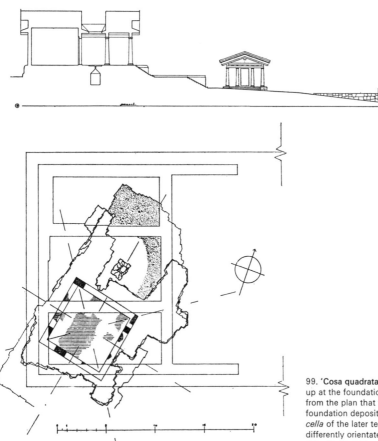

99. **'Cosa quadrata'. Plan of the platform,** presumably set up at the foundation of Cosa in 273 B.C. It is evident from the plan that the hole in the rock in which the foundation deposit was discovered lay in the axis of the *cella* of the later temple, even though this was quite differently orientated
*After Frank E. Brown 'Cosa', II*

have been any first fruit in the new city, in any case, for the territory on which the new city stood had no sort of ritual entity until the rites of foundation had been completed, and, unlike equivalent Indian rites, they do not appear to have lasted long enough for crops or fruit to be grown on the town site within the duration of the ceremonies. Though it would seem that 'fruit' of some kind is exactly what '*Cosa quadrata*' had contained.

To return to the clod of earth. There is evidence of a clod of earth being used in a court of law, when it stood for the whole field from which it was taken; the lore of this custom extends into both Greek and Roman divination,[88] and its 'natural' power was apparently sufficient to extend well into the middle ages, when land transactions were often ratified by the handing over of a clod of earth.[89] It has been suggested that the 'neighbouring land' from which earth was put into the *mundus* in the foundation rite was simply an act of taking possession of the neighbouring fields which provided the town with its agricultural hinterland. But this does not cohere with the other rites, nor is it quite enough to explain the importance of the *mundus*, whether singular or plural, to the city long after its foundation. Many years ago Fustel de Coulanges suggested a convincing interpretation. Each inhabitant of the new city, he says, threw into the *mundus* a piece of earth from his old home town. 'That is where their hearth had been; that is where their fathers lived and were buried. Now religion forbade the abandoning of a place where the hearth had been fixed and the deified ancestors rested. In order to be absolved from all impiety each of them had to make use of a fiction by taking with him, in the form of a clod of earth, the sacred ground in which his ancestors were buried, and to which their *manes* remained attached. No one could move without bringing his earth and ancestors with him. This rite had therefore to be carried out so that each new inhabitant might be able to say, showing the place he had adopted as his own: "This too is the soil of my fathers, *terra patrum, patria*; this is my fatherland, the *manes* of my fathers rest here".'[90] This interpretation has not been bettered, though it deals only with the meaning of the *mundus* in the context of foundation rites. This *mundus* seems a simple ditch, once dug and once filled in, not the vault opened three times a year which Festus mentioned,[91] and to which Virgil (if one of Servius's conjectures is correct) alluded.[92] In spite of speculation, little more is known about it than can be learned from the first author to describe it, Cato.[93] He wrote that, as far as he was able to ascertain, the *mundus* was a vaulted underground chamber, and as it looked like the sky, was called *mundus*, the universe. This etymology is quoted by Festus, though not with complete assent, and he may well have been aware of other derivations of the word. The *mundus* had, for instance, been assimilated to a circular domed basket, a *cista* which was a woman's *nécessaire*, also called mundus but derived from *mundere*, to clean, or tidy.[94] Another opinion derived it from *movere*, to move, as being a representation of the moving firmament.[95] Nowadays it is related to the shadowy, perhaps infernal deity, μυνθυ or μυνθυχ who appears in company with other Etruscan deities—particularly Turan, the Etruscan Venus and a consort, Atunis (Adonis).[96] Very little is known about this deity, or about her relation to the *mundus* of ritual. But it seems clear nevertheless that the word has an Etruscan origin, and that in Etruscan, as much as in Latin, it had a range of meaning almost exactly corresponding to the Greek *kosmos*,[97] except for its ritual implications. Unfortunately for those who wish to interpret the antiquity and meaning of the word, it was dangerous for the uninitiated to see inside the *mundus* and the initiate and priests of its cult presumably did not reveal anything of its mystery.[98]

It was guarded by the fear which surrounded it. The stone which covered it was the 'door of Orcus grisly grim'.[99] As for the thing itself, when it was opened, it was as if the very gate of the sad and infernal gods had opened.[100] It was not only dedicated to death and the dead, but also to Ceres, the great plebeian mother-goddess of Roman religion, although she may, in this context, have been a Romanized Demeter standing-in for the archaic goddess Tellus.[101] Sacrifices were offered to Ceres at the *mundus* periodically by a special priesthood.[102] It has been suggested that the *fruges* thrown into the *mundus* were seed grain, and that the original *mundus* of Ceres or Tellus was an archaic storehouse of seed grain, a primitive village institution which had gradually changed function until it assumed the form under which we met it in the accounts of Festus and Plutarch.[103]

The theme is difficult to interpret because the evidence is particularly vexed. To take the literary allusions first: there was a well-shaped shrine called *Roma quadrata* at least in one place: on the Palatine before the temple of Apollo. It contained objects connected with the foundation or the refoundation of the city.[104] There were also, almost certainly in Rome and in Capua, probably elsewhere, shrines called *mundus* which were dedicated (or were in enclosures dedicated) to Ceres.[105] Whether these were identical with the shrines which were opened three times a year on the *dies religiosi* I have mentioned we do not know. There were any number of underground shrines, practically all dedicated to the infernal gods, some, or most of which may also have been called *mundus*. When they were called that, they most probably consisted of two parts (chambers?), one above the other, and were entered from above.

Finally, *mundus* referred to the circular ditch, dug at the foundation rite—and as far as our sources are concerned, not opened again—which Plutarch, and he alone, says was a bothros called *mundus*. Although Plutarch is often unreliable, there is nothing in other authorities to whom we may appeal to contradict what he says.

There is, however, no particular reason to associate *Roma quadrata* with *mundus*, although both are clearly associated with the town foundation; and *mundus* on its own with the new harvest; and the dead. The connection suggested an explanation of the whole phenomenon to the nineteenth-century mythographer, J. J. Bachofen: 'The open *mundus* into which the founders threw the first of every variety of fruit and all other riches was the maternal *locus genitalis*, from which all blessings spring. Its opening was closely connected with the cereal egg and the funerary function of circus games. As the egg was a picture of the whole universe, so the telluric *mundus* became a representation of what the Pythagoreans were the first to call *cosmos*. As, moreover, the *pyxis* of Proserpine contained, according to the story of Psyche, anything which might be needed for the toilet of Aphrodite, so also the *mundus* becomes an object for the dressing table and the container of all those things which Aphrodite used to heighten her sex-appeal.'[106]

This is not an explanation to be taken quite literally perhaps; but certainly correct in that everything relating to the *mundus* seems to confirm its unequivocally feminine nature. The making of a *mundus* in the course of the foundation rites would surely emphasize—or so it seems to me—in anatomical detail the feminine nature of the urban complex, which was already implicit in other ceremonies and institutions. It is not entirely surprising, for instance, to find the making of the *mundus* confused or identified with the opening of the *sulcus primigenius*, the making of the *pomoerium*. The ploughing ceremony by which this was carried out was a hierogamy in which the *sulcus* became the female counterpart of the male plough. But *mundus* and *pomoerium* are quite distinct. The *mundus* is the hearth of the town and the *pomoerium* its threshold.

*Boundary of the Land and Boundary of the People*

The *mundus* is female: its deities are Vesta, Tellus, Ceres, the *manes* and *lares*. The *pomoerium* is in the tutelage of Deus Fidus, Mars, Terminus. The various rites connected with the protection of the boundary involve the sacrifice of *suovetaurilia*, of a pig, a sheep and a bull—usually sacrificed to Mars;[107] a sacrifice carried out most conspicuously every fifth year on the field of Mars outside the town, when the citizens were drawn up as an army, the sacrificial beasts were led round them, and then offered for the safety of the town.[108] More familiarly, it was carried out by every landowner in May, when he led the three beasts round his fields before sacrificing them.[109] A similar offering went round the town in procession during the *amburbium* of 2 February. In February, too, the *Luperci* 'beat' Romulus's 'bounds'.[110] And in March the Arval brothers sacrificed *suovetaurilia* at the edge of the Ager Romanus, the hinterland of Rome, and sang and danced their hymn, which is one of the oldest surviving Latin texts:

And, Marmar (Mars) do not strike ever more men,
Rage no more Mars, leap the threshold, stand and beat the ground;
*Ne veluere marmar sins incurrere in pleoris*[111]
*Satur fufere Mars limen sali sta berber;*

Finally, the various colleges of the Salian brothers, also worshippers of Mars, moved round the town twice a year, at the beginning and the closing of the war season.[112] We do not know exactly what route they took: it seems to have included the Comitium, the Capitol and the *Pons Sublicius*.[113] To the sound of drumming, they carried—or had carried for them—the *Ancilia*, sacred shields, one of which had fallen from heaven in the reign of Numa, and the others imitated after it by the mythical smith Mamurius Veturius.[114] All the year round these, and the spears of Mars (which were his aniconic representation) rested in the sanctuary of Mars, part of the Regia on the Forum.[115] They were the sacred tokens of the Roman state, and invoked, 'moved' in the case of an emergency, such as the beginning of a military campaign.[116] The Salii, for their dance, wore archaic dress and armour; peaked helmets, breastplates, blood-red cloaks and embroidered tunics (perhaps analogous to the toga of the triumphing general).[117] At set points they stopped and danced rhythmically, clashing swords or clubs on their shields in evident apotropaic fashion. They also sang a *carmen*, which was again of great antiquity and almost incomprehensible, even to the priests themselves.[118]

The days on which the ancilia were taken out of the Regia were observed, much as the days on which the *mundus* was opened, as *dies religiosi*.[119]

The *pomoerium* was male as the *mundus* was female; each was accompanied by a complementary feature of the opposite sex (so the Arval brothers danced in the sanctuary of Dea Dia for instance, and the fire-altar set up by the *mundus* seems to have had a phallic character), but the essential character of each feature was clearly enough defined. As for the *mundus*, I am convinced that the texts are correct in the aggregate, though they have not as yet been given support by archaeological finds.[120]

I take them to mean that sometime in the foundation rite a ditch was dug, probably a circular ditch, and that something was put into it to indicate its dual character of womb and tomb. Like the vaulted *mundus* of Ceres, it was both a passage to the underworld and the spring of fertility, and therefore the source of the town's existence, its *matrix*. And to underline its female character the sacrifice at it, like the sacrifice to Tellus and Ceres and the sacrifice to the *manes*, may have included the immolation of a pregnant sow, *trojanus porcus*.[121].

*Trojan Horse and Trojan Game*  In an attempt to explain the term *trojanus*, 'pregnant', Macrobius suggests rather lamely that the word is derived from *trojanus equus*: the Trojan horse pregnant with Greek warriors. This weird bit of etymology prompts a reconsideration of the Trojan game, the maze dance which was also a musical ride; and which I have described as being danced at the foundations of a town and round a tomb at a funeral.[122]

Virgil tells how after the dance and the sacrifices at the funerary games for Anchises:

> . . . with speckled pride
> A serpent from the tomb began to glide;
> His huge bulk on seven high volumes rolled;
> Blue was his breadth of back, but streaked with scaly gold . . .
> . . . Betwixt the rising altars and around
> The sacred monster sped along the ground;
> With harmless play amidst the bowls he passed
> His lolling tongue assayed the taste:
> Thus fed with holy food, the wondrous guest
> Within the hollow tomb retired to rest.[123]

100. **Cloaca Maxima**: its issue into the Tiber. The masonry, once considered part of the original construction, is now dated to the second century B.C., though of course the drainage channel is much earlier

101. The **Cloaca Maxima** from the modern Ponte Palatino, set in the embankment.

It is not, I hope, absurdly far-fetched to recognize in the seven coils of the serpent a reflection of the seven coils of the conventional labyrinth, and of the Trojan game. The resemblance is noticeable not only in the number of turns and the fact of coiling, but also in the function. Like the labyrinthine dance, the serpent also was ambivalent: death-dealing and regenerating. In many myths it appears as the frightening guardian of the essential mystery of the universe, of the tree of life; and therefore played in all sorts of apotropaic roles. But it also had another aspect: it slid in and out of the ground, and lived in the moist caves sacred to Gea and the nymphs; what is even more important, it could regenerate itself by casting its skin.[124] It was therefore an image of the earth's and of woman's fertility, a symbol of rebirth and particularly of the re-generated soul. Its mirroring of the labyrinthine dance was therefore functional as well as external. The labyrinth, as I have said, had also this double function—apotropaic and regenerative.

It was apotropaic in that it both contained the menace enclosed, and also excluded outside attack; regenerative in that the inwinding and outwinding of the cord which the dancers carried in some forms of the maze-dance, was assimilated to the umbilical cord and to the skin-shedding snake.[125] The dance wound in to a place of death which was also a source of riches and fertility, a place somewhat like the *mundus* in character. Did the Romans perform their 'Trojan game' round the *mundus* at the town foundation? In the absence of evidence, this must remain a conjecture.

I think that I have now gathered enough material from which to infer that like the *templum* the labyrinth was also a synthetic image of the town; and like the *templum* it both protected and regenerated. The elaborate articulation of these rites, the repetition of dances and sacrifices and mysteries—all were performed to this end: to constitute the town as an organic unit and more specifically as protective and regenerating.

*Mundus and Pomoerium*    Some scholars have gone so far as to identify the *mundus* itself as just another altar of Terminus.[126] But I think the identification is too simple. It would perhaps explain certain similarities in Ovid's account of village *Terminalia* and that of Romulus's setting up of the *mundus*; but the notion of *mundus* is too important on its own to be identified with the cult of Terminus—which was itself important enough in Roman religious practice—without any explicit evidence pointing that way. Again, there has been a tendency among some archaeologists[127] to treat the Etruscan provenance of the *pomoerium* with some scepticism. They are right, in so far as the evidence about the *pomoeria* of Etruscan towns is very scanty.[128] We do not really know how the Etruscans demarcated their *pomoeria*, nor at what distance from the actual walls we are to look for them. It may be therefore that such evidence as there is has not always been recognized. It has been suggested, however, that a vocabulary of the matter existed in Etruscan: the words *tular, tularu* seem to mean borderland; and the inscription on a boundary stone, a term at Perugia: *tezan teta tular* has been translated (though not reliably)

102. The Bothros at Agrigento

as meaning *auspicii urbani finis*, the boundary of city auspication.[129] The Umbrian word *tuder*, boundary, which is repeated several times in the Iguvine tables is derived from this Etruscan root.[130] In these bronze tablets of uncertain date (but probably second or third century B.C. if based on older documents or traditions) the boundary stones of the city play a most important part in the city's ritual and therefore in the religious life also.

Unfortunately, we do not know exactly how the earlier Etruscans and Italians demarcated their boundaries. Among the *hermaia* which have survived, for instance, and which were mostly terminal figures of one kind or another, there are a number of Etruscan ones.[131] They are unfortunately too late in date to be regarded as firm evidence of primitive belief, and in any case their actual provenance is rarely known. But there is a good deal of information about the *pomoerium* of Rome itself. Firstly there are the surviving *cippi* which guarded it;[132] then the various variants of the Romulus legend, all of which refer to it; and finally the records of extension of it made in republican and imperial times.[133] The persistence of the rite until the later days of the Empire is in a way another guarantee of its antiquity. Aulus Gellius, whose antiquarian information is always interesting and often reliable, explains that the privilege of extending the *pomoerium* of the city was reserved for those who had extended the limits of Roman rule.[134] Like Roman towns, Greek ones, though they were founded by very different rites, also had a strip of land associated with the walls, on which no building was allowed.[135] Many of the hellenic towns of the classical period only had vestigial walls, and therefore a surviving *abaton*, an inaccessible strip of land connected with the city boundary must have been an important part of the town's image to survive the atrophy of the town's defences. Greek literature is full of echoes of how a *kredemnon*, a magical veil of battlemented walls was established: as at Troy, as at Thebes and Athens.[136] And there are curious echoes, sometimes of how it was done: as when the Telmessian diviners told King Meles of Sardis

103. **The sacrifice of the Suovetaurilia** at the lustration of a military camp and army before a battle with the Dacians. Scene LIII from *Trajan's Column*. There are two further representations of Suovetaurilia on the column and two on that of Marcus Aurelius. The Emperor is represented as a priest as well as a military leader. *From Colonna Traiana . . . nuovamente disegnata et Intagliata da Pietro Santo Bartoli con l'espositione latina d'Alfonso Ciaccone, compendiata da Gio. Pietro Bellori. Rome, N.D. (c. 1675)*
(*This seventeenth century engraving is still preferable to the photographs of plaster cast commonly available*)

104. **The closing of a Lustrum.** A Flavian or Domitianic relief, fragmentary (perhaps one-half of a symmetrical composition, suggested by the two trees and the two altars) and partly restored *Louvre, Paris*

105. **The sacrifice of the Suovetaurilia**; on the Base of the Decennals of 303 A.D. on the Roman Forum

that he will make his city invincible if he carried the lion cub a concubine had born him round the city's wall.[137]

*Boundary, Strength and Fertility*
In Rome, though the sanctity of the *pomoerium* was regarded as an anachronism by the end of the republic, that part of the foundation ceremony by which it was established retained its importance;[138] the part which was performed by the founder himself, ritually dressed, using a curved bronze plough, with a white cow and ox harnessed to it.[139] These elements distinguish it clearly from the ouranian rite of limitation, which had set the city foursquare under the safeguard of the sky. The ploughing was a holy marriage by which earth and sky were united. In a sense, every time the ground was tilled, a hierogamy took place; the earth is the great mother whose fertility is increased by tilling and ploughing.[140] In the foundation rite this fertility was being assured in a figurative and emphatic way. The bronze plough provides the most important clue to its meaning. Since Neolithic times the plough had been a symbol, as well as an instrument of fertilization,[141] and it remained so in classical times. The Greek word ἄρουρα (*aroura*), for instance, meant both 'ploughed land' and 'childbearing woman', and so on. *Amo-aro* was a favourite juxtaposition of Latin poets. Further, the plough is a fertility symbol peculiar to the god of thunder and justice, the sky god as partner of mother earth.[142] That is why it appears in the sky—a part of the Great Bear constellation. In German mythology, thunder clouds take on the shape of ploughs with red-hot ploughshares; and among Germans, too, is found a form of judicial ordeal by stepping over a number of red-hot ploughshares.[143]

The Scythians had been sent four national relics by and from the sky: two of them were a plough and a yoke;[144] in various different contexts the ploughshare was assimilated to a bull's horn and the phallus.[145]

106. **The so-called Plough of Talamone,** a votive bronze plough. Second century B.C.
*After Studi Etruschi, II, pl. 45*
*Museo Archeologico, Florence*

107. Gold **solidus** of **Commodus** coined to commemorate his refoundation of Rome as Colonia Aeliana. *Obverse:* Commodus in his favourite fancy dress, as Hercules (*Aelius Aurelius Commodus Aug. Pius. Felix.*). *Reverse:* Hercules ploughing the pomoerium (*Herc. Rom. Conditori P.M. RP. XVIII/COS. VII PP.*)

And the originator of Etruscan discipline, Tages, had himself sprung from a fresh furrow (ἀπὸ τῆς γῆς (*apo tēs gēs*)), a scholiast noted[146] being a son of the earth and of Jupiter.[147]

As for the rule that the plough should be of bronze, this is hardly surprising. Bronze was associated with the worship of Jupiter, and more generally with archaic rituals. In particular, bronze ploughs have been found among Etruscan ex-votos.[148] As in the case of all rituals which strictly prescribe the use of bronze, it is fair to assume that we are dealing here with a rite which was already practised before the introduction of iron.[149] It may—like everything Etruscan—have been either native or imported; though its presence in such a rite suggests an origin in a plains culture, such as that of the *Terramaricoli* (who indeed seem to have used wooden ploughs)[150] rather than the hilltop Apennine culture settlements: though indeed both cultures were clearly agricultural. The plough may have been a wooden *ard* shod with a bronze shoe, or a proper bronze instrument, as is suggested by the Talamone model.

108. **Statuette of hero or divinity ploughing** with an archaic wooden plough to which two bulls (?) are yoked. Third century B.C. Bronze. Found at Arezzo
*Villa Giulia, Rome*

Ploughs were in universal use in Italy by 1200 B.C.[151] So its use in the rite cannot be considered as evidence about origins. It may well be that the rite of the *sulcus* and the *pomoerium* which it hallowed had taken form in the Bronze Age somewhere in the Po valley or in the Romagna.[152]

Whatever its origins, it became very important in the Iron Age. Classical writers were tempted to derive the word *urbs*, a city, from *urvum*, the curve of a ploughshare,[153] or *urvo*, I plough round;[154] also from *orbis*, a curved thing, a globe, the world.[155] Dionysius of Halicarnassus's remark that the plough described a rectangle is more of a layman's observation on what happened in his day than a comment on the true meaning of the rite.[156] The ploughing, we may take it, was independent ritually of the quadripartite division, and that is why the sources do not tell us where, in relation to the main roads, the founder started his ploughing. I cannot accept Dionysius's remark as evidence; and yet the opinions of ancient grammarians which contradict it cannot be taken literally either, though they are a strong indication of how the mind of the ancient writers worked: the word for city immediately provoked the association with ploughing.

In a sense, too, ploughing round the boundary served to define the town as a legal unit of territory. The most complete colonial law to have survived, that of Osuna in Spain (Colonia Genetiva Iulia s. Ursoniensis) forbids the burial or burning of any corpse within the town boundary, as it is defined by the plough: *intra fines oppidi . . . qua aratrum circumductum erit. . . .*[157] More important for my purpose, an ancient law forbade passing over walls on pain of death for sacrilege, mentioning in particular climbing over them with a ladder; and invoking the death of Remus.[158] This prohibition has been associated with the condemnation of anyone who violated a boundary by driving a plough over it.[159] Though this second rule deals with a ritual boundary, it is concerned primarily with the protection of private land in an agricultural community, while the safeguards of the walls and the *pomoerium* protect the well-being of the whole community directly.

John Lydus,[160] a Byzantine writer, concerned himself with another detail of the rite: 'Having harnessed a bullock and a heifer [Romulus] walked round the walls, keeping the male animal outside, towards the fields, and the female towards the town, so that its men be feared by outsiders and the women be fertile at home.' Modern commentators have dismissed Lydus's reasoning;[161] but, though he may have misjudged the details of the symbolism, he was correct in interpreting the rite as giving the town strength and fertility. Fertility was plainly one aim of the rite, and is in any case something which country people are always trying to insure by means of rituals and incantations and prayers. In fact, wherever sexual rites are found in an archaic setting, it is probably true to say that the more primitive the culture the more generalized their implications are, the more they are concerned with fertility, and the less with personal sexuality, the less 'genital'. Nor is it surprising to find such an agricultural rite in an urban setting; a large proportion of the urban population in antiquity was still engaged in agriculture. In particular, the Etruscans who 'urbanized' north Italy and bequeathed to the Romans their foundation rites were experts in irrigation and agriculture when the Latins were still all but nomadic shepherds. Other peoples had even more explicit references to fertility in their foundation rituals, which involved sowing. The Macedonians sowed barley in a line round the outline of the town.[162]

Indians still plough and sow on the site of a new building several times; under the altar of fire, four furrows are cut with a plough (the celebrant must never turn his back on the east while doing this, so the directions are elaborate) and while cutting each he repeats the ritual invitation to the 'cow of abundance' and to all that lives.[163] Before each phase of a more important temple building the ground has to be ploughed and sowed several times with different cereals (pulse, sesame, rice, kidney bean, etc.); some rituals recommend the grazing of cattle on the site before ploughing the plants in and ploughing again until the earth has become pure and even, 'as flat as a mirror', so that the site of the temple may assimilate much vital energy.[164] This ploughing and sowing, this packing of the earth with new energy before building on it, is quite understandable, if not what is nowadays called 'rational'.

One aliterate modern people has a radical prohibition which reflects on the purpose of this rite: they are forbidden to build their houses or villages on inferior or fallow soil because its hungriness will eat up the satiety of the inhabitants.[165] These same people associate standing stones with the protection of their houses and property, and also the protection of the living from the dead. It is a similar association of fertility and protection to that which is implicit in the rite of the *sulcus*.[166]

## The Boundary and the Gate

The safety, and the sacred, untouchable character of the walls was guaranteed by the union of heaven and earth. Anyone crossing over the place where earth and heaven were united was an enemy of the life which that union had guaranteed. Again, we are dealing with one of the great commonplaces of religious experience. 'He that entereth not by the door into the sheepfold, but climbeth up some other way, the same is a thief and a robber. But he that entereth in by the door, is the shepherd of the sheep. . . . I am the door, by me if any man enter in, he shall be saved, and shall go in and out, and find pasture.'[167] The act of entering through a gate is an act of covenant with those inside the walls through which the gate leads. Knowing this, it is not easy to take Plutarch's statement[168] quite literally. The Romans held their walls to be sacred—*sacra*, ἱερα (*hiera*) and not *sancta*, ἅγια (*hagia*) or taboo, as old-fashioned anthropologists would say,[169] but not the gates because, Plutarch added, through them corpses as well as other necessities had to be carried out.

Plutarch does not tell all; in this context he quotes Varro's opinion that walls were considered sacred so that citizens might fight the harder and defend them by suffering death. Varro's opinion was quoted, I take it, from a text now lost; in his treatise on the Latin language he seems to be saying something slightly different: 'This [Etruscan rite] was performed with a religious motive on the auspicious day, so that

109. **Aes Liberale, Rome.** *Obverse* : Janus. *Reverse* : a rostrum. *Museo Nazionale, Rome (63360)*

[towns] may be provided with a moat and a wall.' The furrowed earth was called 'moat' and the ridge (thrown up by the plough) was called 'wall'.[170] And of course this text makes quite explicit what I had suggested: the nature of the 'wall' which Remus had jumped. What this text implies is that the 'wall' which was sacrosanct was not so much the defence wall, but the ritual wall, the furrow marked out by terminal *cippi*. This ritual wall and its moat were probably at some small distance from the actual defence wall, if the town had one. For the two seem to have been quite independent features; towns founded by the Etruscan rite and provided with a ritual wall may have had fragmentary defence walls, or no defence walls at all,[171] while there were also walled towns founded by rites other than the Etruscans which may not have had a *pomoerium*. As for the width of the *pomoerium*, clearly it could not have been a line, as some have maintained: ritual, and indeed Roman surveying, does not recognize such Euclidian abstractions as a line.[172] The word implies a strip, 'within', not 'outside' the walls, since '*postliminum*' means within the boundaries, not 'outside' them;[173] but within the ritual furrow and ridge, not within the defence walls. Commenting on another surveying book, Agenius Urbicus observed that the pomoerium was a strip of land which ran round the outside of the city walls at a given distance from them, while in some cases there was another such strip inside them. This only means that the defence walls were built in the *pomoerium*, sometimes on its inner edge, and sometimes nearer the middle. It provides no clue either to the word or to the rite.[174]

The *pomoerium*, then, is a strip of land within the ritual 'wall' (the ploughed ridge), and on which the defence wall was to be built. Where gates were to pass through the wall, the plough was raised. The gates, as Plutarch saw, could not be sacrosanct—though they were not the purely civil institutions his text seems to imply. To begin with there were

110. Development of a **Hittite cylinder seal** from Adin, in Lydia. The central figure, double-headed, is also helmeted like certain Akkadian deities on cylinder seals. *Paris, Louvre, after Bossert*

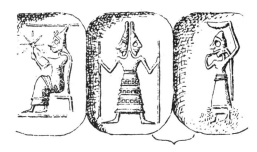

111. Section of eight-sided **Hittite seal** showing double-headed and helmeted figure. *Berlin, Vorasiatische Sammlung, after Bossert*

to be three of them, dedicated to the Etruscan triad: Jupiter, Juno and Minerva.[175] This number of gates is difficult to accommodate with the quadruple division of the town by *cardo* and *decumanus*; some historians have even suggested that the ploughing is independent of the rite of orientation and *templum*. But though their origins may have been different, it is easy to harmonize the two rites if one remembers that north was where the gods were, and that from there they looked down on the town.[176] So that naturally the *templum* end, the north end of the *cardo*, whatever may have actually happened in different towns, did not end in a *ritual* gate.

In addition to their particular protectors, the gates of Roman towns were all in the care of Janus. Despite Plutarch's assertion that they were not sacred, house doors were looked after by another god, Portunus; and the two deities seem to have been related in some way.[177] Now Janus was worshipped in one of the most ancient Roman temples, reputed by some to have been built even before the union between the Romans and Sabines.[178] It was in the form of a passage between two parallel walls, with arched gates at either end—the famous gates which were shut in peacetime and opened in war—all of which indicates that Plutarch's ideas about gates are only acceptable in a modified form. 'Holy (*sancta*) things they are,' the digests say, 'both gates and walls . . . they belong to holy laws.'[179] But Plutarch is right in so far as gates could obviously not be sacred in the sense in which the walls and the *pomoerium* were. The gates were bridges over a forbidden tract of earth charged with menacing power.

112. **The Temple of Janus,** a coin minted to commemorate one of the rare occasions when its gates had been shut. *Obverse:* the Temple of Janus. *Reverse:* Nero

113. **The Arch of Janus Quadrifrons** on the Forum Boarium in Rome. Through the arch is the Basilica of San Giorgio in Velabro and the Via San Teodoro, which skirts the Palatine, leading to the Roman Forum

116. **Cippi of Janus Quadrifrons** inserted into the balustrade of the Pons Fabricius, the one antique bridge which has remained in use in Rome.

114. **Seal** found at Kydonia, Crete. **Minoan** (c. 1700 B.C.). God or Hero between two lions.

115. **Ring-bezel, Mycenae,** c. 1500 B.C. Divinized column guarded by two lions.

*The Guardian of the Gate*    Naturally, to cross over such a bridge is in itself a religious act. The gates were a complex of elements: vault, imposts, hinges, panels, threshold, each separately in the charge of a deity.[180] Janus himself was chief of these: he was the gate personified. He was also the god of all beginnings and openings. As openings in boundaries and walls join two spaces inside and outside, so Janus had two faces. He was also good and bad, and so again two-faced.[181] As watcher of beginnings, and god of the gate-vault he was also called 'universe'. His name is Latin, but his function was more ancient than the Latin language, and rooted in the archaic ground of both Mediterranean and Indo-European mythology. Some scholars have identified Janus with Culsans, the Etruscan guardian of gates.[182] This is hazardous; the association of Culsans (and his partner Culsu, goddess of the underworld) with the Kulshesh, lion-headed and griffin-headed human figures which guarded the gates of the Hittite underworld[183] is even more so. Nor do we know enough about the Hittites' religion to decide whether any of their two-faced divine figures, such as the sword-god of Yazilikaya, belong to the Kulshesh.[184]

The more obvious identification with Ani, more obvious phonetically at any rate, seems to be sanctioned by the analogy between the place Ani occupies among the names of the gods engraved on the sixteen divisions of the skirt of the Piacenza liver, and the one Janus has in a rather different list: that of the gods who preside over the sixteen 'houses' of the divinatory horizon, and which Martianus Capella reports in his curious work 'on the marriage of Mercury and Philosophy'[185] written nearly a millennium after the liver had been made. There is much more to be said about Janus, however, than this simple

117. **Two crouching sphinxes,** facing each other (probably guardians on either side of a door). Painted terracotta plaques, black and brown on white ground. Found in a tomb in Caere. Archaic Etruscan. Sixth century B.C. *British Museum, London.*

118. **Oedipus and the Sphinx.**
Attic Cantharos, fifth century B.C.
*British Museum, London*

correspondence allows.[186] He is the god of beginnings: he is offered the first share of major sacrifices, and is also credited with having invented sacrificing, as well as kingship and many other divinatory, ritual and productive techniques; coinage, for instance. His double face appears on some of the first Roman coins. He is also the master of the first month of the official year, and its first feast, the *Agonium* or *dies agonalis*,[187] and probably as partner of Juno (which their names imply) he patronizes the ides of every new month.[188] He is the god of mornings and watcher of birth.

Sometimes he is presented as a king of the aborigines, or their principal god; also the eponymous founder of the Janiculum village. But the monstrous nature of the two-headed god who is old man and youth, keeper both of war and peace, benevolent senior deity and terror with the face of griffin or lion, assimilates him to the equally mysterious if—physically—less improbable androgyne; as well as to other monsters of classical mythology: to sphinxes and harpies, to the minotaur.[189] And yet later antiquarians consider him a sky-god, as they did some hermaphroditic deities.[190] His temple has a unique form: a passage, apparently vaulted, it therefore inevitably faced two ways, being a passage from one condition to another: as from outside to inside, from war to peace. The passage from war to peace recalls to mind the analogous function performed by the triumphal arch—a short barrel-vault, crowned by one or more statues; and perhaps even the original *Porta*

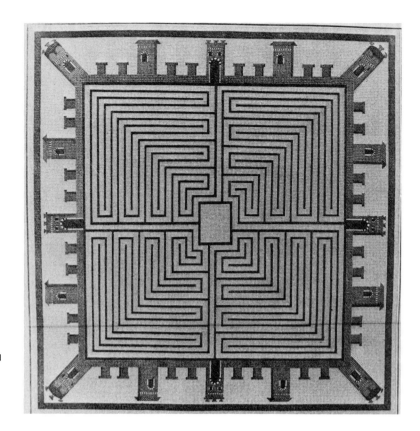

119. Roman floor-mosaic of late republican date showing a fortified labyrinth.
*After Gli Ornati delle Pareti ed i Pavimenti delle Stanze dell'Antica Pompei, incisi in Rame; Napoli, Stamperia Regale, 1796*

*Triumphalis*: it would have been used in this way whether part of the walls or not. The remains of another monument, the *Janus Quadrifrons* of the *Forum Boarium* suggests that such analogies were not altogether unfamiliar in antiquity.[191] However the ambiguity was 'realized' or conceived, its incarnation always had something of the monster about it.

Monsters and fabulous creatures frequently guarded gates: like those of the underworld, so those of earthly cities, towns and forts were protected by carved or sculptured creatures: lions or griffins, bulls, scorpion-men, bull-men and lion-men, lion-women. Lion-women, sometimes winged, are the form of the Egyptian as well as the Theban sphinx.[192]

Such an association is not quite as arbitrary as it may at first seem. I should like to stretch it still further, to invoke one of the most famous of all apotropaic images of antiquity, the relief over the lion-gate at Mycenae. The lions on either side of the column recall the iconography of many Mycenaean and some Minoan ring-bezels on which the column seems to be interchangeable with a tree or hero, and the animals may be griffins: and which may well also have had some apotropaic purpose.[193] Through Crete and through Thebes the motif derives from an immemorially ancient Asian ancestry. If the column-tree-hero may be separated from the guardian beasts (and they sometimes are in such images) it will be seen to play a part similar to some aspects of the complex 'personality' of Janus in Roman ritual and

120. Roman floor-mosaic of late republican or early Imperial date showing **a fret-maze** in projection *After Gli Ornati* . .

mythology: that of the deified and protective or menacing upright. This function associates him with kingship; and the sphinx is also, tantalizingly, associated with it. The sphinx, which has a human head but monstrous other parts, inverts the Janus relation of monstrous to normal. It has been suggested that the sphinx grew these appendages to its normal head, having first been human, and a sacrifice: a buried sacrifice under the threshold or doorpost.[194]

Such human sacrifices, and analogous ones under foundation stones have been examined so often that they need no more attention here.[195] The deified sacrifice, as I have suggested, sometimes became the permanent guardian at the gates, and in many archaic societies he—or she—had to be propitiated by the entering stranger. In the story of Oedipus and the sphinx, Oedipus is the type of such a stranger. If my argument is sound, then the monster sphinx was not abstraction drawn from some foreign pantheon, but the concrete guardian of the gates of Thebes, grown to fabulous proportions, and assimilated to some feature of Theban religious life.[196] Scholars have pointed out that the conflict between hero and monster, such as that between Oedipus and the guardian-sphinx, was not between creatures utterly different in nature, but on the contrary, of cognate beings, of relations almost.[197] The sphinx seems to have been related to the family of Laius in some way, was even said by some to have been Oedipus's sister. Later antiquarians at any rate had such legends.[198] Oedipus, before his death, bequeathed

121. **Theseus killing the Minotaur**: centre roundel of a kylix illustrating the deeds of Theseus. The labyrinth is represented in a meander-and-chessboard pattern round the scene and on the side of the building. The kylix is early fifth century B.C.
In a later kylix (by the painter Aison, late fifth century B.C., *Madrid Archaeological Museum*), the meander is reduced further, while the building is given a pediment. *British Museum, London* (3185)

his body to Theseus, so that it became one of the guardian relics of Athens.[199] His tomb—in spite of the secrecy he enjoined on Theseus—was shown on the Athenian Areopagus among other remains of the earliest past of the city.[200] So that Oedipus took over the functions of the sphinx, played a similar role to that of the monster he defeated. This polarity is perhaps endemic to all guardians, who have both to exclude the enemies and protect their own.

*The Riddle and the Maze*   Again I have touched on a commonplace of mythology and archaic religion: the riddle-setting monster at the gate.[201] But the monster did not always ask riddles. In some cases the approaching hero or soul (this particular monster is met most frequently in the course of the soul's journey to the underworld), whoever it was that wanted to pass the monster, had to find his way through a maze, or show his knowledge of

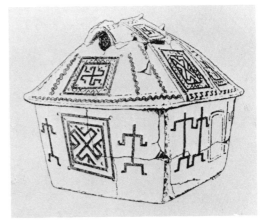

122. **Etruscan hut-urn** decorated with maze patterns found at Salciatello   *After Notizie Degli Scavi (1907)*

a maze-like pattern by drawing it.[202] Frequently, the purpose of initiation ceremonies is to provide the postulant with the knowledge of how to cope with such immediate if unfamiliar matters as the mysterious nature of the other sex and its negative characteristics through a symbolic device; but also, ultimately, how to solve the monster's riddle or draw the maze, and so be able to pass his terrifying questioner. This knowledge is the key of salvation. Often it consists of a statement in which man acknowledges his real nature—as it is in the story of Oedipus: which may indeed refer to some kind of initiation into kingship,[203] particularly into kingship by marriage with the reigning queen.

Mazes and riddles are some of the most ancient apotropaic tokens. Their purpose is to arrest and confuse the intruder faced with them, so that he is not able to go on until he has solved the riddle, or traced his way to the centre of the maze.[204] They appear on doors and walls, by openings, on urns—particularly on funerary ware—or woven into fabrics and so on.[205] By classical times the force of the image had decayed out of recognition.

Here and there its archaic function was recalled. It appeared heraldically, for instance, on the coins of the city of Knossos, or occasionally provided the hall of a Roman villa with a protective pattern. On the whole, though, it was only one floor pattern among others; but it also survived in children's games: *in pavimentis puerorumque ludis campestribus*.[206] So Pliny, recording, nostalgically, the great and important mazes of a half-forgotten past. The most famous of these, the house of the Minotaur in Knossos, has never been satisfactorily identified with any of the remains excavated in Crete.

The first textual description of it, in the *Iliad*, does not speak of that palace with high walls and wandering ways which Virgil knew.[207] Homer's labyrinth, χόρος, though he does not actually name it so, is a dance floor on the shield which Hephaestus made for Achilles, 'like the one that Daedalus designed in the broad city of Knossos for Ariadne of the bright curls.'[208] In a commentary on this passage Eustathius of Thessalonica says that Theseus had learned Ariadne's dance from

123A. Development of the upper register according to Mariani (1881)

123B. Development of the middle register according to Mariani

123C, D, E. Side, back and front views of the jug

# Ballenford Architectural Books
### 98 Scollard Street
### Toronto, Ontario  M5R 1G2
### Tel: (416) 960-0055

ORDER NO. _____ DATE __6-12__ 19__88__

SOLD TO __Goldie Rans__

ADDRESS __109 Victoria Street__

SHIP TO __London   N6A 2B1__

ADDRESS _____439-0808_____

| SHIPPING DATE | | VIA | TERMS<br>CHEQUE | BUYER | | SALESMAN<br>yL | |
|---|---|---|---|---|---|---|---|
| | 1 | Sites 20 | | | NN | 6 | 95 |
| | 1 | Rykwert, Idea of a Town | | | | 20 | 95 |
| | | | | | | 27 | 90 |
| | | | | | | | |
| | | | | | | | |
| | | Visa | | | | | |
| | | 4510 324 086 663 | | | | | |
| | | 06/90 | | | | | |
| | | | | | | | |
| | | | | | | | |
| | | | | | | | |
| | | | | | | | |
| | | | | | | | |
| | | | | | | | |
| | | | | | | | |
| | | | | | | | |

**27415**        SIGNATURE

BLUELINE D 22

Ballenford Architectural Books
98 Scollard Street
Toronto, Ontario M5R 1G2
Tel: (416) 960-0055

123F. The jug seen from the side, showing the maze

123B. Development of the middle register (continued)

123. **The Tragliatella Oinochoe.** Seventh century Etruscan jug found at Tragliatella, near Bracciano. The middle Register, reading from left to right on the developed drawing shows: A woman holding a circular object (mirror? fruit?), with some other objects (chairs? *cippi*? rocks?) on the ground; two coitions; a labyrinth of the usual 'Knossos' type, labelled *ⵍⵉ ⵎ ⵜ* (truia); two horsemen, whose shields bear birds, the second accompanied by a monkey (?); a completely nude man with a baton; seven soldiers who appear to be dancing (?), each armed with three javelins and a shield displaying the front quarters of a boar; a man in a loincloth, holding a round object inscribed ⟨ⵎⵉⵀⵣ ⵜⵀ'ⵎ (mithesathei); a child fully dressed, inscribed ⵍ ⵏⵍ ⵣⵠ ⵣ ⵣ'ⵎ (undeciphered); while a third personage, a woman, inscribed ⵣⵉⵄⵠⵏⵎⵍ'ⵎ (miamnucare) also holds out a round object

While these inscriptions have not been satisfactorily read, and the style of the grafitti is so rough as to leave a great deal of room for interpretation, it seems that certain elements which appear on it suggest a connection with the Trojan dance. The Knossos maze (much earlier here, incidentally, than on the coins shown earlier) labelled the boars and the birds on the shield, and the snake on the handle
*Coll. Titoni, Rome*

Daedalus (here Daedalus is primarily the mythical builder of the palace) and that he danced it to represent his entry into the labyrinth, the killing of the Minotaur and his escape. Eustathius goes on to say—this is about A.D. 1100—that he had actually known an old sailor who could dance it.[209] But Eustathius takes no interest, apparently, in the close connection between the maze and the dance.

Virgil's description of the labyrinth is a part of his account of the Troy game—*Trojae ludus*—which, as he records in the same passage, was danced by the young Trojans at the funeral games commemorating Anchises, and at the foundation of Alba Longa. This dance, later grammarians thought, was called the Trojan game because it had been brought from Troy. Playful *Volksetymologie*, modern scholars say.[210] The words 'play' and '*volk*' are losing the condescending ring they once had. The very connection of words 'Troy', 'maze', 'dance' in popular lore indicates a deep and strong association of ideas. In fact the connection between Troy and mazes is almost as old as the text in *Homer* I have just quoted, and has survived all over Europe as a name for turf and stone mazes.[211]

Its earliest recorded appearance, in such a context, is a *graffito* on a wine jug found in a tomb near Bracciano, just north of Rome,[212] probably of the end of the seventh century B.C. The principal ornament of this pot is a drawing of a procession, led by three unfamiliar personages. They are followed by seven young men who carry shields, each decorated with a boar. Then follow a man and a woman, and behind them two horsemen (one accompanied by an animal, perhaps a monkey) whose shields bear a bird. This procession is coming out of (or is associated with) a maze clearly labelled *Truia*. Beyond the maze are two copulating couples.

This *graffito* may refer to some form of the Trojan legend, even to some epic poem; more certainly it seems to show some kind of a happening like the Trojan game. Perhaps it may already refer to both.

*Maze, Dance, City*    Troy, Ilion, figured in the imagination of the ancients as an ambiguously foreign town (the Phrygians were not *altogether* barbarian) in which the succession of cataclysmic events which fate may reserve to any town were acted or suffered. Its mythical foundation by a divine hero and its re-founding by another hero; its growth, its pride, its wars, its destruction and disappearance. Troy incarnated the paradigm of urban fate. Hence the inevitable association of its epic story with pageants and rites. The Tragliatella *oinochoe* is rather earlier than—by current accounts—the appearance of the Trojan legend in mainland Italy, and more particularly the episodes connecting Ilion with Rome through Aeneas. Some authors have therefore tended to dismiss the *oinochoe* as offering no evidence of the early knowledge of the Trojan legend by the Etruscans, while others have maintained the contrary.[213] It seems to me that the *graffito* cannot offer, unsupported, any definite evidence either way. But it does indicate some relation between the name of the game or the rite, and the name of a town; or whatever of both the *lusus Troianus* first had. The word *truia* seems to describe something in which

124. **Coin of Knossos.** Fifth–
fourth century B.C. *Obverse:*
labyrinth pattern. *Reverse:*
Minotaur
*British Museum, London*

125. **Coin of Knossos.** Second–
first century B.C. *Obverse:* curved
labyrinth. *Reverse:* Apollo (Polchos,
whose name appears on this face,
was probably a mint official)
*British Museum, London*

126. **Coin of Knossos,** Second–
first century B.C. *Obverse:*
rectangular labyrinth. *Reverse:*
Poseidon (?)
*British Museum, London*

127. **Coin of Knossos.** First
century B.C. *Obverse:* rectangular
labyrinth, owl, olive branches.
*Reverse:* Athena (?)
*British Museum, London*

128. The numbers in this illustration show the sequence in which the lines are to be drawn

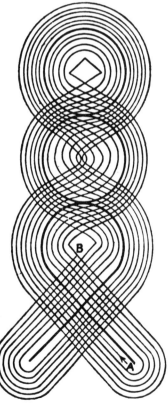

128, 129, 130. Some varieties of the **sand-drawings now made by natives of the New Hebridean Islands** (Molekula, Ambryn, Oba) as games of skill, but based on patterns of the 'way' drawn in the sand by the female devouring spirit of Molekulan eschatology
*After J. Layard, 'The Molekulan Journey of the Dead' in 'Spiritual Disciplines' Papers from the Eranos Yearbooks, New York and London, 1960*

the syllable *tro* was associated with a game, a rite, a dance, a circumambulation; with which the myth of Ilion, and the complex of Trojan legends, including the story of Aeneas's wanderings in Italy came to be associated by a kind of 'folk' metonymy.

However this fusion occurred, the *oinochoe* shows many elements we associate with Troy and the maze: the boars, for instance, remind one of *truia*, a sow, and the birds or perhaps the cranes Theseus and his companions had as their device when they danced the maze dance which Daedalus had taught them when they arrived on Apollo's island.[214] There are two ways out of the maze: by flying out as cranes might, or by having a clue to its windings, the clue with which Ariadne provided Theseus in the form of a red thread. The thread led Theseus to the core of the maze where he killed Minotaur, the son of Pasiphae and Minos, who was King of Crete, but also a judge in the underworld. Pasiphae herself was queen to Minos; but also a manifestation of the ancient Mediterranean moon-goddess.[215] After this peril Theseus returned to the world of the living by following the red thread of Ariadne, the umbilical cord of his rebirth. Ariadne, too, was no simple girl. The sister, or half-sister of the Minotaur,[216] she was identified with Aphrodite in Amathusa and at Delos. And at Delos where Theseus's exploits were danced ritually, the centre of the maze pattern of the dance was an altar built up of bulls' left horns, horns of death; this altar represented the Minotaur's lair.[217] The story of Theseus, Ariadne and the Minotaur was one mythical equivalent of the mystery of death and resurrection, analogous to the one celebrated at Eleusis, with which Theseus was also connected.

Mazes were principally channels of salvation, patterns of initiation; but they were also something humbler: devices for immuring in and exclusion. In this role they appeared on thresholds, doors, windows, and worn about the person; while on tombs they seem to have had the double function of securing the spirits of the dead in their resting places, and of excluding intruders, whether divine or human.[218] Maze dances had much the same function as maze patterns. That is why the *Trojae ludus* was performed in the course of the funerary games for Anchises, and at the foundation of Alba Longa. The meaning of the maze pattern and the maze dance is not reducible to a simple formula. One strand recurring in the story may lead me back to my central theme. Ariadne showed Theseus the way in and out of the maze by giving him a red thread to unwind as he went in and to wind up as he went out. For her pains she was abandoned—perhaps even killed—by Theseus on Naxos.

This abandonment of Ariadne recalls a much older legend: the journey of the Mesopotamian hero Gilgamesh into the maze-forest of the entrail-demon Humbaba (Assyrian form) or Hawawawa (Akkadian), his killing of the Demon, and later rejection of Ishtar, who had helped him in his quest.[219] Variants of this legend recur all over the eastern Mediterranean: all involve the betrayal by an incontinent or rapacious girl of her father's secret and stronghold; the girl is either killed or married (more usually the first) by the besieging hero.[220] The story of

131. **The punishment of Tarpeia.** Terracotta frieze of the Basilica Aemilia in the Forum Romanum. Late Republican (first century B.C.) *Antiquario Forense, Rome*

Rahab the Harlot[221] may perhaps be related to this type of legend.

She had let the Jewish spies down from the wall on a scarlet rope and she hung the same rope out of her window so that her house should be spared. There are other echoes of the legend of Ariadne in the story of Jericho: the conventional picture of the labyrinth has seven turns, which is the number of times the Jews marched solemnly round Jericho to make its walls fall down. Their marching seems to be the 'undoing' of a protective foundation rite, which presumably was also of the circumambulating type; it may even have been the deliberate 'unwinding' of a maze dance: inevitably an incontinent woman was accessory to it.

The most famous legend of this type is that of Tarpeia, who betrayed the Roman citadel on the Capitol to the Sabine king Titus Tatius either for love or money. She was a Vestal, and her corruption—whatever the means—involved a suggestion that she lost her ritual chastity. The Sabines despised her, and suffocated her under the weight of their gifts inside a cave in the rock which bore her name.[222] The myth was echoed in the execution of every Vestal who broke her vow of chastity: she was condemned to be buried alive in an underground chamber on the Campo Scelerato just inside the Porta Collatina and therefore inside the *pomoerium* of the city.[223]

Burial inside the city limits had been strictly forbidden by the law of the Twelve Tables.[224] But the burial alive of a Vestal had something of the nature of a sacrifice rather than of a simple burial. Sacrifices of human victims, by burying them alive, were sometimes practised by the Romans at times of great national panic—as in the crisis of the second Punic war.[225] But the burying alive of legendary maidens, in city foundations particularly, is frequent enough in peace time. In those cases the virginity of the girl, who became the city's tutelary deity, was associated with the city's safety.[226] Vesta was such a maiden goddess: she was both the earth and the city of Rome. The virginity of her priestesses was a guarantee of the safety of the city. Even when their virginity was broken, the greatest care was taken that their bodies should not suffer any damage in the course of their punishment.[227]

*The Guilty Founder*

Though even here there is an element of ambiguity: Romulus and Remus were themselves children of a guilty vestal, Rhea, or Rea (or Ilia) Sylvia and an unknown man, Mars according to some legends. Rhea Sylvia is sometimes associated with the Greek goddess Rhea, mother of the gods, and sometimes with other personages called Ilia, suggesting a connection with the Trojan descent of the Romans. She was often called daughter of Aeneas. In Ennius's version of the annals she trusts herself to her grandmother when her guilt is discovered '*Te nunc sancta precor Venus, te genetrix patris nostri/ut me de caelo visas cognata parumper. . . .*' ('You holy Venus now I pray, you our father's begetter, look down from heaven on me a while, my kinswoman').[228]

The more common version of Rhea Sylvia's parentage is given by Livy: that she was the daughter of the dethroned king of Alba Longa, Numitor, and was forced into Vestal virginity by her wicked uncle the usurper Amulius.[229] Whether her father was Numitor or Aeneas, hers is the earliest name of a Vestal to occur in legend, Tarpeia's the second. And both are Vestals of Alba Longa, not of Rome, and both are faithless, though in different ways.

The Alban cult of Vesta, with many other cults and priesthoods of the original Latin capital, survived the destruction of the town by Tullus Hostilius, and came to be settled to the north of the old Alba, at Bovillae.[230] There were Alban Vestals in office in late imperial times[231] almost as if the survival was a memento of some vow of Tullus, of an *evocatio* of the Alban gods.

The Laurentian cult of the goddess and her priesthood were even more important: since the belief was current in Rome that the '*sacra principia p(opuli) R(omani) Q(uiritum) nominisque Latini . . . apud Laurentis coluntur*'[232] (the sacred origins of the Roman people of the Quiriti and of the Latin race derive from the Laurentians)[233] and the Roman magistrates on taking and on laying down office (dictators, consuls, praetors are mentioned explicitly) sacrificed to Vesta and the Penates at Lavinium.[234] Both Rhea Sylvia and Tarpeia have been connected with archaic Italiot oracular practices.[235] But in these legends it is their faithlessness which they have in common.

Romulus and Remus appear in the legends almost as if they were transformed analogues of a series of eastern Mediterranean hero-founders who were exposed on water as babies: Moses, Sargon and Perseus[236] are obvious instances. Closer home there were other heroes, exposed and abandoned, sometimes suckled by animals.[237] To take an obvious instance, Miletos, was suckled by a she-wolf: son of a daughter of Minos and of Apollo, he became the eponymous founder of Miletus. In Etruria itself, the founder of Tarquinia, which some called the oldest

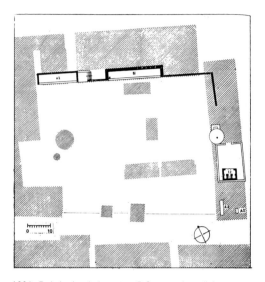

132A. Early in the sixth century B.C. a tumulus adjoins a sacred enclosure (?) on the West side of the forum

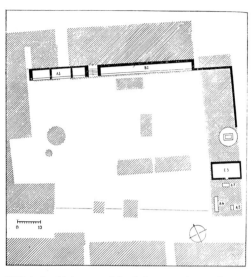

132B. In the third quarter of the sixth century the tumulus is replaced by a cenotaph tumulus, and the enclosure by a chamber

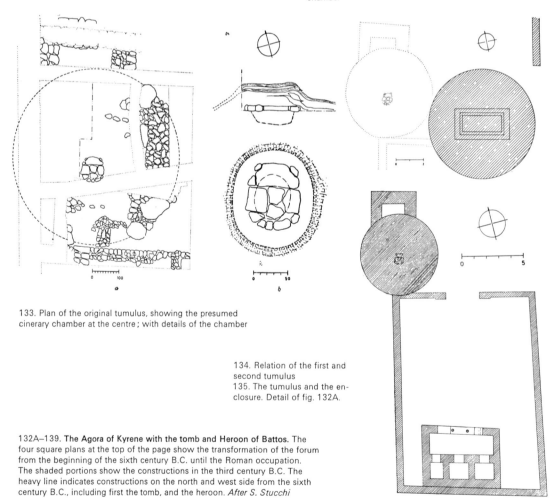

133. Plan of the original tumulus, showing the presumed cinerary chamber at the centre; with details of the chamber

134. Relation of the first and second tumulus
135. The tumulus and the enclosure. Detail of fig. 132A.

132A–139. **The Agora of Kyrene with the tomb and Heroon of Battos.** The four square plans at the top of the page show the transformation of the forum from the beginning of the sixth century B.C. until the Roman occupation. The shaded portions show the constructions in the third century B.C. The heavy line indicates constructions on the north and west side from the sixth century B.C., including first the tomb, and the heroon. *After S. Stucchi*

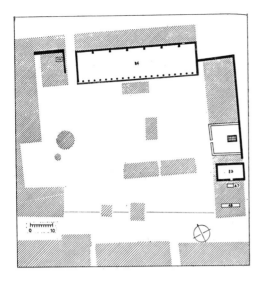

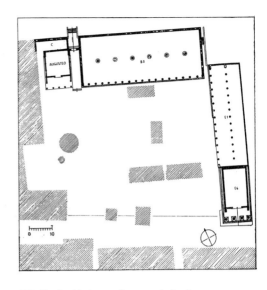

132C. In the fifth century the tumulus is replaced by an enclosed and visible heroon

132D. The Battide heroon disappears in the Roman Imperial town and is replaced by a temple of the Imperial cult.

136. Plan of the first buried Cenotaph. Dotted lines show Byzantine buildings

137. The cenotaph and the sacred enclosure towards the end of the sixth century B.C.

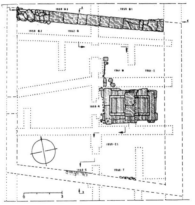

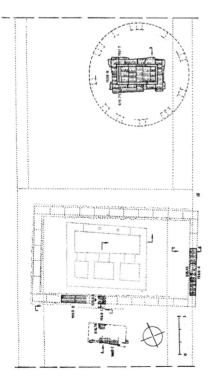

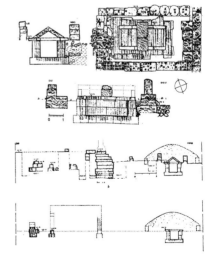

138. Plans, sections and elevations of the later cenotaph

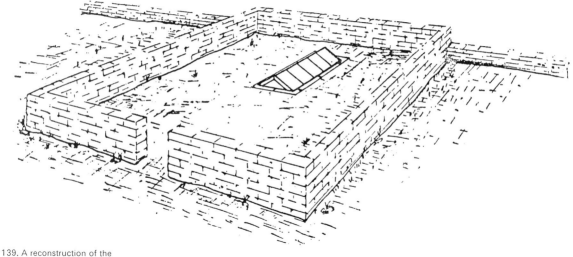

139. A reconstruction of the cenotaph, or box-heroon, as it may have appeared late in the sixth and early in the fifth century
*After S. Stucchi*

of the Etruscan towns, was it eponymous hero Tarchon, the son or father of Tyrrhenus, the eponymous hero of the whole Etruscan nation. In some—rather late—versions of the legend[238] it was his plough which turned up the divine child Tages, who gave the Etruscans their sacred lore. The father of Tyrrhenus and Tarquin, Telephus, is in one version of their legend shown as exposed and nourished by a doe.

The legend of Romulus and Remus only appears in literature with the first Roman annalists: but much earlier, sometime in the first half of the third century B.C. it already figures on Roman coins. The kind of relationship suggested by the legend of Romulus, Remus and their parentage is echoed by the legend of the paternity of Servius Tullius, the sixth king of Rome, the founder of the city's 'orders and divisions' and the builder of its walls;[239] its second founder in short. I referred to it briefly earlier; but here a fuller account of the legend must be given. His mother, Ocrisia is—if not exactly a Vestal—a 'lady at the hearth' where she, worshipping, sees a phallus-penis; in one version of the legend, as the slave of Tanaquil, she is told to put on the bridal veil and submit to the male member:[240] Servius is her miraculous child,[241] either by Vulcan or by some *Lar*. There is a closely parallel story of the birth of the aborigine founder of Praeneste (Palestrina), Caeculus, who was conceived by a slave girl of a spark from a hearth, and found abandoned, a baby, by some virgins seeking water; these recognized the divine nature of the child because of the fire burning by him; on a later occasion Caeculus proved his descent from Vulcan by calling fire down from heaven to surround them with a ring of flames.[242] These legends relate back to the legend of the paternity of Romulus and Remus which Plutarch repeats on the authority of Promathion, a Greek historian: that a wicked king of Alba saw a phallus or penis appear on his hearth; that it remained there a long time. An Etruscan oracle[243] told him that if the phallus were offered a virgin, she would

140. The 'buried' shrine at Paestum from S.–W.

141. The 'buried' shrine at Paestum from S.–E. showing the blocked 'entrance'

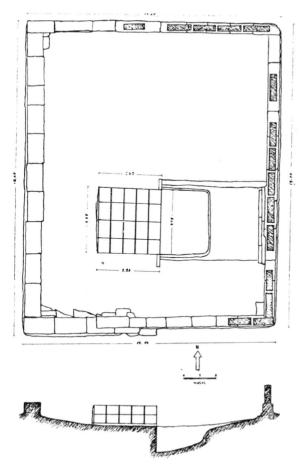

143. The central 'house' of the 'buried' shrine at Paestum showing the 'bed' in the middle and the amphorae against the walls
*After P. C. Sestieri*

142. Plan and section of the 'buried' sanctuary at Paestum
*After P. C. Sestieri*

144. Two of the amphorae from the buried shrine

give birth to a hero. Tarchetius (whose name may be a variant of the Roman rulers' names beginning Tarq-, Tarch-)[244] forced a daughter to mate with the disembodied phallus: she persuaded one of her slaves to do it in her place; the furious king then condemned the two women to death. Vesta persuaded him in a dream to commute to a sentence of imprisonment until they had woven certain cloths; but what they wove during the day he had undone at night. The slave girl was in due course delivered of twins, whom Tarchetius ordered to be destroyed (drowned). The man who was to do it carried them to the riverside, where a she-wolf suckled them, and birds brought them food. When they grew up, they overthrew Tarchetius.[245] In this version of the legend there are curious affinities to the myth of Caecalus, almost as if the two towns, Rome and Praeneste, had symmetrical foundation myths, divided in the way in which Claude Lévi-Strauss describes the symmetrical structuring of the myths of two Dakotan tribes, the Hidatsa and the Mandan. We do not have sufficient information about Praenestan ritual and mythology to allow of such comparative analysis.[246]

But clearly another symmetry is more important in this case. Promathion does not identify (or at least, does not 'personify') the hearth-phallus, nor is the father of Caeculus given a name. But both heroes' mothers are servant-virgins at the sacred or the royal hearth, even if not explicitly Vestals, and both are impregnated by the male principle inherent in it. The Vestals had, among the relics which they preserved in an inner shrine of their 'house', the *fascinus populi Romani*. The *fascinus* was a phallus, perhaps a wooden or bone one, perhaps (though less likely) a metal one. It would be suspended from the back or from the axle of the triumphing general's chariot, to protect him from the envy of onlookers.[247] It may have been the very object kept by the Vestal virgins among the relics of the state, and worshipped by them—in Pliny's phrase—as a god; or a replica of it. But this kind of phallus was a common image; it protected street corners and was familiarly worn by children, (particularly boys) to ward off the evil (particularly the envious) eye.[248] Such objects (Varro's *turpicula res*) are the original of those coral stem amulets worn as pendants or held as rattles by so many children in Mediterranean countries.

The disembodied phallus of the legend, however, has not merely an apotropaic, it has a creative power. Roman matrons worshipped, veiled, an ithyphallic deity Mutunus Tutunus, in his shrine on the Palatine[249] and phalli or ithyphallic statues were used (as the church fathers often scathingly say)[250] in Roman wedding ceremonies. The reference in the Promathean legend is to a male power inherent in the hearth, or closely associated with it, as might by the *fascinus* of the Vestal virgins. The anonymous Alban princess substitutes her servant in a coition to which perhaps the wedding practices also refer. There is here almost a suggestion of a hierogamy. It has recently been suggested that when Heliogabalus married the Vestal Julia Aquilia Severa, he may not only have the conversion of Roman custom to Syrian in mind, but also some antiquarian evocation of such hierogamies preserved in myth and recalled in rituals which promised the birth of a divine child.[251]

The unfaithful, the incestuous Vestal who suffers punishment has the 'divine' Rhea Sylvia as her prototype. Hers is the one type of Vestal corruption. The other is typified by Tarpeia and echoed by that of Ariadne and also, paradoxically, of Rahab the Harlot (who was mentioned earlier). Rahab has been the subject of much speculation on the part of Rabbinic and scriptural commentators. She herself is said to have married Joshua and mothered, through Boaz, a race of kings and prophets; even Our Lord. Her dwelling, built on to the wall of Jericho, suggests a secret entrance into a guarded place; the red thread hanging from it as a sign of her exemption from the dreadful fate of her co-citizens (whose sevenfold protection was unmade by the circumambulations of the Arc) recalls the red thread which showed Theseus the way out of the sevenfold twists of the Minotaur's maze. Like Ariadne, like so many other Greek and Roman heroines (to whom I have referred), she betrays her own people to cleave to the foreign leader. The Patristic commentators saw the red thread as a mark of the salvation by blood.[252]

In the genealogy of Our Lord which St. Matthew puts at the opening of his gospel, Rahab marries a Judean, Salmon, and becomes the mother or the ancestress of Boaz. However the passage is coloured or speculated upon, homiletic writers inevitably compare her case with that of Tarpeia, who betrayed her people not for salvation or through faith in a yet unknown God, but for gold. There are further parallels, echoing the theme of treason for gold (Gullveig in strophes 21–4 of the Volüspa) or for pleasures of the senses (Sukanya in III Mahabharata, 123).[253] These two instances from Indo-European epics show corruption threatening the powerful magic of the divine king. But the corruption of the maiden is associated with a hierogamy, and behind them inevitably looms the shadowy figure of the queen-harlot, whose holy intercourse with the alien here confers kingship on him.

The structures of this relationship are various. In Rome the ritual seems remote, but even in Rome through the virgin at the sacred hearth and her guilty or substitute intercourse with god or hero, as well as its punishment, a new city, a new alliance, a new nation, a new state are founded.

Hence Tarpeia's ambiguous place in Roman history and ritual. She was the traitress of legend; but also the recipient of a yearly libation. According to Mommsen,[254] this sacrifice was very important, as it opened the *dies parentales*, a nine-day festival in honour of ancestors. The *parentatio* to Tarpeia was a state sacrifice, carried out on 13 February at her reputed tomb by a Vestal virgin: there is no reason to question Philolaus's calendar wording: *virgo Vestalis parentat.*[255] Acca Laurentia was worshipped by a *parentatio* carried out at her tomb by the Flamen Quirinalis and the Pontifices.[256] So Acca, the foster-mother of dubious reputation, was associated ritually with Tarpeia, the patroness of the Capitoline rock: a Sabine form, some scholars have thought, of the Tarch-, Tarq- suffix to which I referred earlier.[257] As the harlot and the false vestal are associated in rite, so the harlot is associated with another false vestal in myth, since she is the foster-mother of Rhea Sylvia's children, and forms with her the kind of hero-mother couples which Caeculus and Servius Tullius also seemed to have.

Acca (Wissowa had surmised), was—among other figures— associated with another Sabine figure, the goddess Larunda, whose worship Titus Tatius had—according to Ausonius[258]—brought to Rome; in Ovid's Fasti[259] a sad story is related of her, which also sends her into the underworld, and makes her mother of the twin *Lares*. The divine tomb both in the case of Tarpeia and of Acca received the type of sacrifice to the dead which suggests that they were not tombs in the ordinary sense of the word, but shrines with a sacrificial pit like the Greek βόθροι (*bothroi*): something like the *mundus* in fact.

Some scholars have recently suggested that the word cannot be applied, for instance, to the ritual 'tombs' of legendary figures: Romulus, Acca Laurentia, Tarpeia. The tombs of Acca Laurentia and Tarpeia have not been identified; but the 'tomb of Romulus' on the Comitium has been thoroughly explored; it contained, among other things, an inscribed *cippus* of great antiquity, and which was certainly mutilated in the republican era;[260] a moulded base, roughly square on plan, now much mutilated, which probably carried two lions; various other archaic objects, ex votos, a puteal and a foundation deposit of— presumably—sacrificial animals, which surprisingly enough included the bones of one or more vultures.[261] It is this place, which Festus first called the black, dire stone, a place *funestum*, and which Dionysius of Halicarnassus calls the tomb of Faustulus (Romulus's foster-father, reputed to have fallen there while fighting the Sabines) or of Hostilius.[262] Horace and his scholiasts seem to imply that it was the tomb of the founder himself,[263] while Plutarch suggests that this mournful black spot was the original *mundus* of the first foundation.[264]

Near it stood a number of remarkable monuments of the earliest life of the city: the fig-tree under which the founding twins had been abandoned on the Palatine, moved there by a miracle-working augur;[265] and a bronze statue of the she-wolf, analogous to the one which still survives on the Palatine.[266]

Though the tradition about the Palatine foundation is explicit, it may well be that in Plutarch's day the black stone was known to cover holy and frightening things, and that it was sometimes referred to as *mundus*. As for the mundus on the Palatine, several candidate cisterns have been put forward for that title by various archeologists.[267]

The defensive character of the *mundus*, the protective nature of the whole female body-image in the town's configuration, must now have become evident. But they relate to other female elements in the town's make-up, the *mundus* as *locus genitalis*, as the source of the town's life. But the whole town is often represented as a female being, the town's *tyche*, wearing a mural crown.[268] Moreover the town was protected by the lady of the hearth and her intact priestesses; and all these had some relation again to the town's secret protectress—or protector.

The divine protector or protectress was a part of an elaborate metaphysical defensive apparatus. Some defences were physical: the earthworks and the ditches. Others, such as the formulae and the rites and the apotropaic monuments had a magical function. But all these protective aids, whether physical or magical, were always part of a bigger unity: and the unity was a social and religious (not a magical) phenomenon. Its aim was not just to conserve, but to nourish and to fortify. Even the magical *apotropos* was a function of the greater whole, of the town as a machine for thinking with, as an instrument for understanding the world and the human predicament in it.

Five  **The Parallels**

What is true of the ancient city might more generally be applied to the 'traditional' city (I use the word in Guénon's sense). But I wish to insist on the grandeur and the quickening complexity of the particular Etrusco-Roman example. And to comment on it adequately I need to set it beside instances, sometimes puzzling, of parallel rites, customs, monuments: an exalted Indian one, an epic African one, and an earthbound Amerindian one.

The Indian parallel is the constitution of the *mandala*.

*Mandala*  The meaning of this word has been obscured with its recent use by psychologists as a quasi-technical term. Originally it meant 'circle' in Sanskrit: and included the idea of 'centre' and 'circumference'. In Indian and Tibetan ritual, and particularly in the parlance of yoga, it came to signify a complex design of one or several concentric circles, in which a square is inscribed; the square is divided by its diagonals into four triangles.[1] There are many variations on this basic scheme, and they are usually covered with a whole iconographic system of symbolic figures, plants, animals. Like the *templum* and like the labyrinth it was a cosmography, a diagram of universal order. So the yogi uses it to focus his attention: first to identify parts of his own body with different parts of the diagram, and through this identification to integrate himself into the order of the universe, and so become 'deified'. But like the maze, a painted *mandala* may be simply apotropaic and be displayed in or painted on the outside of buildings to protect them from all evil influences. In that sense its drawing above seems to have an analogous apotropaic and therapeutic function to the repeated recitations of 'creation epics': such as the Babylonian *Enuma Eliš*.

The *mandala* is also drawn ceremonially on a piece of flat ground when a guru wishes to initiate a disciple: then the *mandala* becomes the image of a paradisal state, and entry into it—all this seems to be an echo of the story of Oedipus and Theseus—is guarded by four demons, set at each of the four gates of the *mandala*. In the course of his initiation the probationer has to undergo a number of trials, until he reaches the centre of the *mandala*, which is identified with the centre of the world.[2]

One of the essential rites at the founding of an Indian temple is the drawing of a *vástupurusamandala*.[3] This is a square whose sides may be divided by any number from 1 to 32 (giving between 1 and 1,024 units) which are further apportioned in various combinations to a number of deities.[4] The word itself consists of three parts: on the last, *mandala*, I have already commented; *Vástu* may be taken as the whole extent of ordered being, or more mundanely, as the site of the building;[5] *Purusa* is cosmic man, the origin of existence, and at the same time, manifestation of what is beyond being. The word may also be taken in its coarser meaning: spirit, man.[6] It would be useless therefore to give a single translation of the word which can mean, on the one hand some-

145. **Mandala of Amogha-Pasa.** Nepalese. Dated 1504. *British Museum, London*

PĀPARĀKṢASĪ    PILIPIÑJĀ    CARAKĪ

| ROGA | AHI | MUKHYA | BHALLĀTA | SOMA | BHUJAGA | ADITI | DITI | AGNI |
|---|---|---|---|---|---|---|---|---|
| PĀPA-YAKSMAN | RUDRA | | | | | | ĀPA | PARJANYA |
| ŚOṢA | | RĀJA-YAKSMAN | PRTHIVĪDHARA | | | ĀPA-VATSA | | JAYANTA |
| ASURA | | M | | | | A | | INDRA |
| VARUNA | | R | BRAHMĀ | | | Y | | SŪRYA |
| KUSUMA-DANTA | | A | | | | N | | SATYA |
| SUGRĪVA | | INDRA | VIVASVĀN | | | SAVITR | | BHRŚA |
| DAU-VĀRIKA | JAYĀ | | | | | | SĀVITRA | ANTAR-IKṢA |
| PITARAH | MRGA | BHRNGA-RĀJA | GAN-DHARVA | YAMA | BRHAT-KṢATA | VITATHA | PŪSAN | ANILA |

JAMBHAKA (left)    SARVA-SKANDA (right)

PŪTANA    ARYAMAN    VIDĀRI

146. The Vástupuruśamandala according to the *Brhatsamhita*, LII, 43 f. *After Kramrish, 'The Hindu Temple', I, p. 32*

thing like 'a diagram of cosmic man, summing up the whole of ordered being and so manifesting what is beyond being; and on the other, simply: the *mandala* of the spirit of the ground-plan, or even of the site. But all this remains a bald and dry reduction of a very rich notion'.[7] In the course of a foundation rite of a temple, this diagram is drawn ceremonially and elaborately on the ground; it is decorated with flowers, lights, incense. In such a context it becomes a programme for the building, a metaphorical plan and a prophecy of what is going to be built on the site.

The square form is not an imitation of the form of the earth, but a symbol of it: the earth is round in Indian cosmology. The square form then, 'does not refer to the outline of the earth. It connects the four points established by the primary pairs of opposites'—north, south, east and west—sunset and sunrise, and the two ends of the world axis. 'The earth is therefore called *caturbursti*, four-cornered.'[8] What is more, the method of setting up the ceremonial square always presupposed a circle; it was always constructed by drawing intersecting circles with cords fixed on poles.[9]

The diagram functions inward from the edge of the nine central squares consecrated to Brahma. The primitive *vástupurusamandala* was a much simpler affair, an enclosure round the Vedic fire-altar. All the same, the making of a fire-altar was a capital ceremony of Vedic religion. The ceremony begins with the cutting of four furrows, which make a square. The centres of the sides and the angles are then joined by four more furrows. At the crossing of the inner furrows the officiating brahmin sets a tuft of grass. And there, too, he makes a complicated series of sacrifices before the fire-altar may be built.[10]

The *Satapatha Brahmana* may well have been composed at a period contemporary with the rule of the kings in Rome. There are many other rules relating to building interspersed in the Brahmanas. But the specific skill of architects, the *śilpa*, was codified in *śastras*, in treatises which claim to go back to the architect of the Dewas, Viśvakarma—in one case, to the equivalent master working for the other spirits, the Asuras, Maya. There were many other canonical or quasi-canonical books which dealt in great detail with rituals of building and the proportions of buildings as well as of statues, mostly composed in the Gupta period.[11] The directions, in spite of their prolixity, are never complete, but always refer the reader to oral tradition and local custom, both in the matter of craftsmanship, and of ritual.[12] But the ritual examination of the site, the ploughing ceremonial are always described, as are the required subjects for meditation, while carrying them out: the colouring and the ornaments of the two oxen are discussed in detail by the Manasara, for instance. It goes on: 'The wise architect should meditate on the two oxen as the sun and the moon, on the plough as the boar-god (Viṣnu) and on the builder as Brahma. . . .'[13]

The analogy to the Etruscan rite is clear. It is reinforced by the further steps: the establishing of the north by the use of a *gnomon*, the ritual setting up of the pegs for rectilineal construction, the drawing of the *mandala*.[14] These rituals were not only prescribed for altars and temples, but for cities on the one hand and for private houses on the other.[15]

It would be easy at this point to conclude that Roman and Indian usage—as well as perhaps Etruscan—derive from some common Indo-European heritage. Certainly, the earliest documents relating to limitation and orientation rituals are post-Vedic, inevitably. Nevertheless, wheat and barley were cultivated on artificially irrigated and ploughed land in India long before the arrival of the Vedic invaders, and orientation was practised there on a vast scale. I do not think anyone would maintain that these practices were not carried out ritually in 'Harappan' India: it would go contrary to evidence from all other civilizations and pre-Vedic India seems to have been something of a clerisy. While the rituals which we know as Indian are definitely part of the Hindu tradition, therefore, there is no evidence about whether they did or did not have any connection with earlier practices.

In Hindu tradition, however, the complexity of the foundation rite was carried into the actual occupation of the town. The *vástupurusa-mandala*, which varied in attributing different quarters and 'houses' to different gods, was the basis of the use and caste zoning of the town or village. But even in the description of the fire-altar ritual, as it is set down in the *Satapatha Brahmana*, there is a clear contrast between the

Four of the eight village plan-types specified by the Manasara Silpasastra. *After E. B. Havell*

147. (a) *Dandaka*, the simplest, shows the essential characteristics of the cruciform main streets: W–E the King's street, Rajapatha; N–S Mahakalapatha or Vanapatha (broadstreet or southstreet). Round the inside perimeter is a wide unoccupied space, the Path of Auspiciousness (*Mangalavithi*) which the priest used daily for the rite of circumambulation and which in time of war was used by the sentries. At the crossing of the main streets a banyan or a pipal tree was planted, representing the heaven-tree of Indian mythology and giving shadow to the council meeting of the village

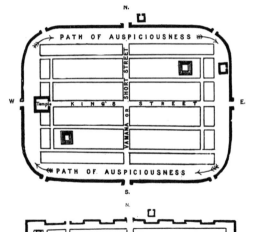

148. (b) The type of plan called *Swastika*

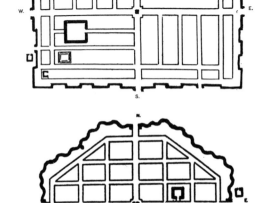

149. (c) The type of plan called *Padmaka*, the lotus-leaf

150. (d) The type of plan called *Nandyavarta*, the abode of happiness. The plan is here shown divided according to the zones of occupation; the innermost given to the brahmins; the second to warriors; the third to craftsmen, the outer to labourers. All other plan-types had similar regulations on the way the different zones were to be occupied
*'The Ancient and Medieval Architecture of India', London, 1915, pp. 9–17*

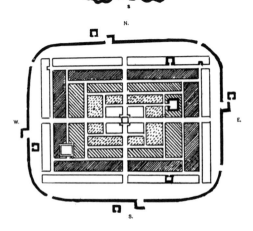

built object and the *mandala*: as the *mandala* functions from the edge inwards, so the building proper functions from the centre outwards—that is from the *gharbha griha*, 'the womb chamber', where the temple's cult statue was. Related as word and as object to the womb chamber was the *gharbha* itself, 'the womb of the temple'; its position may have varied according to such factors as the caste of the founder, but the object was always the same, a brass vessel containing wealth from the earth: gems, metal, soil, roots, herbs: they were the seeds of the building's energy and power.[16]

The guru who supervised the building had to place the vessel in the structure on an auspicious 'night of stars'. The parallel between the *gharbha* and the *mundus* seems obvious enough. The relation *templum-maze-mandala*, though perhaps less evident, is established by the way in which the *templum*, like the *mandala* becomes a 'prophecy' of the building or town, while at the same time it guarantees its stability, its immovability in the uncertain world. A thoughtful Indian, even obscurely aware of the terminology of yoga, can, by looking at a temple, infer the *vástupurusamandala* from it, and identify his body, limb by limb, with its different parts and so with the whole universe which it represented. In a similar way a Roman, however cursorily acquainted with traditional cosmology—certainly without going into any of the finer points discussed by philosophers—should certainly have been able to infer the *templum* from the layout of the town and so have situated himself securely in the world.[17]

I have discussed the most etiolated and 'spiritual' instance of a rite related—or at least similar—to the *ritus Etruscus*; and also the ones which are most elaborate, and have been given the most complex philosophical and theological commentaries first.

*The Mande Rites*   But there are others, more bloody and more barbarous, at any rate in folk memory, and which exist only in the raw state of an anthropologist's report. In 1907–9, on his visit to West Africa, Leo Frobenius was told of a rite practised by a tribe called the Mande:[18] his information was given him several times over by Mande nobles. A Mande town, they told him,[19] would be founded by sons of chiefs who had no heritage. They would leave their home town with chosen representatives of the three classes, warriors, bards and metal smiths and lesser followers. At the first quarter of the moon, the walls and bastions were outlined, and a bull was driven round them three times. He was then driven into the enclosure with four cows. When he had covered three of them, he was sacrificed. His genitals were buried in the centre of the town and covered with a phallic altar, beside which a sacrificial pit was dug. Three animals were always sacrificed on the altar, four in the ditch. It was most important to understand, so Frobenius was told by his informant, that the bull was related to the moon, and that the form of the city (which could be square or circular) in some way represented the sun.

Frobenius had already pointed out the parallels to Roman practice: *ver sacrum, pomoerium, mundus* are all three represented in a rudimentary form.[20] On another occasion Frobenius was given a more circumstantial, epic version of the rite.[21] The auspices were taken on the site; the warriors mounted, and drove the bull round the town circumference three times, the riders and the bull leaping the width of each of the four gates which opened to the four points of the compass. The bull's meat was eaten as a communion meal to seal the compact between the new inhabitants. The dried genitals of the bull were to be buried at the end of the third quarter of the moon; and it was not until another sacrifice had been performed on the altar and in the ditch that the houses could be built and work begin. But even then marriages were forbidden, and so was trade involving foreigners. Huntsmen were not allowed out, and no bull could be slaughtered. This had to continue for three months at least. Frobenius's informants also told him of a second part of the rite; he could not believe that this account dealt with rules, however, but considered it a mythical account of a once-and-for-all foundation. And there is, as he wrote elsewhere, a mythology of the perfect, four-gated and four-faced town in Mandingo mythology: the four-times lost town of Wagadu which the Mandingo bards sing,[22] which has four times been lost because of human weakness and four times rebuilt, four times changed again, and which will one day rise again.[23] It may well be that the second part of the rites of the Horros, the Mande nobles described to Frobenius, were not performed at the frequent town foundations of the tribe, but were—as Frobenius suspected—to be performed only on that great future occasion. This is what he was told, three months later, after the completion of the first lot of ceremonies: a second bull in the enclosure, a brother of the one slaughtered at the first foundation, and similar to him in every way, would break his tethering at the spring solstice, and run into the country, out of the enclosure, run wild until he stopped in front of the hut of a noble nubile virgin. There the representatives of the three classes found him. They entered the hut and brought out the virgin; her virtues were praised by the bards and she was consecrated by having corn poured over her by the workmen. Finally the bull, now docile, rode back to the town with her on his back, circled three times round the enclosure, following the course of the sun. He entered it by its eastern gate.

When they came to the centre the bull was sacrificed on the altar, the virgin in the ditch. Then the bards sang a hymn of the marriage of the sun and the moon. The body of the virgin was buried to the left of the eastern gate, that of the bull to the right of it. Over the two corpses the doorposts were placed, and then the other gates were built. And now the city was open to the world. Since it had gates, people could go in and come out in peace. This elaborate epic account needs an exegesis of its own. But it will be enough for my purpose if I repeat Frobenius's brief comment: 'It is clear that in these [and in similar] classical ceremonies which originated in western Asia, the image of the world becomes a scenario for men, and the temple turns into a mirror of the universe. . . .'[24]

*The Bororo Rites*    There is a parallel with a people who are still more primitive, the

151. Dromenon pattern building. Kejara, a view of the village. The men's house and the dancing floor are in the centre. The elaborate and formal Bororo funeral dance contrasts sharply with the apparent shapelessness of Kejara, the village home of these dancers. What reconciles the two is the elaborate structuring, both social and clannish, of the village plan (figs. 152 and 153) *After Lévi-Strauss*

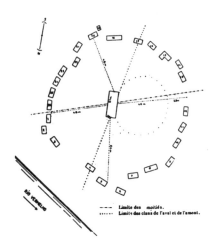

--- Limite des moitiés.
...... Limite des clans de l'aval et de l'amont.

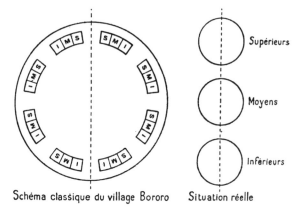

Schéma classique du village Bororo    Situation réelle

Supérieurs

Moyens

Inférieurs

152. **Survey plan of Kejara,** marking the divisions of the two moities as well as the upstream and the downstream clans. *After C. Lévi-Strauss*

153. The real and the apparent structure of **the Bororo village** *After C. Lévi-Strauss*

Bororo of Mato Grosso in Brazil. We know nothing of their foundation rites, but quite a lot about the actual shape of the village. It was organized in a rough circle round the men's house and the dancing ground, and divided into four quarters by two axes—north–south and east–west. These divisions governed the whole social life of the village, its system of intermarriage and kinship; in former times, it seems it was even further complicated by a division of the village into eight tribes vertically and into three classes horizontally.

In spite of this elaborate social structure and a corresponding religion

154. A funeral dance at Kejara
*After C. Lévi-Strauss*

the Bororo were a primitive people. They did not use metal and had only the most rudimentary notion of agriculture: they were almost a Stone Age people. Such a hybrid term as a 'modern Stone Age people' is misleading; it may be better to describe them (a Brazilian sociologist did[25]) as a band 'of grown-up children with an incipient, unripe culture; or, to vary the figure, a culture that was still cutting its teeth, was without the bony framework, the development or the resistance of the great American semi-civilizations. . . .' The Salesian missionaries who first dealt with this people found that the only way to approach them was to persuade them to leave their traditional village and settle in a new village of rectangular huts set out in parallel rows. This completely destroyed the complex Bororo social system which was so closely tied to the layout of the village that it could not survive transplantation into a different environment. What was more radical even was that the Bororo, in spite of their quasi-nomadic way of life, felt completely disorientated in the world, once they were divorced from the traditional cosmology demonstrated in the village plan. And so they accepted eagerly any other plausible explanation of the confusing universe which was offered them.[26]

The Bororo conceptions were relatively elaborate, and their villages intended to last for several years. But even when villages were moving, for longer or shorter periods, they maintained the order of the organized village, and its rough geometry, even when they stopped only for a night encampment.[27] Nor was the order broken when the villages became—as they were reputed to have done—very large, in the early years of this century.[28]

*The Sioux*     The social and geometric organization of the Bororo village had many equivalents in Indian America. Unfortunately, a great deal more is known about the mythology of these builders than about their ritual procedures. Much more is known about the Northern American Indians. The conception of a space which is divided and apportioned in a manner which unites the order of the sky to that of the earth, the quartering of the circle as the essential element of such ordering, appears sometimes in wholly nomadic conditions. So for instance, Black Elk, a shaman, a Holy Man of the Oglala Sioux—one who had been a follower of Chief Crazy Horse—complained that his people had been treated by the Middle West settlers as the Salesians had treated the Bororo:

> We made these little grey houses of logs that you see, and they are square. It is a bad way to live, for there can be no power in a square. You have noticed that everything an Indian does is in a circle, and that is because the Power of the World always works in circles, and everything tries to be round. . . . Birds make their nests in circles, for theirs is the same religion as ours. . . . Our tepees were round like the nests of birds, and these were always set in a circle, the nation's hoop, a nest of many nests where the Great Spirit means for us to hatch our children. But the Wasichus[29] have put us in these square boxes. Our power is gone and we are dying. . . .[30]

And yet Black Elk, so contemptuous of the square houses, divided the circle into its four quarters: during the great Horse dance which is carried out by the Oglala as a result of Black Elk's vision, the following ceremony is carried out in the sacred tepee: 'Right in the middle of the tepee the Grandfathers made a circle in the ground with a little trench, and across this they painted two roads—the red one running north and south, the black one, east to west . . .'[31] and this division by quarters marks the whole ceremony. On another occasion, when Black Elk had his messianic dog vision, the ground for his ceremonial lamenting— which led to the vision—was prepared by an older Shaman, Few Tails: 'We went to the highest point of the hill and made it sacred by spreading sage upon it. Then Few Tails set a flowering stick in the middle of the place, and on the west, the north, the east and south sides of it he placed offerings. . . .'[32]

The six powers, whom Black Elk calls Grandfathers, represent the four directions, the sky and the earth, and the symbolism of the four quarters seems repeated almost obsessively in Sioux ritual and myth. The Sioux 'religious' universe, to use Black Elk's word, is squared, 'quadratus' and circular: much as the world of the Roman augurs.

*The Tiwi*   The circle is of course a universal figure in the religious world of 'primitive' people; preceding even the ability to draw a circle by means of a peg and a piece of string. Preceding—I hasten to add—conceptually rather than temporarily. J. P. Mountford, an English anthropologist, describes the ritual 'ground' of a yam 'secret society' of the Tiwi on Melville Island, north of Darwin, Australia:

155. Copy of a Tiwi drawing of a mythical Kulama ceremony.
a The yam-oven: dots represent upright sticks enclosing the fire-wood. The darker circle is the mound of earth surrounding the ceremonial ground. The figures show men chanting ceremonial songs
b the leader of the group of men
c initiates not taking part in the ceremony
d women and children
*After J. P. Mountford, The Tiw*

'The men walked towards an open space in the forest and with low cries beat the ground with sticks, while the leader, pulling up a tuft of grass threw it into the air. Where it fell, the men dug a small circle (which they call) the *tumaparari* or the navel in which the yams are to be cooked; then sitting down, the men pushed the grass outward with their feet until the enclosure, about 15 ft [4.6 m] in diameter, was surrounded by a low mound of earth and grass. Dry sticks were pushed round the navel-oven, kindling wood was laid between them, and the yams were cooked . . .'[33]

The eating of those yams is a type of the '*première communion du genre humain*' anterior to the eating of those '*gâteaux*' of which Rousseau spoke.[34] And the rucking up of that grassy earth a forerunner of the drawing up of a *pomoerium*.

In a specific but simple operation (whose order the *Ritus Etruscus* seems, remotely, to echo) its constituent parts are listed so brutally as to make a caricature of the Roman one: the opposition centre-outline, the geometry of the form, the intimate link of the geometry of the 'object' (that is the ritual 'field') and the human body are explicitly present. Even the 'mundus' at the centre, the yam-oven, provides a foreshadowing of the great ceremonies of imperial Rome.

*Separation, Guilt and Reconciliation*

But the Tiwi yam-ritual sets out another consideration which has perhaps not been adequately emphasized: the separation of the ritual 'field' from the secular, the unknown, the unregistered ground. The separation of known and unknown, of holy and profane, of cultured and uncultured recalls those binary opposites in which the structural anthropologist rejoices. The separation, in the case of the Tiwi, is temporary. But for most of our contemporaries the act of separation, the original act of separation which makes it possible for us to think *about* that from which we are separated, is embedded in the history of our consciousness, perhaps formed in the very structure of the brain: 'The ascent towards consciousness is the "unnatural" thing in nature. . . . The struggle between the specifically human and the universally natural constitutes the history of man's conscious development.'[35]

And yet this separation is always felt as a loss. 'Separateness . . . is the fall—the fall into division, the original lie.'[36] Separation however is both an evil, a falling-off and a necessity. Therefore separation has to be punished and to be atoned for. Some anthropologists have posited the temple of the dead as the original building: a temple of the dead which had the body of the ancestor, of the dead ancestor as its image: 'The killed deity is the first to make the journey of the dead, and transforms itself into the underworld, whose image on earth is the cult-house. . . . The Temple as the image of the world of the dead and the first killing as the origin of cosmic order are therefore closely connected in myth. It is therefore hardly surprising, that under varying forms, the cult-repetition of the drama of origins recollects the original murder and further the construction of a holy house.'[37]

And indeed building—every act of building—is necessarily an act against nature: it is an unnatural act in the sense in which Neumann talks of the development of consciousness being unnatural. When you choose a site you set it apart from nature. However frail your structure, the act of choosing a site for it, of setting it up is different from the animal's choice of nest or lair. A man knows that he is doing it, the animal does not. Therefore the setting up of it, and the choosing must also contain the act of explaining the action to the actor, and also—since it is in some way an action *against* nature—of justifying it.

It is all part of this terrible world in which we are always doing the things which we ought not to do and leave undone those things which we ought to do. 'Primitives consider it a sinister and grievous act to kill their quarry, yet they have to do it, but then surround themselves with rites of atonement meant to placate their victims. Our predicament, properly speaking, remains inextricable. . . .'[38] And building, like owning—since in some sense you always own the site on which you build—is part of the predicament.

'Cain means "ownership". Ownership was the originator of the earthly city.'[39] Cain from √knh, to own; perhaps related, as the Book indicates, to √kna, to envy. Cain, the owner, the first city founder ('and he—Cain—builded a city, and called the name of the city after the name of his son Henoch').[40] The first fratricide is the first founder of cities. The Rabbinic legends tell of the blight which Abel's death brought on the whole of nature.[41] Ownership and blight: the farmer's curse. As Cain was, so Romulus is the fratricide founder; there are parricide founders, like Theseus, and child-murderer founders. Town foundations always seem to carry the burden of guilt. That is another reason for the ceremonial structure which I have described. Again, there is a terrifying range of parallel customs. The Chinese child sacrifice at the house is a custom to which only shadowy references remain: but sacrificial heads under the threshold or on the gable were a familiar theme.[42] The fear of cutting the ground, of cutting the first sod with the plough was also powerful: the first ploughing of the season seemed to require the sacrifice of a couple.[43] But on a vaster scale, at the origin of the first three Chinese dynasties there is the self-sacrifice of the dynastic ancestor for his people in a holy place. The Ancestor also founds a dance which becomes the dynasty's heraldic device. The dance, the holy place and the cult of the ancestor become the symbols of dynastic power. 'But the three are as one: for the dance of the ancestor is the holy place which dances and which is danced.'[44] Marcel Granet takes this theme and its variations as the guide in his *Danses et Légendes de la Chine Ancienne*; and with it he considers another curious tradition: the distribution of the victim's body after a sacrifice. When the dynastic virtues had weakened, these weakened virtues were expelled from the holy place, or from the city, by shooting arrows in the four directions, as well as by quartering a sacrificial victim, and carrying out the four parts through the four gates of a city.[45]

*The Quartered Body as a Picture of the World*

An execution and a quartering of the victims is even attributed to Confucius by a number of early historians and his first biographies: Kong-Yang, Kou-Liang, Sin-You, Kia-Yu, Sseu-Ma Ts'ien.[46] This identification of the city with the world-picture, and the world-picture with the victim is implicit in many divining systems: in haruspicinium and entrail-divining; it is immanent in the Enuma-Eliš, since the monster's (or victim's) body is transformed into the world fabric. This analogy is carried down to a commonplace by many African peoples.

*The Hausa*

The Hausa, for instance, a powerful and numerous people who occupy northern Nigeria and southern Niger, have, in spite of their Islamization, preserved a very explicit sacrificial 'theology'. The victim is often divided into a male and a female half—whatever its sex—down the spine; at other times (at a birth, for instance) it is split into four joints; the hindquarters are given to the Marabout and the father, the forequarters to the mother and the midwife; and this kind of division is extended to unbloody sacrifices, such as the marriage sacrifice of bread and salt. But of this unbloody sacrifice, as well as of the others, a recent writer says: 'Nevertheless the contemporary sacrifices . . . are explained by the substitution of animals for man. There is every reason to believe that the division of victims nowadays follows the conception of the human body which guided the priests of the old times, and still guides the way in which people perceive their bodies.'[47]

The Hausa have both an elaborate cosmological system, and a standard, orthogonal town plan to which it relates.[48] This division is carried through into the normal land-division, and accompanied by many rituals.[49] But their identification of body—human or substitute animal—with an orthogonally quartered world is not as strange as it may seem at first. It is the basis of many ritual and religious practices.

156. The central panel of a Dogon 'Red Ally' blanket, worn by a totemic priest during sowing ceremonies. The large checkerboard pattern represents the layout of fields, the diagonal squares, various orientated buildings. The coloured, thin edges, various races, while the small checkerboards are the vegetable and the animal world, there are alternative interpretations of the symbolism. *After G. Calame-Griaule La Parole chez les Dogon, Paris, 1965*

Some—those connected with the *mandala*—I have discussed above; but there are many more common ones. To take a banal instance, the Christian practice of making the sign of the cross 'in' one's own body. Or again, the widely diffused custom of orientated burial refers to it: some late Palaeolithic burials seem to have been roughly orientated east–west;[50] it is exhibited in its most elaborate and developed ritual and pictorial form in the Egyptian Pyramid Texts.[51] So that the identity of body and quartered city is established through its divisions: whether the outline of the town is rectangular or circular has little relevance.

Hausa mythology has a further interesting variant. The body is variously divided into male right and female left, into male front and female back corresponding to a division of each person according to his own sex, but also of his body between his parents' clans: so that he knows his right side to belong to his paternal clan, the left to the maternal.[52] This insistence on identifying one's own body with clan divisions, as well as with the totality of the settlement, may suggest the notion of androgynous origins, such as are found elsewhere in Africa.

*The Dogon*    The Dogon, who live well to the west of the Hausa, provide an elaborate description of the standard village layout, which presupposes a knowledge of it transmitted through both myth and ritual. 'The village' said Ogotemêli, Marcel Griaule's venerable informant, 'should extend from north to south like the body of a man lying on his back. The village called Lower Ogol is almost correct. The head is the council house, built on the chief square which is the symbol of the primal field.'

Clearly, as in all such cases there is a familiar schema which circumstances or local conditions may debar the builder from following. But the scheme is nevertheless known, and deviations from it registered.

Indeed Ogotemêli had explained that the village, if built on the plain, should be a square, with the streets running north–south, east–west.[53] But on the cliff and the plateau on which the Dogon lived this was not possible. At the very north end of the village was to be the smithy, as the place of the culture-bringers. To the east and west of the village boundary were the circular, womb-like houses for the menstruating women, representing the hands. The actual housing are the chest and belly of the village. The communal altars at the south end of the village are its feet. The mill for crushing the sã fruit, the main source of fat, at the village centre is the female genitals; 'beside it should be set the foundation altar which is (the village's) male sex organ; but out of respect to the women this altar is erected outside the walls'.[54] Thanks to Marcel Griaule, the Dogon symbolism is known in much more detail, and is much more explicit than that known for most African societies.

It is not only the village plan which is seen in such organic terms, but the individual house is also an androgynous figure: 'The vestibule, which belongs to the master of the house, represents the male partner of the couple, the outside door being his sexual organ. The big central room is the domain and symbol of the woman; the storerooms on each side are her arms, and the communicating door her sexual parts. The central room and the store rooms together represent the woman lying on her back with outstretched arms, the door open and the woman ready for intercourse.[55]

The room at the back, which contains the hearth and looks out on to the flat roof, shows the breathing of the woman, who lies in the central room under the ceiling which is the symbol of a man, its beams representing his skeleton . . .'[56] and much more in this vein.[57] Not only are the features of the house understood in this way, but behaviour within it is regulated by this understanding, both intimate and working behaviour. Parallels between the house façade, the village plan, the shroud commonly used and the schema of the Dogon mask reveal yet other parallels; and they all refer back to the myth of the world origins: when the creator-god Ammu having made the sky by throwing lumps of clay at it, finally flung some spreading clay northward; this clay spread out 'and from there stretched to the south, which is the bottom of the world. . . . The earth lies flat, but the north is at the top. It extends east and west with separate members like a foetus in the womb. It is a body, that is to say, a thing with members branching out from a central mass. This body, lying flat, face upwards, in a line from north to south, is feminine. Its sexual organ is an anthill, and its clitoris a termite hill. Ammu, being lonely and desirous of intercourse with this creature, approached it. That was the occasion of the first breach of order in the universe. . . . At God's approach the termite hill rose up, barring the passage and displaying masculinity. It was as strong as the organ of the stranger, and intercourse could not take place. But God is all-powerful. He cut down the termite hill, and had intercourse with the excised earth . . . from this defective union was born [a] jackal, symbol of the difficulties of God.'[58] The creation myth provides—among other things—an etiology of excision, which the Dogon practice widely, though, unlike circumcision, not universally.[59]

Another world model is represented by a creation legend, lower on the demiurgic scale, that of the 'third world' which is a curious object, circular at the base and square at the top, with four stairways, one on each side: the object is oriented in the legend, and of course it represents the cross-in-circle plan: Dogon granaries in fact are circular and quartered internally.[60]

*The Everyday Microcosm*     This multiplicity of world plans, each explained by its own aetiological myth, is often confusing to a modern occidental reader, who expects one of these accounts to be preferred to another. They never are. In the same way, world models co-exist, supplement each other, sometimes—as in the case of the Dogon body-model and oriented basket-model—are imposed on each other.

The Bambara, the Hausa—many other African peoples are known to have similar explanations of their bodies, the world and their methods of building. The Hausa method of making a clearing, from the way the site is set out, through the method of burning the cleared plants and the sowing, are all related to ritual patterns of this nature.[61] Their towns were square, walled, with four gates opening to the compass points; the modern surveyor's land-divisions are often contaminated by old custom.[62] Some of the rituals sound familiar. When the town of Maradi was instituted in 1946, for instance, pots containing various 'medicines' were buried at the centre and at the four corners, the 'medicines' including four puppy heads and a black dog, sacrificed by a local non-muslim grandee, the *durbi*, who told an anthropologist that the puppies were substitutes for his own children; the durbi who founded the town of Katsina, he said, had laid the gates of the town on the bones of his children.[63]

The Bambara, whose villages are planned symmetrically round their chief's house, describe them in terms analogous to those of the Hausa and the Dogon.[64] The Akkan of the Gold Coast, who had emigrated to their present settlements some time before the fifteenth century, and whose capitals were destroyed in the seventeenth and the eighteenth century, maintain traditions about their regularly planned towns. Some speak of towns of seven districts, others of properly quartered towns; there is even an account of a town divided into eight. All speak of a main north–south road, laid out accurately—presumably by *gnomon*—'crossing the sun's path'. At the centre, there seems to have been a baetyl stone and a sacred tree, which were related to the town's prosperity. These two sacred tokens were related to the main gate of the king's palace. A daughter of the queen-mother, and niece of the founder-king, was sacrificed, dressed in splendid ornaments and buried in gold dust in front of the gate of the king's palace at the foundation ceremonies of Bono-Mansu and also at Bono-Takyiman; in Akwamu, a son and a niece of the Omonahene were sacrificed, and buried, impaled to the sacred stools. But information about the Akkan rituals is fragmentary, and the sites of their cities have not yet been excavated.[65]

Nevertheless, the settlements, particularly those further inland, are marked by such ideas, and the vernacular Ashanti house, which—as a type at least—is a square courtyard with four shallow chambers opening off it, reflects these beliefs *in parvo*; the shrines and palaces of the Ashanti are often agglomerates of such clearly individuated units.[66] Unfortunately neither students of African architecture, nor even anthropologists have always registered what the inhabitants said about their houses. For instance, in the study of the variants of Cameroon housing by the group of architects done in 1949–50 for French official sources, a study which is a model of lovingly recorded detail, not a word is said about the mythology surrounding building or even the work-songs which appear to be sung by some of the workers in the photographs; nor do they comment on obvious 'classificatory' plans: as of the Mundang, who have quite distinct and explicitly characterized house plans, for men and for women, or of the Mofu of Lake Chad who seem to build houses of circular huts interconnected to form a plan shaped like a human body.[67] Curiously, an observer as acute as Frobenius does not remark on this same feature of an underground Gurunshi (W. Sudan) house.[68] Frobenius does, however, consider in some detail the cross-in-circle schema in African divination.[69] These are customs of hamitic or sudanic speaking peoples, who had never passed through a stage of urbanization. It is of course conceivable that these peoples inherited or imitated—many of them are people who moved westward in relatively recent times—some aspects of the Romano-Etruscan world picture. Though why people who had no cities in the Roman sense of the term, should emulate, as it seems, the *Ritus Etruscus*, is more difficult to explain.

*The Great Plan*   But analogous customs are found at the other end of the ancient world, in ancient China. I have already remarked on the quartering of the sacrificial, sometimes human victim in relation to the town plan.[70] This quartering had its aetiology in a cosmic schema different from the ones which I have so far described. The skeletal form of this cosmic schema, the *Hung fan*, the 'Great Plan' specified the five elements and the five numbers which the first (mythical) dynastic emperor Yü received from heaven.[71] The present redaction of the literary text by Ssen-Ma Ts'ien in the Shih Chih (Early Han, c. 100 B.C.) probably bears an analogous relation to the belief of the Hsia people—if there were ever Hsia people[72]—as do the beliefs Plutarch attributes to them have to the actual notions of the Homeric heroes.

In this late redaction the plan relates the five elements and numbers to a ninefold square. Yü had measured the world and had divided it into nine regions; he had channelled the turbulent waters; he was the originator of metal crafts. But his prime mythical work was that of the surveyor and after he had divided the world it was possible to cross the nine marshes, the nine rivers and the nine mountains without danger. Yü possessed nine tripods which were an image of the world; and heaven added to his power by having a tortoise bring him on its back the nine numbers which signified universal order.[73]

The tortoise is a mysterious animal. As the underside of its shell is square and the top domed, it is an image of the universe. It is long lived because by its anagogic form it participates in the life of the cosmos. And that is why its shell is one of the main instruments of the diviner. Among the vast quantities of oracle bones which must have constituted a library—or even libraries—of omen literature, analogous to those which have been found in Mesopotamia (and of which the *Sibylline Books* are a much later example) there were found many inscribed tortoise shells, some of them complete.[74] The diagram which provides the clue, and which underlies much Chinese divination—all forms of geomancy for instance—is the nine-fold square made up of all the numbers up to ten enclosed in a magical square, so that any line of three digits adds up to fifteen, like this:

| 4 | 9 | 2 |
| 3 | 5 | 7 |
| 8 | 1 | 6 |

Various Chinese emperors built calendar houses in their capitals. The calendar house, *Ming t'ang*, was based on the schema of the Great Plan. But it was also shaped like a tortoise shell, and therefore like the universe, with a square base and a circular thatched roof. Those emperors who could not—unlike Yü the Great—measure and circumambulate the world, or even—as was their duty—their empire which was its essence—would content themselves with a progress through the *Ming t'ang*, occupying appropriate parts of it throughout the year and performing the appropriate ceremonies dressed in the appropriate robes.[75]

This building, and all Chinese building for that matter, was further governed by elaborate numerical games and proportional rules in which the opposition 9/6 and 8/7 (a fifth and a tone) related buildings to the microcosmic opposition of male and female, of *Ying* and *Yang*, by which the universe was constituted (by which token the venerable

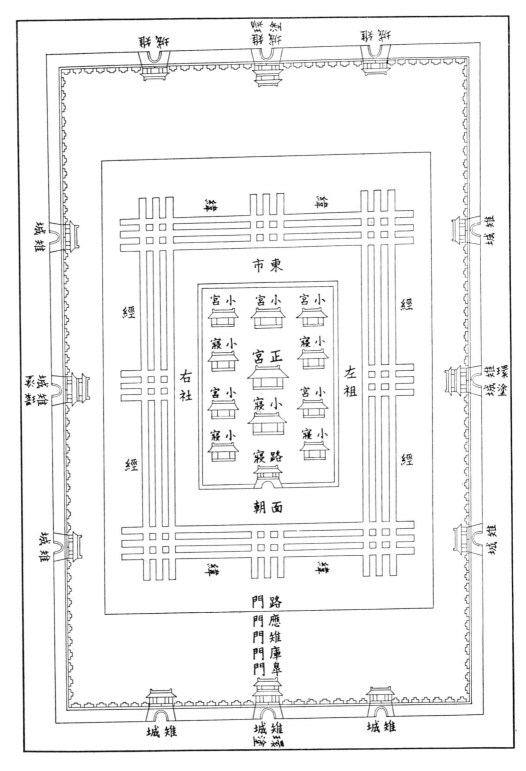

157. **Wang-Ch'eng.** The representation of the plan of the city according to the canonical plan.
*Redrawn from the 'Yung lo Ta-tien', written in 1407 A.D. After Wheatley*

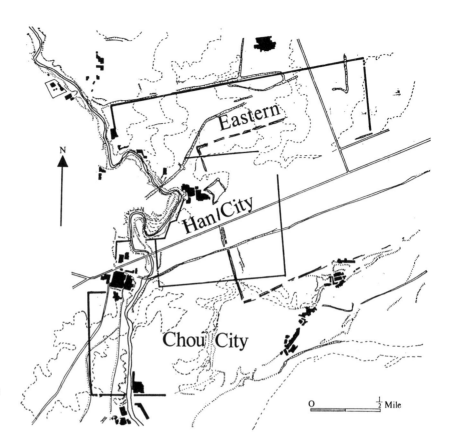

158. Wang-Ch'eng, the royal
capital of the Eastern Chou.
Excavation plan.
*After Wheatley*

Within the map: Eastern, Han City, Chou City, N, O ½ Mile

cosmic tortoise could also be an emblem of unchastity).[76] And in
fact, the Chinese thought of space as made up of their opposition,
and time of their alternating.[77] The ninefold division of the square
remains a staple of Chinese surveying, its privileged figure, and formed
the basis of the many orthogonal town plans which, since the prehistoric past, have been built in China. As may be expected from all
this, the rituals surrounding the choice of a site and the founding of a
new town are suitably elaborate. A town, in China, did not exist without a lord, and every townsman was a lord's vassal. The lord's dominion,
his virtue, distinguished the townsman in his own eyes from the villa-
gers' subsistence ways, their unreflective existence. And yet the city's
orthogonal plan depended on the archaic ordering of the field, the
system of well-fields described by Mencius, and which may be as old
as the Shang dynasty.[78] The city was founded by the ancestor of a noble
family or of a dynasty. From the crest of a hill he observed the light and
the shadow of the land, its *ying* and *yang*, the rivers and hills. He chose
a hilltop for his foundation generally.

'On the third day he (the Duke of Chou, founder of Lo-Yang) took
the (tortoise) oracle (as bearing) on the site. When he had obtained the
oracle, he planned and laid out the city. . . .'[79]

The plan was always, as far as possible, the scheme of orthogonal
streets with a northern palace quarter, the walls a rectangle orientated:

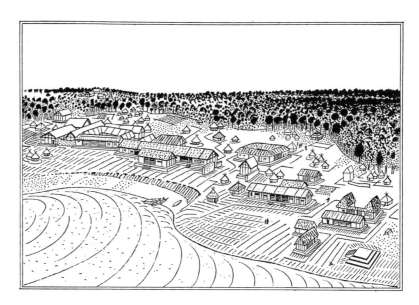

159. **The ceremonial enclave of the Shang at Hsiao-T'un** from the N.E. The main buildings, orientated and raised on hang-t'u foundations, are those excavated; the dwellings and workshops are shown conjuncturally. *After Wheatlev*

> The Ting star was at its zenith
> He began work on the palace of Ch'u
> When he had set it out by the sun
> He started work on the Ch'u mansion . . .
> . . .
> The tortoise shell oracle was auspicious
> It was truly good all through[80]

The *Chou-Li* (the Chou book of rites) prescribes the method of orientation using a *gnomon* and a plumb line, and a circle drawn round the *gnomon*, the shadows being measured when they cut the circumference: a method analogous to the Roman, as well as the Indian one.[81]

This book of rites prescribes, too, how a special functionary 'finds' the centre of the world: the place where earth and sky meet, where the four seasons merge, where *ying* and *yang* are in harmony. A *gnomon* erected there was held to cast no shadow in the summer solstice.[82] But although the *Chou-Li* seems to demand the setting down of the *gnomon* in one particular place on the flat face of the earth, we know that innumerable peoples and even high civilizations sought the centre repeatedly, and found it in many places. *Stat crux dum revolvitur mundus* has its echo in many an '*obscure espérance*'. But China more particularly was the 'middle kingdom'. Within it, however, the centre moved every time a new imperial capital was set up: and there were many of these. It is clear that in spite of the elaborate calculations and the astronomical researches, it is the centre of a space 'for the time', of what has been called an 'existential', not of a geometrical space that is being sought in each case; and sought in fulfilment of an immemorial tradition:

> He made his capital at Feng. Hail King Wên!
> He built the wall with a moat,
> He raised Feng on the pattern
> Not hurrying to whim, but in conformity, filial,
> Hail sovereign, King!

The King's work was glorious
The walls of Feng placed where the quarters joined
The walls where the peoples came together
A sure shelter was our lord and king
Hail, sovereign, King!

. . .

Our King cast oracles
To build Hao the capital for his dwelling
The tortoise confirmed it, King Wu completed it
Hail King Wu![83]

The Chinese, and therefore the whole world, depended on the imperial virtue; the imperial virtue shows itself by the correct and seasonal carrying out of ceremonies. Among the greatest imperial ceremonies were the spring and summer sacrifices on the altar of the earth, and the worship of the imperial ancestors. The altar of the earth was a square hill heaped up of earth in the five colours of the great plan. A Chinese feudal grant was made by the handing over of a handful of earth from this hill, of the colour corresponding to the district in which the granted land lay.[84] And any danger to the sacred space is a signal for a rallying to this altar, 'so that the space may be restored in all its dimensions (even unto the sphere of the stars) by the sole force of the correct disposing of the emblems in the holy place of the federal reunion.'[85]

As the altar of the earth represents the whole order of space, so the temple of the ancestors is the guarantee of the recurrent ordering function in time. For the order of space was dependent on its periodic renewal: the succession of seasons, of generations, of dynastic virtues, all had their proper liturgical place. And the plan of the town was concerned with the relation between the space ordered in the 'Great Plan' of the altar of the earth, and the renewal of time guaranteed by the temple of the ancestors. Between them, in the calendar building which was the centre of the palace, and therefore of the empire, and therefore of the universe, the emperor's passage through its pavilions guaranteed the harmony between the empire and the celestial order. On the borders of the empire, in Cambodia or Burma, the rituals, the circumambulations were carried out with even greater elaboration: and in Cambodia particularly they received the most elaborate architectural incarnation in the Khmer buildings at Angkor Vat and Angkor Thom, where the great King Jayavarman VI attempted to concentrate the whole universal complex of forces and, by harmonizing, master them.[86]

But this apparent stability was constantly contradicted by the need for change. Each prince wanted his own capital: and the ritual in many cases dictated change. Even within the town a son was not to occupy the same house as his father. The cult of the ancestors was—as a rule— broken at the fourth generation. But changes of riverbed, of the fortunes of war or rebellion, of dynastic alignment, or the configuration of the visible stars all imposed shift of site.[87] None of the ancient peoples— except the Egyptians perhaps—practised such changes as frequently. It

160A, B. **Two Chinese mirror-backs.** From the Han period onwards circular mirror-backs were used to illustrate cosmological ideas and the mirror had, particularly in Taoist magical practice, an apotropaic function. *British Museum, London*

was a tribute to the power of the Great Plan in the Chinese conceptual scheme that it could be applied with such ease at a great variety of localities.

According to tradition, the great plan was granted by heaven to the Emperor Yü, sometime therefore between 2,200 and 1,990 B.C. Yü is the first metalsmith, which places him at the beginning of the Chalcolithic period; and yet in absolute chronological terms his reign would correspond to the beginning of the Babylonian reign in Ur, to the eleventh or twelfth dynasty in Egypt, to the beginning of Middle Minoan in Crete, and the passage from Harappa II to Harappa III in India. The notions of orientation, even in strict connection with orthogonal planning, had therefore been current in the Eastern Mediterranean for a millennium. But when comparing the outline excavations at An-Yang with Western equivalents, they seem more like a Hallstatt centre than a Hittite or a Minoan settlement. The technique of fortification, of caissoned earthwork, is also reminiscent of proto-Celtic works, even of *Terramare* building, rather than of anything else.[88] The *Book of Odes* describes a foundation:

> . . . Our people
> living in stone caves, in stone hives
> before they had a house with eaves
>
> Old Prince Tan Fu galloped his horses
> . . . To the slopes of Mount K'i
> The plain of Chou was fertile
> . . . Here T'an began to plan,
> to notch the divining tortoise-shell.
> 'Time: now; place: here; all's well,'
> said the shell 'Build your houses'

So he rested, so he settled,
He went to the left, went to the right,
made boundaries, divided plots,
measured with a rod, from east to west

He called the master of works,
He called the master of lands,[89]
To build the houses.
Their plumb-lines fell straight,
The boards were lashed into frames
And raised the temple of the Ancestors
On the cosmic order.

They queued to scoop the earth
They measured it out
They rammed it down
They scraped and beat
As the hundred cubit wall rose together
Moving faster than the drum beat

He built the outer gate:
The outer gate was strong.
He built the inner gate
The inner gate was splendid.
He raised the earth-altar mound
From which the armies would march.

Then King Wen brought to civility
the lords of Yü and of Ju-i;
taught 'em to bow and stand aside
say: after you, and: if you please,
and: this is no place for barbarities.[90]

King Wen, the founder of the Chou dynasty, was the son of Prince Tan: the description is of the founding of the Chou capital.[91]

From other sources we know of the elaboration of the attendant ritual: the founder—as it might be Prince Tan in the ode—'decked out in all his jewels, jades, girded with a splendid sword inspects the site. He fixes the north–south axis (with a *gnomon*?) observes the sunlit and shadowed places in order to balance the *ying* and *yang* and observes the water courses. And finally he consults the tortoise shell to know the divine will.[92]

Then the order to build is given and work begins at the propitious moment, which is when agricultural work has a respite. The order of the work is fixed: first—as the ode indicates—the ramparts, then the temple of the ancestors, then the tree for the ancestor-offerings (hazel and chestnut) as well as those which will serve for coffins and for musical instruments (paulownia)[93] must be planted; then the houses can be built.

The altar of the earth may well have been established virtually when the site was chosen, before anything else was established. It contained—the ritual directions are not very explicit, unfortunately—the original handful of earth which the founder had received to signify his being granted the territory, and as a sign of his vassalage. The handful of correctly coloured earth, and a tablet, a stele of the correct wood (or of stone), at which trophies, both human and animal, would be consecrated, constitute this rustic and elemental shrine.[94] Its earthbound, female character, its 'central' position, suggest a character like that of the Roman *mundus*: mother earth.[95]

The altar of the earth and the wooden temple of the ancestors were part of the lord's palace. The *Tse Chouan* classifies towns and settlements according to the way they are built. No capital city is worthy of the name if it has no *Ming t'ang*;[96] If the town has earthen walls and no temple of the Imperial ancestors, it is not a city, *Tsong*, but a borough, *Yi*. An important town has masonry walls: then it can be called *Tou*, the capital.[97] The prestige of the lord (his 'face' in modern parlance) depends on the rank of his city and the splendour of its gates; he possesses it not only by a feudal handing down, but by a kind of synoical pact with the inhabitants, which specifies the classification of quarters.[98]

All this is formulated long after the first Shang 'cities' had disappeared. Often, reading the documentary material and comparing it with the archaeological evidence, the conflict is strident. Words like 'great' and 'splendid' hardly seem to apply to the rather ramshackle grouping of buildings, correctly orientated though they are, of the Shang capital—if that is what it is—at An-Yang. Modern writers often neglect or ignore the vast effort which the first urbanization involved.

There is little doubt that Chinese urbanization, like the Mesopotamian and Egyptian (perhaps also the Mesoamerican ones) was a fresh start. Nor could it be a gentle, gradual improvement: clearly the ode about Prince Tan[99] shows a revolution. Prince Tan is imitating the Shang rulers. But at some point, perhaps under some Hsia lord, perhaps at the beginning of Shang, a radical change came over Chinese society, the change which came over the central Italian peoples soon after 1,000 B.C. At An-Yang, the orientation of the buildings of the 'ceremonial centre' of Hsiao-T'un is explicit; the great pit-tombs at Hsi Pei Kang are equally obviously orientated, even if the exact orientation is rather puzzling. The principal buildings of the city—you may see this elaborately developed in the 'forbidden city' of Peking—face south, down a main avenue. The principal palace echoed by the gate building, the succession of spaces (as those of a scroll painting, says Paul Wheatley)[100] paralleling the world model. The central avenue, the *cardo*—if I may, without pressing the parallel, use the Latin word which expresses a similar notion—running south from the palace was always (though it was not invariably correctly orientated) the image of the meridian, and hence more important than any east–west road. The built form was paralleled by ceremonial: the lord always addressed his inferiors facing south; consequently the emperor only faced north when addressing divine powers or his ancestors.

The insistence on the sacrality of space, the identification of the space demarcated with your home city, as well as your behaviour and the intimate form of your body may seem to a modern reader to impose a crushing weight of observance on the city dweller. Siegmund Freud took this problem as a paradigm of Hysteria in his five lectures on psychoanalysis delivered at Clerk University, Worcester, Mass., in 1909.

> *Our hysterical patient suffers from reminiscences.* Their symptoms are residues and mnemonic symbols of particular traumatic experiences. We may perhaps obtain a deeper understanding of this kind of symbolism if we compare them with other mnemonic symbols in other fields. The monuments and memorials with which cities are adorned are also mnemonic symbols. If you take a walk through the streets of London, you will find, in front of one of the large railway termini, a richly carved Gothic column—Charing Cross. One of the old Plantagenet kings of the thirteenth century ordered the body of his beloved Queen Eleanor to be carried to Westminster; and at every stage at which the coffin rested he erected a Gothic cross. At another point in the same city, not far from London Bridge, you will find a towering column which is simply known as The Monument. It was designed as a memorial of the Great Fire which broke out in that neighbourhood in 1666. These monuments, then, resemble hysterical symptoms in being mnemonic symbols. What should we think of a Londoner who paused today in deep melancholy before the memorial of Queen Eleanor's funeral instead of going about his business, or instead of feeling joy over the youthful queen of his own heart? Or again what should we think of a Londoner who shed tears before The Monument that commemorates the reduction of his beloved metropolis into ashes although it has long since risen again in far greater brilliance? Yet every single hysteric and neurotic behaves like these two unpractical Londoners. Not only do they remember painful experiences from the remote past, but they still cling to them emotionally. . . .

Later on in the same lecture Freud exemplifies the nature of the psychoanalytic 'cure':

> One was driven to assume that the illness occurred because the effects generated in the pathogenic situation had their normal outlets blocked because 'the patient . . . was obliged to *suppress* a powerful emotion instead of allowing its discharge in the appropriate signs of emotion, words or action.' And consequently the essence of the illness lay in the fact that these strangulated effects were then put to an abnormal use . . .[1]

In this very simplified—and very early—account of psychoanalytic procedure Freud treats the citizen's familiarity with the specific mnemonic nature of his city's monuments as an analogue of a pathological condition. It seems almost as if he were advocating an indifference to one's environment.

The burden of this book seems to be quite the opposite: I have been concerned to show the town as a total mnemonic symbol, or at any rate a structured complex of symbols; in which the citizen, through a number of bodily exercises, such as processions, seasonal festivals, sacrifices, identifies himself with his town, with its past and its founders. This apparatus of exercises was, however, not repressive. On the contrary, it seems in some sense conciliatory and integrative, what Freud implies the 'normal' relation should be in this situation. That is, the attachment to one's environment allows for emotion to be discharged 'in appropriate signs: . . . words and action.'

But Freud is ever the pathologist: 'There is a dictum in general pathology'—he says in the fourth of these lectures—'which asserts that every developmental process carries with it the seed of a pathological disposition. . . .'[2] And it is highly symptomatic therefore that Freud, very much the bourgeois, the urban dweller, never had a vision of the continuity of urban pattern: not even in the Paris he so much enjoyed. The magnificence of the Acropolis for him were the amber-coloured columns and its associations;[3] the London which he describes in this passage is a complex of historical anecdote. Even to Freud the inveterate visitor of museums, the indefatigable sightseer, the city yields either isolated 'aesthetic' experience or the fascinating obscure conundrums, to dwell on which would get in the way of 'going about one's business in the hurry modern working conditions demand'[4] or the experience of private emotion. It is worth reconsidering this passage: in it the sensitive pathologist lays bare the essential symptom of the diseased condition. The fabric of the model had decayed: the city, as it is presented to the visitor, to the inhabitant, is the mere tissue of anecdote, impeding the individual in the proper prosecution of his duty or his development. Anecdote without a conception of the structure beyond it: Freud's city is the city after Haussmann, the Vienna girt by the Ring: 'the agglomerate had to be transformed' writes Françoise Choay 'into an efficient instrument of production and consumption', and in this context, quotes Haussmann's own words: 'What municipal bonds link the two million inhabitants who crowd into Paris? . . . For them Paris is a great consumers' market, a vast workshop, an arena for ambitions.'[5]

Haussmann's driving force was not merely the desire for increasing the smooth flow of traffic, nor yet the opening of wide avenues for the blowing of the whiffs of grapeshot down them, as his enemies sometimes suggested;[6] not even the raising of the—occasionally appalling—housing standards and the provision of open spaces. All these were considerations. But Haussmann saw himself as an artist. Whatever denigrating remarks he may have made about buildings as a mere *décor de la vie*, he was totally devoted to the *culte de l'axe*. The arteries he opened were not merely the shortest passages from one point to another, he also required them to have, wherever possible, 'grand prospects' and he arranged the planting of the streets to create junctions, to articulate the joints in the long boulevards.

But the pattern was not considered—ever—metaphorically. Poets later may have identified the Ile de la Cité with the sexual organs of the female personage, the Tour St. Jacques with the male:[7] such identifications are easy enough; but they are inevitably fragmentary, because Haussmann's work had indeed been conclusive. A metaphoric understanding of the city structure is impossible. It is not only that the city-dweller does not allow himself to reflect on the great (traumatic?) incidents of the city's past. As he drives along a boulevard, he will not naturally reflect on the origin of both the word and the roadway in the medieval or the seventeenth-century fortifications.

Not that in doing so he would remedy the pathological situation which Freud revealed in the passage I quoted. Though the alleviation of symptoms is a respectable therapy, it has limited uses. The problem therefore remains. The city's monumental structure, in so far as it has an impact on its inhabitants, is seen as an analogue of a pathological condition: since the city should facilitate the circulation of goods and of persons in their pursuit of wealth, duty and ambition—and also personal gratification, Freud would certainly have wanted to add. The legitimate demands of the libido were not to be denied: otherwise the human as well as the social organism would simply collapse.[7a] But of course the matter which I here propose, the problem and the instance are much more far-reaching. They bring me back to the Etruscan rite and the parallel ceremonies and monuments I have invoked.

The parallels—to begin with them—were deliberately widely chosen, but the choice was made from an overwhelming mass of material. The Indian and the Chinese parallels present a highly complex cosmology and social condition embodied in urban form; the Mande have a highly dramatic pantomime of this same kind of belief; so do the Sioux. They and the Bororo show most intimately man's dependence on the immediate shape of his home, his tangible environment. These instances belong to different continents and highly diverse cultures. No doubt, some readers will want to explain certain similarities (as for instance the striking parallels between the Mande custom and the Roman) by a simple act of diffusion; but the parallels extend across the ancient world to China,[8] and further into Mesoamerica and even the Amazon forests: and I dare say, if total coverage was wanted, it would be possible to find adequate instances from the Bantus of South Africa to the Canadian North-West Territories. In time, too, the stretch seems inconceivable. From Paleolithic times the concepts of orthogonality and of orientation persist extraordinarily.

*The First Builders*　　The discovery of the painted caves has tended to inspire theories about the origins of art, the origins of all figuration, and planning with it, in simple figural 'imitation'. But more recently it has become clear that the oldest 'human markings known are the bare expression of rhythmic values'[9] These first signs appear about the same time as the first known human habitations: sometime between 50,000 and 30,000 B.C. The two phenomena are not independent. 'The foundation of man's moral and physical comfort is the wholly animal perception of the perimeter of security, of the close refuge, or of the socializing rhythms.'[10] All these belong to the animal aspect of human behaviour. It is the faculty of conceptualizing, parallel to linguistic ability, and perhaps to the growth of material industries. But while the stone industries of the cutting edge are relatively easy to explore, the problem of origins of shelter is much more obscure: it is sometimes difficult to distinguish certain animal shelters from those presumed to be of the early hominids. It has been assumed that such a passage occurs at the period when the first signs of a human type related to Homo Sapiens appear. That they coincide with the acknowledgement of the rhythms of seasonal change and of the closer recurrences of the moon's alterations and of the succession of night and day; also of the simple geometries which sticks first, sticks and strings perhaps in the second place, allowed these first men to construct. The aborigines of most Australian tribes acknowledge the power of such abstractions, and identify them with their own body. They are capable too, of conceiving figurative—as well as abstract—images in plan: these are images of great size sometimes, involving whole settlements.

Neanderthal men may well have used cave mouths as their dwelling; but the evidence is 'statistically overhelming'[11] that the first men constructed their dwellings. Constructed them with, around them, the carcasses of the great herbivores whose tusks seem everywhere to have acted as guardians or supports of these houses. From the outset there is the association with the animal body, so powerful an image of the house, which was to recur in many initiation and funerary ceremonies, and was to survive in the high civilizations: in the ceremonies of the coronation of the Pharaoh, for instance.

By 30,000 at Arcy in central France, as at the lowest levels of the Ukrainian and Moravian sites, a new factor appears: the midden and the hearth.[12] The passage of 20,000 years, until the late paleolithic age, shows no clear developments. But in the Mesolithic settlements, at the end of the last glaciation, revolutionary features appear: elaborations of burial customs and ceremonious religious practices connected with human and animal remains, particularly skulls.

While we knew very little about the building of the Paleolithic peoples until recently, it has become apparent from the finds at Haçilar, at Çatal Hüyük, at Jericho and elsewhere in the western Mediterranean, that peoples who did not possess ceramic techniques, and perhaps not even a settled agriculture, nevertheless built quite considerable settlements, of predetermined plan, enclosed by some form of enceinte which may have been the outer walls of some houses, as at Çatal Hüyük or a wall proper, as at Jericho. Recent datings have put these buildings in the seventh millennium B.C. They were, of course, the work of pre-literate peoples, and it is fruitless to attempt at this point (it is probable that much more evidence will come to light in the future) to draw up a reasoned catalogue of these constructions, or make any convincing surmises about the cultural allegiances of their builders, though clearly, these peoples had already arrived at a fairly elaborate division of labour.

Urban settlements are not thinkable, however small they are, without a certain stability: stability requires a continuity of cultivation. Continuity of cultivation in turn requires preservation of seed-grain, particularly in hungry times. And this in turn requires the sanction which only an established authority (whether individual or collective) may maintain: even if this authority is granted and withdrawn by common consent.[13]

Delegation is of the essence of the division of labour, as is the elevation of the tribe above subsistence food-production. Certainly, such a level must have been reached long before the urban settlements of which I have here spoken were initiated. They were built of mud, sometimes of brick, with timber roofs. Their interiors were plastered and painted: all this presupposes a much longer development, stretching perhaps into the ice age.

But another and very interesting piece of evidence has come to light very recently (1965–8) at Lepenski Vir, a promontory on a turning of the Danube, to the east of Belgrade.[14]

Lepenski Vir was inhabited seven millennia ago by people who belonged apparently to the familiar late Paleolithic Starčevo culture. Their settlement is of a wholly unknown form: the houses are symmetrical trapezoids in plan, the wide end being curbed; otherwise they are sixths (truncated) of a circle. Within this plan, whatever the size— and there is considerable variation between them—the houses are built on a strange and elaborate geometrical schema. Moreover, the village seems to have had, at various stages in its development, a public place facing the river of a shape very similar to the house-plan.[15]

It is too early to say whether the settlement is isolated or part of a larger, and perhaps even older culture. But even at the present time it is becoming clear that the men of the late paleolithic period were certainly able to conceptualize a rhythmically articulated plan-shape: and that however rudimentary their building techniques may appear, we must credit them with a highly developed way of thinking about them.

*The Sign for a Town*    The geometrical figure at Lepenski Vir presupposes the use of a measuring rod, or perhaps measuring string, and a conception of quantity related to rhythm. In these constructions there is already implicit the notion of a circle, perhaps of the orthogonal joint, and of designing with a module. And when some 3,000 or 4,000 years later the concept of collective dwelling was translated into written term, it was to appeal to this very technique. The Egyptian hieroglyph ⊕ : nywt, is the familiar sign of cross-in-circle, the sign which was discussed earlier in connection with templum.[16] But the sign is also written in another way: like a grid, without the 'main streets'. It is singularly like the sign for a net in a predynastic cylinder seal found at Naga-el-Der. It is not really surprising. The concepts of rope and net are closely associated in Egyptian thinking with orthogonality and with planning generally: the king has spread out his net, the king has cast his net, are a common euphemism for the planning, the laying out of a settlement or a fortress.[17]

The same concept may well underlie the foundation of the Sumerian cuneiform: 𒌷 *er*, *ur*, city, town. Whatever its etymological root (and its connection with the Semitic $\sqrt{Ir}$), the words for the most primitive 'towns' seem associated with the idea of orientation and orthogonality.[18]

The *Ya-hing* sign of the Chinese oracle-bones must be some 400–500 years later than the Egyptian or the Sumerian signs.[19] Nevertheless it seems to be associated with a similar conceptual configuration. The cross in an enclosure seems a kind of abbreviated allusion to a whole world of ideas made much more explicit in the forms and monuments of the early Chinese towns, and in their poetry.

Clearly, this deep-rooted and immemorially hoary notion is not only associated with the Roman system of colonization; nor can it be taken as mere evidence for European or eastern Mediterranean influence.

The whole matter is too ingrained in human experience to be reduced to a simple matter of cultural diffusion. Even when the explanation appears plausible (say in the case of a Roman influence on the Hausa or the Mande), it is not so much the pressure of the cosmology of a more developed people on its less developed neighbours, which is impressive, but the latter's readiness to accept this influence, to base their whole conception of space on it, and to continue its rituals for two millennia in spite of changes of location and religion.

But the reduction of the urban experience to a simple diagram, to a cosmic plan which is universally, or nearly universally known to all planners, is in itself dangerous.

# Conclusion

If it is that universal, why are the towns different? And if they are different, then what does it matter what the remotely guiding simple diagram was like? To consider it, I must go back to the specific instance of my Etruscan rite. When, some time before 800 B.C., some central Italian Villanovan peoples, and some of their Apennine neighbours adopted or had grafted onto them that stock which called itself Etruscan, they assumed—or again imported, or had imposed upon them—the oriental culture to which their arts bear witness. The Greeks at this moment also relied much on oriental manufactures and motifs. We do not know much about the Etruscan religious world: but it does not seem to be too close to that of the Greeks; at times it seems closer to that of the western Semites, the Phoenicians in particular. But it is difficult to unravel this particular skein. However, by the early sixth century, and perhaps even earlier, about the same time as the western (Italian and Sicilian) Greeks, they began to adopt the orthogonal plan for their settlements. It may well be that their earlier settlements, which look so untidy to a modern observer, were demarcated into caste and tribal or family divisions as strictly as a Bororo village; and that the true orthogonal plan in a sequence was a late development: much as it probably was in Egypt.

There is some fragmentary evidence about the passage from one form to another: the fully orthogonal walled city of El Kab was laid out over the earlier walled but roughly shaped oval—and much earlier —settlement sometime during the third dynasty. But earlier orthogonal *mastaba* fields had appeared, forming true necropoles, and orthogonal forts appear in representational reliefs.[20] In Italy such evidence is very hard to come by. The one truly orthogonal plan which can surely be ascribed to the Etruscans is that of Marzabotto[21] and there, although there was certainly an earlier and non-orthogonal settlement underlying the last town which had been destroyed by the Gauls, very little is known about it.

But it is possible that even that earlier settlement, which seems to have been little more than a village, may, like all Etruscan settlements, have been founded by the procedure which the Romans and the Etruscans probably shared in some way with the whole of the ancient world: it consisted of the following elements: (1) the acting out, at the founding of any settlement (or temple maybe, even a mere house) of a dramatic show of the creation of the world; (2) the incarnation of that drama in the plan of the settlement, as well as in its social and religious institution; (3) the achieving of this second aim by the alignment of its axes with those of the universe; and finally (4) the rehearsal of the foundation cosmogony in regularly recurrent festivals, and its commemorative embodiment in the monuments of the settlement. Such a powerful complex must have roots in the biological structure of man, and it must receive support in the formal movement of natural recurrence: day and night, the phases of the moon, the seasons, the changes of the night sky.

In each civilization this apparently atomic element of human make-up had to be incorporated, grafted on (I am aware of the inevitably misleading nature of any analogy in this context but use it because the usual construction has not enough force). How this happened I have tried to describe in the case of the Etrusco-Roman custom; and have used the comparative material to indicate the nature of the phenomenon, outline its limits and allude to the problems: which, in a sense, in Freud's sense, was related to the Romans' obsessive need to harmonize their actions with the will of the gods through augury. But that is only the inevitably negative aspect of the phenomenon, an indication that it is after all properly human. For its essence was, as it always is, to reconcile man to his fate through monument and ritual action. The schema is a construct deduced from the specific example I have given. I claim no universal validity for it. It is only a diagram.

There is a sense in which—as I have already suggested—urban life is a parasitical form of existence, a form of social disease. It is a particular form of the general human predicament, which was summed up in a somewhat rhapsodic form by a French psychiatrist:[22]

> In the beginning environment was a moving ocean. It is becoming. From this becoming the human personality detaches itself to affirm itself in the face of it. The person does it as it might; that is: by modelling environment in its own image, according to both individual and generalized characteristics. But for this very reason it does it almost regretfully, and nurturing deep within itself the nostalgia of the union, of the intimate fusion with becoming which had enveloped it; being constantly pulled by these two forces: the need to affirm and the need to deny itself, the human personality always finds itself wanting when confronted with the wholeness of becoming.

Urban man is exposed not only to the personal predicament, but to that of the social personality, of the society to which he belongs as a person: a person androgynously incarnate in the city founder and its unknown protecting deity. It is this person which is guarded against the dangers inherent in the urban situation by the powerful defences of which I have spoken; the individual was guarded against it even more powerfully in prehistoric times, by the regenerative and reconciling pattern of the town itself. The theme of reconciliation runs insistently through the rituals described: male with female, supernal with infernal gods, town and country, people and land: as when the communities which come together to make the town mix earth from their hearths in the *mundus* to make a common fatherland. Maybe the Etruscan rite was only a ragbag of imported and indigenous usages. But it was robust enough to have survived the disestablishment of paganism by centuries. It turns up in a vestigial form in an 'index of superstitions and paganisms' compiled about the middle of the eighth century.[23] Traces of customs that have echoes of it still survive in certain parts of Europe.[24]

161. **The legendary origin of the city of Mexico,** the Tenochtitlàn of the Aztecs. The site was located when an eagle, the bird-symbol of the god Huitzilipochtili, landed on a cactus among the reeds of a salt-water lake surrounding the city. The figure on the left of the omen represents Tenoch, the hero-founder of Tenochtitlàn *Codex Mendoza, Folio 2 recto.* The manuscript was prepared for Louis de Mendoza, Viceroy of Mexico for the information of Charles V. It was captured at sea and passed to André Thevot, the French geographer who was historiographer to Henri II, whose signature appears in the top left-hand corner *Bodleian Library, Oxford*

Many medieval princes, or at any rate their literate advisers, knew of the antique traditions about town-founding and town-planning. The Christian princes of Spain founded a considerable number of towns, of varying size, which followed an orthogonal plan. First in the south, and later—beginning with Briviesca, near Burgos—also in the north, such towns were outward signs of princely power and order.[25] Briviesca itself was a Roman foundation, which was re-sited in 1208, and replanned about 1315. This tradition was continued by Ferdinand and Isabella. With the very first settlers in the New World this policy was extended to the vast and as yet unknown territories. Even Santo Domingo, the first urban settlement planted over the Atlantic by Bartolomé Colon in

162. **The City of Mexico.** An engraving based on travellers' descriptions
*From G. Braun and F. Hogenberg, 'Civitates Orbis Terrarum', Brussels,
1598, vol. I, p. 58*

163. **Briviesca,** near Burgos. Typical Castilian checkerboard town of
the fourteenth century *After E. A. Gutkind, 'Urban Development in
Southern Europe: Spain and Portugal', The Free Press, New York, 1967*

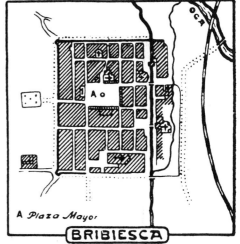

A *Plaza Mayor*

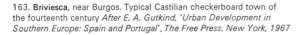

BRIBIESCA

1496, was orthogonally re-planned by Nicolas de Ovando in 1502.[26]
From then on, the consistent policy of *poblaciòn* which the conquerors
were obliged to follow by the central government in the New World,
relied on the rapid and extensive founding of urban centres, for which
standard regulations were drawn up and published.[27]

The conquerors found, as is well known, an autonomous urban
civilization, or perhaps even two separate civilizations. To both of
these, planning, even closely-knit orthogonal planning, was familiar.
La Venta, the great Olmec ceremonial centre, with an axis just 8 degrees
off the true north–south line, may even have been conceived as a vast
figure on plan, a jaguar masque. La Venta must have been founded
about the same time as the city of Rome. Teotihuacàn, the great and
truly urban centre, the capital of a civilization whose exact characteristics have not yet been fully established, was not only orthogonal and
orientated, but also followed a gridiron plan in general. The Aztec
capital, Tenochtitlàn was founded in 1344–5 on a lake island in fulfilment of a legendary prophecy, in the place where an eagle holding a
snake would alight on a cactus.[28] The orientated sacred enclosure of

164. **The Legendary Fall of Snow** on 14th August, which showed Pope Liberius the site and the outlines of the new basilica of St. Mary (*Sta. Maria Maggiore*) which he was to build
*Attributed to Filippino Lippi. By courtesy of the National Trust, London*

Tenochtitlàn stood over this spot; and when it was razed by Cortes in 1521 the new city of Mexico was laid out over the ruins, with its main streets parallel to those of the Aztec capital and its cathedral rising on the site of the temple-pyramid of Xipe Totec, the flayed god.

The miniature which illustrates the foundation myth of Tenochtitlàn in the Codex Mendoza (a tribute-roll, made at the time of the conquest) shows the rectangular city traversed by two diagonals:[29] an unexpected image, considering the persistence elsewhere of the checkerboard. Clearly, the diagonally quartered square or rectangle had a great importance for Mesoamerican thinking. It recurs in calendar images, but is also inherent to Mesoamerican planning. Casual examination of a Maya site, Tikal or Uxmal, or Chichen Itza, will show the way Mayan external space is built up by enclosing it within independent buildings, which line the four sides of a quadrangle, while the corners are left open. This kind of enclosure is evident also at Tiahuanaco, in several of the palaces, but also—in a rudimentary way—in some of the major spaces. The relation between this division of space and the Mesoamerican division of time, so important in the different civilizations of Mexico, Honduras and Guatemala, was clearly most important, though it is as yet only partially understood.[30]

The conquering Spaniards grafted the tradition which was derived, however mediated, from the Roman-Etruscan stem onto a powerful, and apparently quite independent system of practices and beliefs, in which orientated and orthogonal planning had a most important part.[31] The life of cities, and even the development of rural planning in Latin America, cannot be understood without some reference to this superposition. But further study of Maya, Toltec and even Aztec practice will have to wait for the decipherment of more documents and a closer

165. Giorgio Vasari, 'The Foundation of Florence'
*Detail of a ceiling painting in the Salone del Cinquecento, Palazzo Vecchio, Florence*

acquaintance with legendary literature, before a clearer idea can be formed of the ritual practices and the practices related to the surviving buildings.

In Europe, the Etrusco-Roman usages were so firmly part of men's imagination, that they were adapted to both civic[32] and church uses: the ceremony of consecrating a church and an altar according to the Latin rite are both marked by them. Occasionally too, princes would improvise a more elaborate form of foundation rite. During the fifteenth and sixteenth century in Italy, there was an attempt to revive also these ancient practices. Antonio Averlino, called il Filarete, describes the lengthy foundation ceremonies of an ideal town, Sforzinda, in the greatest detail. The foundation stone of the city was to be accompanied by a bronze book and allegorical figures: but also by pots of various grain (millet and wheat) as well as oil, water, wine and milk. After the proper deposition and the benedictions, the lord himself will start digging the foundations, followed by his sons and his principal followers.[33] The day on which this rite was to be performed was calculated by an astrologer to be an auspicious one: this kind of calculation was a matter of course. When Alessandro de' Medici had built that Fortezza da Basso in Florence, which was so hated by the

166. Constantine's Porphyry column, known as the burnt column or (in Turkish) *Chemberli Tash*, the ringed stone. Photograph taken about 1900. *After Aldenham*

Florentines (and perhaps was also the indirect cause of his death) both the elaborate ceremony of laying the first stone and the handing over were carried out at precisely the moment calculated by the astrologers. At the laying of the stone indeed the portable altar at which the officiating bishop had just celebrated a mass was lowered into the foundation ditch, until the signal from two astrologers (who, as it happened, had not synchronized their instruments) to lay the stone,[34] was given.

Naturally, when it came to illustrating ancient history, the details of the rite were observed more closely. The ceiling painting for the Salone del Cinquecento, which Giorgio Vasari did for Cosimo de' Medici in 1563–5 represents the foundation of the colony by the Triumvirs and shows the leader of the colony performing the Etruscan rite according

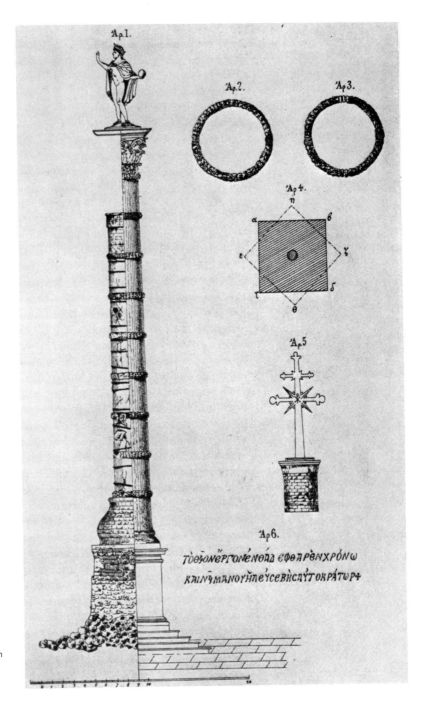

Ἀρ.1.

Ἀρ.2.　　　Ἀρ.3.

Ἀρ.4.

Ἀρ.5

Ἀρ6.

ΤΟΘΥΟΝΕΡΓΟΝΕΝΘΑΔ ΕΦΘΑΡΘΝΧΡΟΝΩ
ΚΑΙΝ<sub>Y</sub>ΜΑΝΟΥΗΠΕΥΣΕΒΗΣΑΥΤΟΚΡΑΤΩΡ+

167. A restoration of the Porphyry
column with its statue of
Constantine which was removed in
1105. On the left, the restoration
carried out by Manuel II and his
inscription. *After Aldenham*

to the texts; it may well have been based on an earlier painting in the
cycle of pictures celebrating Florence's Etruscan past, which was done
for the conferment of Roman citizenship on Giuliano de' Medici in
1513;[35] and the ancient texts are illustrated by many antiquarian
engravers.[35a]

But even later when the Farnese fief Castro was besieged and destroyed by Papal troops on the orders of Innocent X in September 1649, a plough 'passed' over the town, and the ground sown with salt; on the site a column inscribed 'Qui fú Castro' (which has since disappeared) was erected.[36]

Long before all these revivals, the Etruscan rite had a splendid, grandiose, syncretic finish: when Constantine had attempted to revive the Trojan and Hellenic past of the city of Rome and to lay a new capital near the Tomb of Ajax, on the place where the besieging Achaeans had beached their ships and set up camp, a dream warned him to move away, to found it on the site of Byzantium.[37] Zosimus uses the pregnant phrase: that he had decided to move the palladium from Rome to Byzantium, another echo of the new Troy. Constantine consecrated, 'founded' his city in A.D. 326 or 328. Although he had gone some way to Christianity, the foundation ceremony took place in the first year of the 276 Olympiad, when the sun was in the constellation of the Bowman and at an hour dominated by the crab. It may well be that the name of the city was triple, as had been that of Rome, and that Constantinople had been given the same secret protective deity.[38] The legend further tells of Constantine, like Romulus (not a fratricide, but was he not guilty of his son's blood?) walking behind the plough: it is said that he departed from the previously staked-out route. When his followers attempted to make him return to the shorter route he said 'I shall go on until he who is walking ahead of me stops.[39] Whom did Constantine claim to see ahead of him—Christ or an Angel (as the Christian historians, Sozomen and Eusebius claimed)? his genius? or the Tyche of the new city? or perhaps even Apollo himself, the sun-god, whose incarnation Constantine sometimes thought himself. It was all summed up in a monument of which there is a rump still standing: the great column of porphyry set up in the Forum of the new city on a high base of white marble and crowned with a statue of Constantine under which—as in a *mundus*—was buried the original Palladium of Troy, while the orb carried by the statue contained a piece of the true Cross.[40] The rite was powerful enough to be absorbed into the new faith. Its echoes were to sound until our time.

It is difficult to imagine a situation when the formal order of the universe could be reduced to a diagram of two intersecting co-ordinates in one plane. Yet this is exactly what did happen in antiquity: the Roman who walked along the *cardo* knew that his walk was the axis round which the sun turned, and that if he followed the *decumanus*, he was following the sun's course. The whole universe and its meaning could be spelt out of his civic institutions—so he was at home in it. We have lost all the beautiful certainty about the way the world works—we are not even sure if it is expanding or contracting, whether it was produced by a catastrophe or is continuously renewing itself. This does not absolve us from looking for some ground of certainty in our attempts to give form to human environment. It is no longer likely that we shall find this ground in the world which the cosmologists are continuously reshaping round us and so we must look for it inside ourselves: in the constitution and structure of the human person.

168. **The camp of Assurbanipal.** Relief on an orthostat from the throne room of Assurbanipal's Palace at Nimrud. Late Assyrian, *c.* 900 B.C. The camp is shown as two crossing roads inside a fortified circle; in each quarter cooks and servants are preparing for the army's return. *British Museum*

# Notes

## Preface *(between pages 23 and 26)*

1 C. A. Daviler, 'Explication des Termes d'Architecture', *Cours d'Architecture*, II, Paris, 1691, s.v. *Ville*, p. 336: 'C'est par rapport à l'Architecture civile un compartiment d'Isles et de Quartiers disposés avec symétrie et décoration, des Rues et Places publiques percées d'alignement en belle et saine exposition avec pentes nécessaires pour l'écoulement des eaux. Voyez Vitruve, *liv.* I, chap. 6'.

2 Pierre Lelièvre, *La Vie des Cités de l'Antiquité à nos Jours*, Paris, 1950, p. 11.

3 *Thucydides*, trans. Thomas Hobbes, VII, 63, pp. 308–9.

4 P.-H. Chambart de Lauwe, with S. Antoine, L. Couvreur, J. Gauthier, *Paris et l'Agglomération Parisienne*, Paris, 1952, I, pp. 247ff.

## Town and Rite: Rome and Romulus *(between pages 27 and 40)*

1 Plutarch, *Life of Romulus*, ed. John Dryden, rev. A. H. Clough, London, 1927–28, I, p. 36.

2 Genesis 4: 17.

3 Apollod., I, 18; but see Sch. ad. Stat. *Theb.* I, 282, for the variant in which Tydeus kills Toxeus.

4 Plutarch, G.Q., 37, where two further legends are quoted. Miltiades was badly hurt as he climbed the wall of the sanctuary of Ceres Thesmophoros, felt a 'nameless dread' and died soon after (Herod. VI, 134). But the sanctuary was in any case forbidden to men, and the climbing of the fence was here part of a larger act of sacrilege, so the incident is not strictly relevant. Again, Capaneus, the second of the 'Seven Against Thebes' (Aeschylus, *Seven Against Thebes*, 420ff.) and inventor of scaling ladders, who swore to overcome Thebes against the will of Zeus, was struck by lightning while climbing the wall. His desecration of the wall was also part of a larger act of defiance against the gods. Cf. also Hyg. *Fab.*, 71; Flav. Veg., IV, 21.

5 Plutarch, *R.Q.*, 27.

7 Varro, *de L.L.*, V, 143; cf. Fest., s.v. *urvat*, and Serv. in Virg. I *Aen.* 16.

8 In 340 B.C.; Livy, VIII, 9.

9 On Tarchon, see below, p. 156; Pliny, *N.H.* (XIII, lxxxiv) describes how Cn. Terentius, ploughing his field on the Janiculum in 181 B.C., came upon a chest containing the 'books of Numa'; Numa had a similar authority in Roman religious practice to that enjoyed by Tages in Etruscan lore; cf. S. Weinstock, 'Libri Fulgurales', *Papers, Brit. Sch. Rome*, 1951 (XIX) pp. 142f.

10 Cic. *de Div.*, II, 50; Ovid, *Metamorphoses*, XV, 533; Amm. Marc., XVII, 10, ii: 'The Greeks called him Ἑρμῆς Χθόνικός (Hermes Chthonikos)', John Lydus, *de Ostentis*, 3.

11 On Vegoia-Begoia and her relation (as its *las*) to the *gens* Vecu, see C. Clemen, *Die Religion der Etrusker*, Bonn, 1936, p. 31; cf. also J. Heurgon, 'The Date of Vegoia's Prophecy', *J.R.S.*, XIX, 1959, pp. 41–5.

12 These seem with time to have acquired many accretions: see S. Weinstock, 'C. Fonteius Capito and the Libri Tagetici' in *Papers, Brit. Sch. Rome*, 1950 (XVIII), pp. 44ff.; that is, if they can be said to have had an 'original' form.

13 The nature of Etruscan lightning-learning and its interpretation, particularly on its relation to Roman lore on the subject, was discussed by S. Weinstock in 'Libri Fulgurales' (op. cit.) pp. 122ff. This learning was not static, and by historical times had been much 'adulterated'. Nevertheless, Weinstock says: 'A fundamental difference divided the *haruspices* from the Romans: whereas the Greek spirit made the Romans receptive to a secular culture for its own sake, it influenced the Etruscans only in so far as it helped them to improve and modernize their sacred books; and because the Greeks, for good reason, could not satisfy them fully, they turned to the writings of Hellenised Orientals' (op. cit., p. 123). What Weinstock says of lightning-learning and the *haruspices* may be applied more generally to the *interpretatio graeca* of other Etruscan lore.

14 C. O. Thulin's *Die Etruskische Disziplin*, Göteborg, 1906–9, is still the most detailed study of this matter; see also C. Clemen, op. cit., and A. Grenier, 'La Religion des Etrusques et Romains' in *Les Religions de l'Europe Ancienne*, Mana 2, III, Paris, 1948. For a curious note on Begoia as a recent witch or wicked spirit in Tuscany, see L. G. Leland, *Etruscan Roman Remains in Popular Tradition*, London, 1892, pp. 112ff. A brief note on Tages, ibid. pp. 96ff.

15 Fest., s.v. *Rituales*.

16 Fustel de Coulanges, *La Cité Antique*, Paris, 1880, pp. 198–9.

17 The first real fixed date on which the annalists and the Fasti agree is not the foundation of the city, but the dedication of the temple of Jupiter Optimus Maximus on the Capitol by the consul Marcus Horatius Pulvillus on 13th September 509, the year after the expulsion of the kings. The story of the dedication is told by Plutarch in the 'Life of Poplicola'. The reckoning of time was maintained by the driving of a nail into the wall between the *cella* of Jupiter and that of Minerva on every *dies natalis* of the temple (Livy, VII, 3). This was done, according to Livy, by the *praetor maximus*, an office about which the antiquarians seem to have been undecided: see Fest., s.v. *Major*. The rite, as Livy insists, was of Etruscan origin, and had a propitiatory function. In fact nails seem to have been fixed by dictators specially named for that office at times of emergency. The three known *dictatores clavi fingendi causa* are discussed by Krister Hannell in *Das Altrömische Eponyme Amt*, Lund, 1946, pp. 125ff. This rite has led Th. Mommsen, in *Römische Chronologie bis auf Caesar*, Berlin, 1859, to question the regular nail-fixing as a method of time reckoning: pp. 176ff., 217. Mommsen would not accept the evidence of the annalists, which, in the form transmitted, could not be earlier than the third century B.C., since by that time the nail-fixing ceremony had been discarded and perhaps replaced by an *epulum Jovi* (a banquet for the god given on the *dies natalis*). But the twin method of time-reckoning by nail-fixing and eponymous office-holders was rehabilitated by Oscar Leuze in *Die Römische Jahrzählung*, Tübingen, 1909, pp. 293ff. The traditional date has been completely 'restored' by R. Bloch: see 'Le Départ des Etrusques de Rome selon l'Annalistique, et la Dédicace du Temple du Jupiter Capitolin' in *R. Hist. Rel.*, 1961 (159) pp. 141ff., esp. p. 149; who has followed by A. J. Pfiffig *Einführung in die Etruskologie*, Darmstadt, 1972, p. 50.

18 I rely here mostly on Thulin, op. cit., III, pp. 8–9, and K. O. Müller, *Die Etrusker*, Stuttgart, 1877, pp. 146ff. But see also Fustel de Coulanges, op. cit., pp. 152–7.

19 *R.E.*, s.v. *Colonia* (III, Beschreibung der Coloniegründung).

20 R. Bloch, *The Origins of Rome*, London, 1960, p. 36.

21 See in general *R.E.*, s.v.; also G. Wissowa, *Religion und Kultus der Römer*, Munich, 1902, pp. 54, 132 and passim; Kurt Latte, *Römische Religionsgeschichte*, Munich, 1960, pp. 124, 253, 378; and also W. Warde Fowler, *The Religious Experience of the Roman People*, London, 1911, pp. 240ff.

22 In 217 B.C., just after the Roman defeat at Lake Trasimene. The vow was accomplished in 195 B.C.; but after a pontifical declaration of its invalidity it was repeated the next year: Livy, XXII, 10, iii; XXXIII, 44, i; XXXIV, 44, i. This vow was made after a consultation of the Sibylline books (a *graecus ritus*), and unlike other vows of this nature, made to Jupiter instead of Mars.

23 So Fest. (Paulus), s.v. *Ver sacrum*.

24 Serv. in Virg. XI *Aen.* 785; Strabo, V, 4, 12.

25 Strabo, V, 4, iii–xii, and in particular about their capital Bovilium (a curious name, since the bull is not at all associated with Mars); Strabo, V, 6, xii.

26 Pliny, *N.H.*, III, 110; Strabo, V, 4, ii; Fest. (Paulus), s.v. *Oscinum*.

27 Corruption of Martii; but no foundation ritual recorded in ancient sources. See *R.E.*, s.v.

28 Mamers is the Oscan Mars; on the origin of the Mamertini, Fest. (Paulus), s.v.

29 Sacri, *Sacrani*; Fest. (Paulus) s.v. *Picum, Sacrani*; also Serv. in Virg. VII *Aen.* 796.

30 Strabo, VI, 56.

31 Dion. Hal. I, 12; also I, 16 and II, 1. The tithe in honour of Apollo and the *ver sacrum* in honour of Mars present some parallels, but modern authors have identified the *ver sacrum* with the Greek sacrifice of a Φάρμακος (*pharmakos*), which had a purely purificatory function, and is much nearer the Semitic scapegoat than the Italiot *ver sacrum*. This is made clear in Eisenhut's article (s.v. *Ver sacrum, R.E.*), and further commented on by J. E. Harrison, *Prolegomena to the Study of Greek Religion*, London, 1922, pp. 94–114. There is, however, a Roman custom, the 'Expulsion of Mamurius Veturius', also a March ceremony, closely associated with Mars. It is only described by a late authority, John Lydus (*On the Months* IV, 49) and may therefore be a hellenistic and archaizing interpolation, in spite of its innocently primitive air. It echoes the yearly Athenian custom at the Tagelia, but its use of skins suggests a somewhat different emphasis. On Mamurius Veturius as the 'Old Year' being expelled for fertilizing purposes, see J. E. Harrison, *Themis*, 2nd edn., London, 1963, pp. 195–7, following Sir J. G. Frazer, *The Golden Bough*, London, 1911–15, III, 122ff.

32 Cic. *de Rep.*, II, 2.

33 Below, p. 44.

34 *Mythe et Pensée chez les Grecs: Etudes de Psychologie Historique*, 2nd edn., Paris, 1966, pp. 233ff.

35 Plutarch, *Life of Pericles*, pp. 230–1.

36 Strabo, VI, 269–70.

37 H. W. Parke and D. E. W. Wormell, *The Delphic Oracle*, Oxford, 1956, I, pp. 68ff. Cf., however, Jean Bérard, *La Colonisation Grecque de l'Italie Méridionale et de la Sicile dans l'Antiquité*, Paris, 1957, pp. 117, 153ff. The important discussion of the oracular literature as evidence, and the selective survival of texts in M. Miller, *The Sicilian Colony Dates*, Albany N.Y. 1970, vol I pp. 43ff came to my attention when the book was in proof.

38 Cf. Strabo, VI, 262; Bérard, op. cit., p. 151 n. 4 and p. 152 n. 1; Parke and Wormell, op. cit., I, p. 70 n. 44. Cf. also Hippys of Rhegium in *F.G.H.*, III B, p. 554.

39 Bérard, op. cit., p. 323ff.

40 Aristotle, *Constitution of Athens*, XXI, 6; Herod., V, 66. Cf. Parke and Wormell, op. cit., pp. 147ff.; P. Lévéque and P. Vidal-Naquet, *Clisthène l'Athénien*, Paris, 1964, pp. 23ff.

41 Paus., I, 5, 1–3. Cf. J. E. Harrison, *Mythology and Monuments of Ancient Athens*, London, 1890, pp. 57ff. See also, H. A. Thompson and R. E. Wycherley, *The Agora of Athens*, Princeton, 1972.

42 On this matter and Theseus as the mythical antitype of Cleisthenes, see Lévéque and Vidal-Naquet, op. cit., pp. 119ff. On the shrine of Theseus and the eponymous gods and heroes see Al. N. Oikonomides, *The Two Agoras of Ancient Athens*, Chicago, 1964, pp. 64, 70, 98; also 69ff., 87ff.

43 Plutarch 'Life of Cimon', VIII.

44 V. Tscherikower, *Die Hellenistische Stadtgründungen von Alexander dem Grossen bis auf die Römerzeit*, Leipzig, 1927, pl 113.

45 Plutarch, *Par.*, 6.

46 Sch. Vet. (in Pind. *Car.*), ed. A. B. Drachman, Leipzig, 1903, 149 b.

47 Pindar, I Ol, 92.

48 Pausanias, V, 13.

49 A. Boetticher, *Olympia*, Berlin, 1886, pp. 82, 322ff. For recent literature, see H.-V. Herrmann, *Olympia*, 'Heiligtum und Wettkampfstätte', Munich, 1972, pp. 50ff., 226ff.

50 Below, p. 152. cf. E. Rohde, *Psyche*, pp. 166ff.

51 At Megara: Paus. I, 43, 3; cf. Parke and Wormell, op. cit. vol I, p. 351; II, p. 222. For other Megaran traditions about hero-burials in towns, see op. cit. vol I, pp. 62, 346f. A Tarentine tradition of a similar oracle is cited by Polyb. VIII, 28; cf. Parke and Wormell, op. cit. vol II, p. 222.

52 R. Martin, *Recherches sur l'Agora Grecque*, Paris, 1951, pp. 195 n. 2, and 200 n. 5; also pp. 194–201 passim. And *R.E.*, s.v. *Ktistes*; also Brelich, op. cit., p. 130, ns. 169–70 for comparative material.

53 A. Brelich, *Gli Eroi Greci*, Rome, 1959, p. 263.

54 Brelich, op. cit., passim. I have followed Brelich's interpretation of the hero as a mytho-ritual figure.

55 Brelich, op. cit., pp. 8off.

56 Above, p. 34.

57 Thuc., V, 11.

58 On Hagnon, cf. A. J. Graham, op. cit., p. 37ff.

59 On honey as a sacrificial substance in the classical world, see *R.E.*, s.v. *Opfer*, and S. Eitrem, *Opferritus und Voropfer der Griecher und Römer*, Kristiania, 1915, pp. 102ff. Much comparative material is in Claude Lévi-Strauss, *Du Miel au Cendres*, Paris, 1967, Cf. H. Usener, *Milch* and *Honig* in *Rh. M.* (N.F.) 57, 177–92.

60 For the excavator's description and interpretation see Paulo Claudio Sestieri, 'Il Sacello-Heroon Posidonate', *Bolletino d'Arte*, XL, 1955, pp. 53–61. He suggests that the shrine is dedicated to Hera as the avatar of 'The Great Mother'. This interpretation rests, too heavily in my view, on a single ostrakon, and the 'female character' of the hydriae of which there are two in the tomb. An interpretation based in addition on the iconography of the material is offered by Bernhard Neutsch in ταs νυνφαs εμι ηιαρον, 'Ein Vasengrafitto: zum unterirdischen Heiligtum von Paestum' (*Abh.Heid.Ak.Wiss. Ph.-Hist.Kl.*, 2 Abh.), Heidelberg, 1957, who suggests (interpreting the same ostrakon as Sestieri) that the shrine is dedicated either to the nymphs in general, to a particular nymph whose cenotaph it is, or to the nymphs connected with some other funerary cult. While there is no doubt about the interpretation of the ostrakon, I find Neutsch's general treatment of the iconography unsatisfying, and prefer on the whole that of Paola Zanconi-Montuoro in 'Il Poseidonion di Poseidonia', *Archivio Storico per la Calabria e la Lucania*, XXIII, 1954, pp. 165ff. On private prayer at a hero's tomb see W. K. Guthrie, *The Greeks and their Gods*, London, 1950, pp. 232ff. Other interpretations of this monument are suggested by Mario Napoli in his *Paestum*, Novara, 1967, p. 43

61 Sandro Stucchi, *L'Agora di Kyrene*, Rome, 1965, I, pp. 58ff., 139ff., 278ff.

62  F. Chamoux, 'Cyrene sous la Monarchie des Battides', *Bibl. des Ec.Fr.d'Ath. et Rome*, 177, Paris, 1953, pp. 131, 285ff.

63  For this and the various mythological accounts of the foundation of Kyrene as well as the personality of Aristoteles-Battos, see Chamoux, op. cit., pp. 69–114; cf. Bérard, op. cit., pp. 367, 416f.; and Parke and Wormell, op. cit., I, pp. 70, 73ff., 155ff, II, pp. 18f., 32, 168, and more recently, C. M. Bowra, *Pindar*, Oxford, 1964, pp. 137ff., 329f.

64  Pind. *Pyth.*, IV, lines 33ff. I have used the translation (slightly modified) by H. T. Wade-Gray and C. M. Bowra, London, 1928.

65  On the 'mouth of hell' and the shrine of Poseidon at Taenarum, see *R.E.* s.v. Taenarum.

66  Apol. Rhod., IV, 1537–71 and 1731–72.

67  Cf. R. W. B. Burton, *Pindar's Pythian Odes*, London, 1962, pp. 135ff.

68  Plutarch, 'Life of Romulus', 11.

69  Cf. above, p. 59.

70  *S.E.G.*, IX, 3. Cf. also Chamoux, op. cit., pp. 105ff.

71  On Apollo as Archegetes, cf. *R.E.*, s.v. *Ktistes*.

72  Herod., I, 165. Cf. Marcus N. Tod, *A Selection of Greek Historical Inscriptions*, Oxford, 1933, nos. 23, 25.

73  *S.E.G.*, IX, 3.

74  Cf. Vernant, op. cit., pp. 258f.

75  S. Ferri, 'La Lex Cathartica di Cirene', *Notiziaro Archeologico*, Rome, 1927, IV, pp. 93ff.

76  Cf., however, Plato, *Laws*, 738.

77  Tod, op. cit., no. 24.

78  Tod, op. cit., no. 44. For the translation and commentary, I have followed A. J. Graham, *Colony and Mother City*, Manchester, 1964, Appendix II. A much later inscription records the extending of the boundaries of the city of Colophon which had regained its independence. The ceremonies and the administration of this extending, which was carried out sometime before 300 B.C., were treated almost as a new foundation. See R. Martin (op. cit.) pp. 55ff.

79  More properly orichalkos, probably mountain-copper. The word is sometimes used for bronze. But Plato's stele is of mythical metal, in a mythical city.

80  Plato, *Critias*, 119dff. On the background of this passage, see Platon, *Oeuvres Complètes*, vol. X, pp. 244ff.; see also Paul Friedländer, *Plato*, London, 1958, vol. I, pp. 314ff.

81  Herod., I, cxlvi 2.

82  Sch. *Vet.* in Pind. XI *Nem.* I. On the issue of carrying an 'old' flame, on the continuity of the sacred fire; as against the 'new' fire which Romulus lit on the Palatine, see G. Devoto, *Tabulae Iguvinae*, pp. 175f.

83  For a case in which these customs were flaunted, with dire consequences, see the case of Dorieus the Spartan, below p. 43.

84  Thuc., I, xxiv, 2; elsewhere (VI, iv, 2, 3) he records the same customs being followed in the founding of Selinus (628 B.C.) from Megara Hyblaea by an oecist sent from Megara proper, Pamillus.

85  For a specifically Macedonian rite, followed by Alexander the Great, see below pp. 135.

86  Herod., III, 19. A great deal is known about the rites for founding temples and tombs in ancient Mesopotamia and Egypt. At Jerusalem too, the building and dedication of the temple (with Phoenician aid) were sacral activities (I Kings, V–IX; II Kings, V–IX; Chronicles, I–VIII). But parallel customs about whole towns are unfamiliar.

## City and Site *(between pages 41 and 71)*

1  See above, p. 37.

2  Aristotle, *Politics*, VII, 11, 276, 1330a.

3  Hippocrates, *Aphorisms*, III, 4 and 5; also *Airs, Waters* (ed. Littre), II, p. 130. While this short treatise may not have had any direct influence on town planning, it certainly sets out clearly Greek medical attention to the nature of place as a direct cause of health or disease.

4  Vitruv., I, 4, i. Vitruvius's insistence on the importance of wind follows classical doctrines on the subject as set out for instance in the short Hippocratean book 'on winds' (most recent version in R. Joly, *Hippocrates*, Paris, 1964, pp. 26ff.). But it goes back to earlier thinkers, who considered the air as the primary 'substance' of the world, such as Anaximenes of Miletus or Diogenes of Apollonia. Cf. G. S. Kirk and J. E. Raven, *The Presocratic Philosophers*, Cambridge, 1957, pp. 151ff., 434ff.

5  Aristotle, *Politics*, 1345 a.

6  Xenophon, *Economics*, IX, 4.

7  Vitruv., I, 4. viii.

8 Vitruv., I, 6, i–v and ix–xiii.

9 Oribasius, ed. Daremberg, II, p. 318f. Cf. also Max Neuberger, *History of Medicine*, Oxford, 1910, pp. 298–303; and T. Clifford Owen, *Greek Medicine in Rome*, London, 1921, pp. 324ff.

10 Roland Martin, *L'Urbanisme dans la Grèce Antique*, Paris, 1956, pp. 12–29. The second edition (Paris, 1974) appeared when this book was in proof.

11 Plato, *Laws*, p. 747, trans. Jowett.

12 Ibid.

13 Lévêque and Vidal-Naquet, op. cit., p. 120. Cf. Plato, *Laws*, loc. cit.

14 Herod., V, pp. 42–3. Cf. Parke and Wormell, op. cit., I, p. 152; II, p. 72; also Bérard, op. cit., p. 259.

15 Herod., V, 44–5; Bérard, op. cit., pp. 156 and 259.

16 De Coulanges, op. cit., p. 153.

17 Parke and Wormell, op. cit., I, pp. 49–81; Bérard, op. cit., p. 100ff. and passim; also Martin P. Nilsson, *Geschichte der Griechischen Religion*, Munich, 1941, I, pp. 604–7.

18 The site of the Delphic oracle: Bouché-Leclercq, op. cit. *De la Divination*, I, p. 146.

19 Many instances; see G. R. Levy, *The Gate of Horn*, London, 1948, pp. 250–1.

20 Capua: Serv. in Virg. X *Aen.* 145 and C. Clemen, op. cit., p. 52.

21 As Platea: A. B. Cook, *Zeus*, Cambridge, 1924–40, II, p. 898, n. 6 (Strabo).

22 Pythopolis in Mysia, founded by Theseus. See Plutarch, *Life of Theseus* and Levy, op. cit., p. 251.

23 The oracle of Trophonius at Lebadea: Paus., IX, 40, 1–2. Cf. Bouché-Leclercq, op. cit., III, 321ff.; for other incidents with bees leading colonists, ibid., I, p. 146.

24 The Cretans were led to Delphi by Apollo incarnate in a dolphin. Hom.*Hymn.* to Apollo, I, 397ff. Apollo Delphinios as the eponym of Delphi in Bouche-Léclercq, op. cit., III, pp. 55ff.; cf. also A. B. Cook, op. cit., II, p. 189.

25 Bouche-Léclercq, op. cit., I, 143.

26 Varro, de *L. L.*, V, II, 144. At Delphi, the centre of all divination, many such oracles coincide. There is Pytho the serpent, the eagles released by Zeus, the Cretans' dolphin, the goats which first found the chasm, etc.

27 De Coulanges, op. cit., p. 153.

28 Plutarch, 'Life of Romulus', p. 35. Dion Hal. I, 79. Cf. also G. de Sanctis, *Storia dei Romani*, Rome, 1907, I, p. 187, For a description of the Lupercal, see G. Lugli, *Roma Antica*, Rome, 1946, pp. 420–30.

29 Plutarch says that Romulus went up on the Palatine, and Remus on the Aventine (Plutarch, op. cit., 35; also Ovid, *Fasti*, V, 145ff.); this second, inauspicious station was later consecrated to Bona Dea, whose cult and mysteries are closed to men (Plutarch, 'Life of Cicero', 28; and 'Life of Caesar', 9f.; Cic. *ad Attic.*, I, 12). Whatever the connection, the Aventine was left outside the *pomoerium* (a term I shall discuss later) of Rome until the reign of Claudius. See Aul. Gell., XIII, 14. Also L. Homo, *Rome Imperiale et l'Urbanisme dans l'Antiquité*, Paris, 1951, p. 94. Cf. E. Gjerstadt, *The Fortifications of Early Rome: Opuscula Romana*, Stockholm, 1941, I, p. 56, esp. n. 1.

30 The prayer distinguised *inauguratio* performed by an augur on an *auguraculum*, esp. the Capitoline *auguraculum* (*ex arce*, as Livy, IV, 18, vi; X, 7, x), and *inauspicatio* which could be performed by many other magistrates. So Serv. on Virg. I *Aen.* 398 on that and other differences between the two rites. For the legal and institutional aspects of the distinction, see P. de Francisci, *Primordia Civitatis*, Rome, 1959, pp. 518ff. Cf. also Werner Müller. *Die Heilige Stadt*, Stuttgart, 1961, pp. 38–9.

31 Varro, de *L.L.*, VII, 8. The text used here is the one restored and interpreted by Eduard Norden in his *Aus den Altrömischen Priesterbüchern*, Lund and Leipzig, 1939, pp. 71ff.; further corrected by Kurt Latte in 'Augur und Templum in der Varronischen Auguralformel', *Philologus*, XCVII, 1948, pp. 143–59, and 'Römische Religionsgeschichte', op. cit., p. 42, n. 3. As against that see R. G. Kent's reading in *Varro on the Latin Language*, London and Cambridge, Mass., 1958, I, p. 275; P. Goidanich, 'Il Tempio Augurale.', *Historia*, XII, 1934, pp. 579–93; and Müller, op. cit., pp. 40ff.

32 The actual *lituus* with which Romulus inaugurated Rome was preserved in the *Curia Saliorum* on the Palatine. So Plutarch ('Life of Camillus', 216); and Cic. (*de Div.* I, 30), who also remarks on the double meaning of the word *lituus*: a trumpet and wand which, he says, is due to the resemblance of a crooked staff to a trumpet. In fact the *Tubilustrium* (23 March) coincided with the feast of the finding of the *lituus Romuli* after the *Curia Saliorum* had been burnt by the Gauls. This, and a remark of Lydus (*de Mens.* IV, 42) suggested to Mommsen (*Römisches Staatsrecht*, III, Leipzig, 1881–7, p. 386) that the wand was in fact a trumpet. G. Wissowa is not quite committal (*Religion and Kult der Römer*, p. 482, n. 1) 'sog. *Lituus Romuli* der tatsächlich viel mehr (als baculus) eine Tuba war'. This argument is dismissed a little summarily by N. Turchi, *La Religion di*

*Roma Antica*, Bologna, 1939, pp. 82–3. On the Etruscan origin of the *lituus* as a crooked staff, see Latte, op. cit., 157, n. 3. Müller, op. cit., attempts to prove the exclusively Indo-European origin of the augural staff, and discounts its Etruscan origins, to my mind inconclusively. On the *lituus* and rod symbolism generally, see Cic. *de Div.* ed. A. S. Pease, Urbana, III., 1920, pp. 190ff. and, more generally, F. J. M. de Waele, *The Magic Staff or Rod in Graeco-Italian Antiquity*, The Hague, 1927; also E. Benveniste, *Le Vocabulaire des Institutions Indo-Européennes*, Paris, 1963, I, pp. 29ff. (trans. E. Palmer, *Indo-European Language and Society*, London, 1973).

33 Livy, I, 18; for a detailed commentary on this passage see H. J. Rose, 'The Inauguration of Numa', *J.R.S.*, XIII, 1923, pp. 82–90.

34 *Signum . . . animo finivit:* this seems to be technical terminology of divination; see Norden, op. cit., p. 84.

35 Both Varro, loc. cit., and the Iguvine Tables (VI a, 1, ff.), specify such signs.

36 Serv. in Virg. III *Aen.* 89; Fest., s.v. *Templum*.

37 Livy, I, 18. Another, much more elaborate formula of an augural *lex* survives in the text of the Iguvine tables; this incomplete set of bronze tablets inscribed with ritual formulae was discovered in Gubbio in 1444, and much has been written about them. The most recent edition of the text with a commentary is by Ambrose Josef Pfiffig, 'Religio Iguvina', *Osterreichische Akademie der Wissenschaften, Philosophisch-Historische Klasse, Denkschriften*, 84, Vienna, 1964. But see also *Tabulae Iguvinae*, I, ed. G. Devoto, Rome, 1937; I. Rosenzweig, *Ritual and Cults of Pre-Roman Iguvium*, London, 1937.

38 These vultures were often identified with the Roman eagle. But although the appearance of a bird identified with the protective divinity of the city (as the eagle was with Jupiter) might have been expected, it seems that the vulture appears here as a bird of good omen generally. Omens from eagles and from vultures were quite distinct. So Serv. in Virg. I *Aen.* 398; see also Plutarch, *R.Q.*, 93, 286; also Apollod., I, 9, xii and Sch., Hom., *Od.* XI, 287–90; and A. Bouché-Leclercq, *Histoire de la Divination*, I, 134. A curious echo of the legend was the identification of some of the bones which Boni found in the 'Tomb of Romulus' (i.e. under the *Lapis Niger*) on the Forum in 1899 as those of a vulture, a bird which, as Plutarch observed, was very rare in Italy; see G. A. and A. C. Blanc, 'Bones of a Vulture, etc.', *Nature*, CXXVIII, 5 July 1958, p. 66. On the vulture as a bird of good omen in Roman augury, see Plutarch, 'Life of Romulus', p. 35.

39 On this term see Latte and Norden, op. cit.; also V. Pisani, 'Cortumio', *Glotta*, XXXIV, 1955, p. 296; 'Demnach wird c. in der Auguralsprache das Koordinieren der verschiedenen Zeichen oder der fines usw seitens des Augurs bezeichnet haben'.

40 The demarcation of *contemplatio* as a ritual entity is not very clearly outlined by any authority in antiquity.

41 Varro, *de L.L.*, VII, 6.

42 S. Weinstock, 'Templum', *Mitt.Deutsc.Arch.Inst., Röm.*, XLVII, 1932, pp. 95–121; pp. 100ff., taking up the Vitruvian use of *templum* to mean a cross-beam.

43 Though this did not apply to all such places; not to the temple of Vesta, for instance: *Aul.Gell.*, XIV, 7.

44 *Aul. Gell.*, loc. cit.

45 Cic. *de Leg.*, II, 8, xxi. The term *effatus* is almost untranslatable. Fest., s.v., suggested that the words *liberatus* and *effatus* were almost equivalent; they were certainly complementary. Servius explains it more closely (in Virg. III *Aen.*, 463; Virg. VI *Aen.*, 197), and before him Varro, *de L.L.*, VI, 53. Perhaps the word 'consecrated', which I have used here, involves some anachronism—and of course there is the Latin word *consecratus*, to which the modern 'consecrated' is closer.

46 Varro, *de L.L.*, VII, 13.

47 Aul Gell., XIII, 14. Cf. also Wissowa, *Religion und Kultus der Römer*, pp. 455f.

48 K. Latte, *Römische Religions Geschichte*, p. 41

49 Fest. 38 M. On the destruction of the block of flats which Titus Claudius Centualis sold to Publius Calpurnius Lanarius, and which obstructed the view from the Capitoline *auguraculum* (though it stood on the Celian hill, i.e. 1½ km away!), see Cic. *de Off.*, III, 66.

50 For an extended discussion of this system, see H. Nissen, *Das Templum*, Berlin, 1869. More recently it has been re-considered by S. Weinstock in his 'Martianus Capella and the Cosmic System of the Etruscans', *J.R.S.*, 1946, pp. 101–9. There is a criticism of Weinstock's views in Grenier, op. cit. The divisions forward-backward and left-right were usually associated with cardinal directions. According to Goidanich (op. cit., pp. 25ff.), the Augur stood on the *decussis* of the *templum*. It is much more likely that he stood just 'north' of it, facing 'south', that is, along the Cardo. I find it very difficult to reconcile the idea of the augur standing at the centre of the *templum* with all we know

about their practice. The augur observed the signs with his head veiled, and all the texts agree that he had to pay the closest attention to all he saw. Moreover he had to stand or sit absolutely still (Serv. in Virg. VI *Aen.* 197): the *templum* could not, therefore, be all round him; it had to be right in front.

50a Varro, *de L.L.*, VII, 6ff.

51 See for instance, R. Eisler, *Weltmantel und Himmelszelt*, Munich, 1910, passim; or E. Baldwin Smith, *The Dome*, Princeton, 1950.

51a Varro, *de L.L.*, VII, 7.

51b Julius Frontinus, *de Limit.*, I (ed. Thulin, p. 11). On the difference between the two directional systems, see O. A. W. Dilke, *The Roman Land Surveyors: an Introduction to the Agrimensores*, London, 1971, pp. 32ff. See also below, no 51e.

51b(i) See above, p. 48.

51c Even if many details of augural practice and lore survive, Varro comments, not without some asperity perhaps, that *augures augurium agere dicuntur, quom in eo plura dicant quam faciant*; augurs are said to *practice* augury, though they say more in it than they do (Varro, *de L.L.*, VI, 42). In his advocacy of plebeian rights against the patricians, the tribune C. Canuleius, speaking in the senate in 445 B.C., attributed the foundation of both the native augural and pontifical colleges to Numa: presumably, as the chroniclers suggest, until then diviners and ritual practitioners were either foreign or trained out of Rome. Livy, who reports Canuleius's speech (IV, 4, ii), also reports the inauguration of Numa quoted in the text as a 'type' of augural practice. This text has been analysed in great detail by S. Weinstock in 'Templum', *Mitt. Deutsc. Arch. Inst. Röm.*, 1932, XLVII, pp. 99ff.

The assumption has been made by several authors—on the authority of Wissowa (*Religion und Kultus der Römer*, p. 452) that the augur faced east, while the king faced north. But a glance at the map of Rome, and the place of the Capitoline *auguraculum* in it would show that this was impossible. And neither the Capitoline, nor the other known *auguracula* (at Cosa, Iguvium, Norba), faced the cardinal points. The drawing of the templum therefore was not the recognition by the augur of the world-order and the calling down of it on to the auguraculum. So that a more accurate translation of the literal 'he declared the part to the south to be 'right' and the part to the north to be 'left' (*dextras ad meridiem partes, laevasque ad septentrionem esse dixit*) is its reversal: he called the parts on his right 'south', and those on his left he called 'north'. Livy is therefore following Frontinus's, not Varro's, ordering of the *templum*. The whole matter has been discussed in another context by A. J. Frothingham, in 'Ancient Orientation Unveiled', *A.J.A.* 1915, (XIX) pp. 55–76, 187–201, 313–36 and 420–48. He seems to have a valid point when he suggests that the words *sinistra dextra postica antica* referred, not to the spectator and his position, but to an abstract division of the world. This is echoed in many ways and in many parts of the world: see L. Frobenius, *Kulturgeschichte Afrikas*, Zürich 1933, pp. 232ff. The system of quartering is familiar to the older forms of divination as to the newer: to crystal-gazing, tea-cup reading, if dispensed with in statistical projection and other forms of futurology. The generalized practice of 'quartered' divination has led some authors to suggest a generalized scheme. Frothingham's depended on two principal directions: a northward one, implying a 'lucky' right (Indian, Greek, Gothic) while a southward one would imply a 'lucky' left. In both cases the luck would come *ex oriente*. Frothingham hesitated to draw this conclusion, however. More recently it has been suggested that the east-west is the most 'primitive': so O. Meneghin, *Weltgeschichte der Steinzeit*, Berlin, p. 100; so also Levy, *The Gate of Horn*, pp. 146ff. Perhaps the most useful basis for discussing the religious conception of space and the related value of orientation remain the few paragraphs in E. Durkheim's *The Elementary Forms of the Religious Life*, New York, 1961, pp. 23ff.

51d So at Rome it faced E.S.E., at Norba S.S.W., at Iguvium S.E., at Cosa E.N.E. The surveyor's system, as recorded by Frontinus, was not normative however: quite often the *agrimensores* seem to have used a mirror-image version of it. See A. Piganiol, *Les Documents Cadastraux de la Colonie Romaine d'Orange*, Paris, 1962 (*Gallia*, supplement 16) pp. 42ff. The textual references in *R.E.*, s.v. Auguratorium, Auguraculum.

51e Fest. s.v. *Posticum* (276). On the difficulty of translating these terms see, however, Piganiol, op. cit., p. 44, n. 3.

52 Serv. in Virg. IX *Ecl.* 15; in Virg. VII *Aen.* 187

53 See above, note 51c.

54 In the *Codex Arcerianus* see fig. 6.

55 Varro, *de L.L.*, VII, 8.

56 Varro, *de L.L.*, VII, 13.

57 Fest. s.v. *Minora templa*; cf. Bouché-Leclercq, *Divination.* IV, 197, n. 1.

58 Polyb. VI, 27, ii; also Flav. Veg. I, 23. Compare Nissen, op. cit., pp. 25–53; F. W.

Wallbank, *Commentary on Polybius*, Oxford, 1957, I, p. 712; U. Antonelli, 'Sull' Orientamento dei Castra Praetoria', *Bull. Com.*, XLI, 1913, pp. 31ff.; more recent material in G. Zanghieri, 'Castro Pretorio', *Bull. Ist. Stor.*, 1948, p. 30f. F. Castagnoli, *Ippodamo di Mileto*, etc., Rome, 1956, pp. 94–103, insists on the Greek origin of the camp plan which Polybius explicitly denied.

59 Pliny, *N.H.*, XVIII, 326.

60 Vitruv., I, 6, 12; and fig. 9.

61 See S. Weinstock, 'Martianus Capella and the Cosmic System of the Etruscans', *J.R.S.*, XXXVI, 1946, p. 101ff. (part n. B); M. Pallottino, *The Etruscans*, Harmondsworth, 1956, pp. 164–6.

62 This could be related further to the sixteen compartments of the Pantheon and the sixteen heads of the Florence Gorgon lamp, etc. See L. Hautecoeur, *Mystique et Architecture*, Paris, 1948, pp. 167–8; E. Lefebvre, *Rites Egyptiens*, Paris, 1890, p. 38; and below, p. 53.

63 Vitruv., I, 6, vi and vii.

64 Hyg. Grom. *de Const. Limit.*, ed. Thulin, p. 102.

65 The methods of orientation are illustrated in the manuscripts of the Agrimensores; cf. Thulin, *Corp. Agr. Vet.*, figs. 102–6. A stone tablet, presumably part of a surveying instrument, was found in Rome (?) and is now in the Prague Museum (*Philolog.* 1931, p. 199). It is divided into sixteen sections and carries twelve wind-names.

66 On *groma-gnomon*, see O. A. W. Dilke, op. cit., p. 66, where the most recent account of Roman surveying instruments may be found; cf. A. Piganiol, op. cit., p. 44 n. 2, and *R.E.*, s.v. *Groma*.

67 Fest, 351. See also W. Müller, *Die Heilige Stadt*, Stuttgart, 1961, p. 44.

68 *R.E.*, s.v. *Limitatio*; Müller, op. cit., p. 43, n. 32.

69 The feasts connected with the foundation of Rome did not occur on the same day; the official birthday of Rome, the Parilia, was on 21st April while Remus's death was commemorated by the Remuria (Lemuria) on 9th to 13th May; Ovid. *Fasti*, IV, 8064, and V, 455 H.

70 See, e.g., Strabo, III, 3, vi (Lusitania); Cristobal de Molina, *Fables and Rites of the Incas*, London, 1933, p. 48; J. Warneck, *Religion der Batak*, 1909, p. 110f.

71 G. Furlani, 'Epatoscopia Babilonense' and 'Epatoscopia Etrusca' in *St. M. St. R.*, VI, 19–28, p. 251; also W. Warde-Fowler, *Rom. Essays and Interpretations*, 1926, pp. 146ff. (on parallel with Borneo) and on Mesop. origin of Indonesian Hepat. A. L. Kroeber, *Anthropology*, 1923, p. 209; also H. Lowie, *Primitive Religion*, 1924, p. 183.

72 M. Jastrow, *Aspects of Religious Belief and Practice in Babylonia*, 1911, p. 159ff.; also H. E. Siegrist, *History of Medicine*, New York, 1951, I, 488ff.

73 A. Grenier, op. cit., p. 19.

74 M. Rutter, '32 Modèles de Foies', *R. d'Ass.*, XXXV, 1, 1938, pp. 36–70; J. Nougayrol, 'Textes Hepat.', *R. d'Ass.*, XXXVIII, 1941, pp. 77–81. Also G. Furlani, *La Religione Babil. e Assira*, Bologna, 1929, II, pp. 102ff.; B. Hrozny, *Histoire de l'Asie Antérieure*, Paris, 1947, pp. 132ff.; A. Boissier, *Choix de Textes Relatifs à la Divination*, Paris, 1905, p. 877; and Michelangelo Cagiano de Azevedo, *Saggio Sul Labirinto*, Milan, 1959, pp. 13–14 and 21.

75 The relevant text: Martianus Capella, 'de Nuptiis Mercurii et Philologiae', is given with a commentary by C. Thulin, *Die Gotter des M.C. und die Bronzleber von Piacenza*, Gieszen, 1906. See also C. Clemen, op. cit., pp. 27–36, and M. Pallottino, op. cit., pp. 163ff. (Bibl. p. 177, n. 13); and, most recently, G. Dumézil, *La Religion Romaine Archaique*, Paris, 1966, pp. 618–27. The sixteen-fold division is much more important than I have been able to suggest: the Pantheon, which represents the horizon, is divided into sixteen 'houses'. And the sixteen-fold division was adopted as a basic division of geomancy throughout the Near East and Africa. See Robert Jaulin, *La Géomancie, Analyse Formelle*, Paris and The Hague, 1966.

76 L. Cefate of Pesaro; see A. Fabretti, *Corpus Inscriptionum Italicarum*, 69. See also Antistus Labeo in Placidus Fulgentius, *de Expositione Priscis Sermonis*, s.v. *Manales*. On the congruence of the liver-divining and thunder-interpreting system, and the oriental, archaic origin of the sixteen-fold division, see S. Weinstock, 'Libri Fulgurales', op. cit., esp. pp. 145f.

77 G. Furlani, loc. cit.; R. M. Th. Bohl, *Zum Babylonischen Ursprung des Labyrinths*, *Miscellanea Orientalia (Deimel)*, Rome, 1935, 13f. and 20ff.

78 Bohl, op. cit., p. 22. See also Karl Kerenyi, *Labyrinth-Studien*, Zurich, 1950, pp. 14f.

79 The examination began with simple inspection, but was lengthy and elaborate; it included the boiling of the examined entrails and observation of their behaviour during the boiling. It was often repeated more than once, as recommended (though not for the reasons given) by Vitruv., I, 4, ix and x; for a very rationalized adaptation thirteen

centuries later, see L. B. Alberti, *De Re Aedificatoria*, I, 6. Alberti, curiously enough, does not mention Cicero's contemptuous dismissal of this kind of rationalization in *de Div.* II, 13ff., together with the whole machinery of entrail-divination.

80 Ager Subsicivus, 'Julius Frontinus', in *Corp. Agr. Vet.*; and Varro, *de R.R.*, I, 10. Cf. O. A. W. Dilke, op. cit., pp. 99, 107; and A. Piganiol, op. cit., p. 61.

81 Surviving Roman plans in Ch. Huelsen, 'Piante iconographiche incise in Marmo', *Mitt. Deutsc. Arch. Inst. Rome*, 1890, V, pp. 46ff.; and H. Th. Bossert, *Architektur-Zeichnungen*, Berlin, 1922, pp. IX–X; more recently, A. Piganiol, op. cit., pp. 66ff., who remarks on the Roman *custom* of placing large stone maps in porticoes.

82 Cic. *de Div.*, I, 17.

83 Legends collected by David Lathaud in his 'Consécration et Dédicace de Constantinople', *Echos d'Orient*, Paris, 1924, pp. 294ff.

84 Dion. Hal., I, 88; comment by De Coulanges, op. cit., p. 153; Wissowa, op. cit., p. 166; Latte, op. cit., p. 141; G. Dumézil, op. cit., pp. 344–6.

85 So J. G. Frazer in his comment on Ovid. *Fasti*, VI, 780–806 (III, 373); though such rites are far too generalized for Frazer's rather dismissive explanation. They figure importantly in rites of initiation as well as those of purification, as had already been noted by E. B. Taylor, *Primitive Culture*, II, pp. 431 and 434, etc. There is much literature on the subject. See for instance M. Eliade, *Shamanism: Archaic Techniques of Ecstasy*, New York, 1964, p. 112; B. Bettelheim, *Symbolic Wounds*, London, 1955, pp. 180ff. There is no *a priori* reason in fact why fire-leaping or the passage between two fires should not have at some or at all stages been part of the rite.

86 Plutarch, 'Life of Romulus', 36.

87 Ovid. *Fasti*, IV, 821.

88 Fest., s.v. *Quadrata Roma*; cf. Tac. *Hist.*, IV, 53.

89 Ovid and Plutarch, loc. cit.; also John Lydus, *de Mens*.

90 Fest., s.v. *Mundus, Mundum*; also generally Grenier, op. cit., pp. 57–8. Festus quotes C. Ateus Capito's *De Pontificio Iure* (fr. 11, L. Strzelecki, *C. Atei Capitonis Fragmenta*, Warsaw, 1960), and M. Porcius Cato Licinianus's *De Iuris Disciplina*, see below, p. 124, n. 93.

91 So Y. Hedlund, 'Mundus', *Eranos*, XXXI, 1933, p. 55; also H. le Bonniec, *Le Culte de Cérès à Rome*, Paris, 1958, p. 183, n. 5; G. de Sanctis, *Storia*, 193, n. 255.

92 S. Weinstock, 'Mundus Patet', *Mitt. Deutsc. Arch. Inst. Röm.*, XLV, 1930, pp. 112 and 122.

93 Ovid. *Fasti*, loc. cit.; Fest. 258

94 Plutarch, loc. cit.

95 *C.I.L.*, X, 3926 (Dessau 3348); see also Le Bonniec, op. cit., pp. 175, n. 2 and 182, n. 5; also G. de Sanctis, *Storia*, 193, n. 255.

96 As E. Täubler, Terramare und Rom.', (*Abh. Heid. Ak. Wiss. Ph.-Hist. Kl.*), Heidelberg, 1932, pp. 58–9; Thulin, *Disciplina*, III, p. 59.

97 A. Piganiol, *Recherches sur les Jeux Romains*, Strasburg, 1923, p. 9.

98 So Täubler, op. cit., p. 63, n. 1. A. Szabo, 'Roma Quadrata', *Maia*, 1956, p. 271, suggests that the *bothros* of the archaic sanctuary at Agrigentum was a *templum* with a *mundus* built in: an elegant notion, but fanciful. See also Müller, *Die Heilige Stadt*, p. 30f. The buried cippi at the crossroads of Marzabotto (see below, p. 80) may have echoed this idea.

99 Ovid. IV, *Fasti*, 823.

100 On the *Lituus*, see n. 32 above, p. 208.

101 Lydus, *On the Months*, ed. Bekker, 1837, pp. 85–6 (ad XI Kal. Maias).

102 Plutarch, *R.Q.*, 61. Pliny, *N.H.*, III, 65; cf. also Serv. in Virg. I *Aen.* 277; and G. Dumézil, *La Religion*, p. 489, n. 3; Latte, op. cit., p. 125.

103 A. Brelich, *Die Geheime Schutzgottheit von Rom*, Zurich, 1949 (see esp. pp. 49–56).

104 Above, pp. 49ff.

105 Above, n. 51b.

106 So Pliny, *N.H.*, XVIII, 331; Hyg. Grom., *Corp. Agr. Vet.*; Siculus Flaccus, *Corp. Agr. Vet.*

107 See above, p. 50.

107a Fragment (ex Libris Magonis et Vegoiae auctorum) in *Die Schriften der Römischen Feldmesser*, eds., F. Blume, K. Lachman and A. Rudorf, Berlin, 1846, p. 349, is the only reference in surveying literature; but see Varro *de R.R.*, I, 1; Col. *de R.R.*, I, 1. Columella quotes him very copiously; the much later Palladius seems to take his quotations of Mago from Columella. Varro gives the information about the translation of a large part of the book into Greek by one Dion Cassius of Utica, a Greek-speaking African, and of a digest, while Columella reports the *senatusconsultum* about the Latin translation. On the Roman attitude to Carthaginian traditions, see G. Charles-Picard, *Les Religions de l'Afrique Antique*, Paris, 1954, pp. 100ff.

107b *Philo of Byblos*, Fr. II, 1–4 (Eusebius, Prep. Evan); cf. M.-J. Lagrange, *Etude sur les Religions Sémitiques*, Paris, 1905, pp. 420f. Other authors on Carthage and Phoenicia know him only as the author of the treatise; cf. B. H. Warmington, *Carthage*, London, 1960, pp. 128f., and O. A. W. Dilke, op. cit., pp. 34, 126.

107c O. A. W. Dilke, op. cit., pp. 96f., summarizes this procedure. A more extensive treatment in A. Piganiol, op. cit., pp. 47ff. The drawing of lots was a common practice in Roman juridical procedure (Serv. in Virg. VI *Aen.* 431), and the apportioning of the rule over different parts of the universe between the sons of Saturn was done by the drawing of lots: so Serv. in Virg. I *Aen.* 139.

108 So F. Castagnoli, *Ippodamo di Mileto e l' Urbanistica a Pianta Ortogonale*, Rome, 1956, p. 70.

109 Below, p. 112.

110 Wissowa, op. cit., pp. 124ff.

111 Simone Weil, *La Pesanteur et la Grâce*, Paris, 1947, p. 174.

112 Lévi-Strauss, *Le Totémisme Aujourd'hui*, Paris, 1965, p. 128.

113 Latte, op. cit., p. 41.

114 Plutarch, 'Life of Romulus', 11; Serv. (Dan) in Virg. IV, *Aen.* 212, Macrob. *Sat.* V, 19.

115 Cato in Serv. ad Virg. V, *Aen.* 755; without specifying the placing of the cow and ox, most accounts mention them as Varro, loc. cit.; Ovid, *Fasti* IV, 826; Col. *de R.R.*, III, 1; Fest. 236; Dion. Hal. I, 288; the sources quoted above, p. 29.

116 See Tac. *Ann.* XII, 24; Solinus I, 18; Dion. Hal. I, 79. The routes indicated are compared by G. Lugli, *Roma Antica-Centro Monumentale*, Rome, 1946, pp. 400ff. and chartered, pl. VII.

117 Cato in Serv., loc. cit.; Plutarch, 'Life of Romulus', loc. cit. Cf. also Varro, loc. cit.

118 Ritu Gabino (Varro, *de L.L.*, V, 143); Sabino, *id est togae parte caput velati, parte succincti* (Serv. in Virg. V *Aen.* 755). Gabino is the more convincing reading.

119 Grenier, op. cit., p. 23; Clemen, op. cit., p. 54.

120 Serv. in Virg. II *Aen.*, 730; Cato apud *Isid.* I, 15.

121 Plutarch, *Q.R.*, 27.

122 Ennius, *Annals* 48–54; in Cic. *de Div.*, I, 48.

123 Polyb. VI, 27, iii.

124 Hyg. Grom. *de Cast.* a 3.

125 Hyg. Grom.

126 Flav. Veg., *Epitome*, I, 23.

127 Claudii Salamasii (Claude Saumaise) *Plinianae Exercitationes in Caii Julii Solini Polyhistoria* . . . Utrecht, 1689, pp. 472f.

128 Livy, VI, 41.

129 For these changes, see E. Feldman, *Das Römische Lager, insbesonderes aus Livius*, Leipzig and Berlin, 1916, pp. 5ff.

130 Julius Frontinus, *Strategy*, IV, 1, xiv.

131 Plutarch, 'Life of Pyrrhus', 16.

132 Livy, XXXI, 34, 7–8.

133 Adolf Schulten, *Geschichte der Stadt Numantia*, Munich, 1933, pp. 107ff. Cf. App., Sp., XV.

134 Wissowa, op. cit., p. 479; Latte, op. cit., p. 122; Dumézil, op. cit., p. 563. The *Pater patratus* was chief priest of the Fetiales, a priestly sodality of twenty members (Serv. in Virg. *Aen.* IX, 53). On their duties, Cic. *de Off.*, I, 36; Cic. *de Leg.*, II, 9. Their foundation by Ancus Marcius, their rituals and formulae are described by Livy, I, 32. On the *campus hostilis*, cf. Ovid, *Fasti*, VI, 205ff.; Serv. in Virg. IX *Aen.*

135 See p. 23, n. 3.

136 Virg. IV *Aen.*, 212.

137 Cf. W. F. Jackson Knight, 'The Wooden Horse', *Classical Philology*, XXV, 4, Oct. 1930, pp. 358ff.; also *Cumaean Gates*, Oxford, 1936, pp. 90 and 95ff.

138 *Culex* 324; quoted by Jackson Knight, loc. cit. Cf. infra p. 123.

139 On the unknown tutelary deities, cp. Roman custom referred to above, n. 101.

140 Macrob. III *Sat.* 19 gives the text of the complete *carmen* and directions about the ritual to be followed. Appian records, as does Livy, that Scipio Aemilianus destroyed Numantia, as he had done Carthage, but without senatorial authorization, in order to get the suffix Numantinus. It may well be that he followed the same procedure here as he had at Carthage.

141 Jackson Knight, loc. cit. St. Jerome is sometimes quoted in this context as showing that salt was used in Roman destruction rites. St. Hieron. in Matthew, V, 13 (Migne, Pat. Lat. vol. XXVI, 35). But he is referring back to the destruction of Shechem, not to any known Roman ritual.

142 Modestinus Jurisconsultus in *Isid.* XV, 11.

143 Judges IX, 45.

144 Xenophon, *Hellen.*, V, ii, 5.
145 Seneca, *de Clem.*, I, 26; Manilius, *Astron.*, IV.
146 Hor. Car. I, Ode 16: *Palinodia ad Amatam Puellam.*

## Square and Cross *(between pages 72 and 96)*

1 Summaries of the discussion are available in Pallottino, *The Etruscans*, pp. 46–73, and, more recently, R. Bloch, *The Etruscans*, London, 1958, pp. 52–64. See also E. Richardson, *The Etruscans*, Chicago, 1964, pp. 1–10. For another and more recent view see Hugh Hencken, *Tarquinia and Etruscan Origins*, London, 1968. For a brief summary of the problems see C. F. C. Hawkes, 'The Origins of the Archaic Cultures in Etruria' in *St. Etr.*, 1958 (XXVI), pp. 363ff. The most recent addition to the literature is A. J. Pfiffig's *Einführung in Die Etruskologie*, Darmstadt, 1972, which analyses new material.
2 Serv. Virg. *Aen.* II.
3 Most conspicuously at Marzabotto, on which the most recent material is published by G. Mansuelli in *Guida alla Città Etrusca e al Museo di Marzabotto*, Bologna, 1966; and more extensively in 'Una Cittá Etrusca dell' Appennino Settentrionale', *Situla*, 8, Ljubljana, 1965, pp. 75–92. Much other recent material is summarized by Axel Boethius in *The Golden House of Nero*, Ann Arbor, 1960, pp. 26–54; and some comments in his 'The Old Etruscan Town', *Studies in Honour of Berthold Louis Ullman*, Rome, 1964, pp. 3–16. Cf. also Müller, op. cit., pp. 46–51. On Marzabotto, see below, p. 79.
4 A corruption of *terra marna*, marly earth. 'The word *marna* appears to be of northern origin, or is perhaps an independent form of Pliny's word *marga*, which he uses in speaking of red and white marls. . . .' (Pliny, *N.H.*, XVII, 42, etc.): C. H. Chambers in his preface to B. Gastaldi, *Lake Habitations and Prehistoric Remains . . . of Northern and Central Italy*, London, 1865. The decayed timber structures of these settlements made excellent humus, and the use of this earth as fertilizer over a period of time has made further work on these settlements almost impossible.
5 The latest attempt was made by Täubler, op. cit., quoting most of the relevant earlier material.
6 G. Säflund, *Le Terramare delle Provincie di Modena, Reggio Emilia, Parma, Piacenza*, Lund and Leipzig, 1939.
7 Säflund, op. cit., p. 221.
8 A more recent and more balanced view of the problem in the context of the Emilian Bronze Age set out in G. A. Mansuelli and R. Scarcani, *L'Emilia prima dei Romani*, Milan, 1961, pp. 151ff. On the end of the *Terramare* see also *Civiltà di Ferro*, Documenti e Studi, Dep. di Storia Patria, Provincia di Emilia, IV, Bologna, 1960; esp. Pia Laviosa Zambotti, 'Le Origini della Civiltà Villanoviana', pp. 73ff. and Hermann Müller-Karpe, 'Sulla Cronologia Assoluta della tarda Età di Bronzo', pp. 447ff.
9 L. Pigorini, 'Terramara dell'età del bronzo situata in Castione de' Marchesi', *Atti della Reale Accademia dei Lincei*, Rome, 1883, pp. 265ff.; R. Munro, *The Lake Dwellings of Europe*, London, 1890, pp. 252–6; Säflund, op. cit., pp. 96f., 220ff.
10 Säflund, op. cit., ibid.
11 Stuart Piggott, *Ancient Europe from the Beginning of Agriculture to Classical Antiquity*, London, 1965, p. 204.
12 Piggott, op. cit., pp. 202ff.
13 So, for example, F. Castagnoli, *Ippodamo di Mileto*, op. cit., passim; or even G. A. Mansuelli, *Una Città Etrusca*, op cit., p. 91. For *quadratus* see below, p. 98.
13a So far, eleven 'houses', single-room dwellings in the centre of the town, have been identified by the excavators, some of which are orientated, while others seem to be aligned on the later street-lines. But no general plan, let alone an orientated one, may be deduced from it. However, the regularized plan, neither orientated, nor wholly regularized like that of Marzabotto, probably dates to the last years of the seventh century. See G. Vallet, F. Villard and P. Auberson, 'Expériences coloniales en Occident et Urbanisme Grec: les Fouilles de Mégara Hyblaea' in *Annales*, 1970, (IV) pp. 1102ff.; cf. an earlier excavation report in *Mélanges d'Archéologie et d'Histoire*, Paris 1970, LXXXII, pp. 527ff.
14 P. C. Sestieri, in 'Rendiconti della Accademia di Archeologia', *Lettere e Belle Arti*, ns., XXIII, Naples, 1947–8, pp. 255. For a discussion of the evidence, see *Catalogue of the Mostra della Preistoria e della Protoistoria del Salernitano*, Salerno, 1962, pp. 39ff., and G. Vosa, 'Ultimi Scavi nella Necropoli di Gaudo', in *Istituto Italiano di Preistoria e Protostoria, Atti della VIII e IX Riunione Scientifica*, Florence, 1964, pp. 265ff. Vosa has recently thrown doubt on Sestieri's 'reading' of the orthogonal streets or channels in a letter to the author, but no satisfactory alternative interpretation of this feature has yet been offered.

15 P. C. Sestieri, 'La Necropoli Preistorica di Paestum', in *Atti del I Congresso Internazionale di Preistoria e Protostoria Mediterranea*, Florence, 1950, pp. 195ff. The preliminary study by Sestieri, 'Nuovi risultati degli Scavi nella Necropoli preistorica di Paestum' appeared in *Rivista di Scienze Preistoriche*, I, 4, 1947, pp. 283–90, together with a study of the human remains: P. Graziosi, 'I resti scheletrici umani nella Necropoli preistorica di Paestum', *Rivista di Scienze Preistoriche*, Florence, II, 1947, pp. 291–322.

16 G. A. Mansuelli, *Marzabotto: Dix Années*, pp. 113ff., 124.

17 Mansuelli, op. cit., pp. 114ff.

18 R. Bloch, 'Urbanisme et Religion', *La Città Etrusca e Italica*, pp. 11ff.; Christian Peyre 'L'Habitat Etrusque de Casalecchio di Reno, Bologna', ibid., pp. 253ff.; F. H. Pairault, 'L'Habitat Archaique de Casalecchio di Reno près de Bologne: Structure planimétrique et Technique de Construction', *Mélanges de l'Ecole Française de Rome (Antiquité)*, LXXXIV, Paris and Rome, 1972, pp. 145ff.

19 Mansuelli, *Guida*, pp. 49ff.; more recently Mansuelli, *Marzabotto: Dix Années*, pp. 120ff.

20 Mansuelli, ibid.: '. . . les cippes ne peuvent pas avoir eu *stricto sensu*, un caractère religieux . . . mais ils en sont le témoignage de façon indirecte'.

21 Romolo A. Staccioli, 'A proposito della Casa Etrusca a Sviluppo Verticale', *La Città Etrusca e Italica*, pp. 129ff.; cf. G. A. Mansuelli, 'La Casa Etrusca di Marzabotto', *Römische Mitteilungen*, LXX, 1963, pp. 44ff.

22 Leandro Alberti, *Descritione di Tutta Italia*, Bologna, 1550, f. 305.

23 Filippus Cluverius, *Italia Antiqua*, Leyden, 1624, p. 133.

24 A full report on the earlier necropole excavations, in Salvatore Aurigemma, *La Necropoli di Spina in Valle Trebba*, Rome, 1960, I, 1 and 2. This and much further material is summarized in 'S. Aurigemma and Nereo Alfieri', *Il Museo Nazionale Archeologico di Spina a Ferrara*, Rome, 1961; in N. Alfieri, P. E. Arias, and M. Hirmer, *Spina*, Munich, 1958, and in *Mostra dell'Etruria Padana e della Città di Spina*, Bologna, 1961.

25 Alfieri, Arias, and Hirmer, op. cit., p. 21.

26 Ibid.

27 Alfieri, Arias, and Hirmer, op. cit., p. 12.

28 On the economic and ethnic background of Spina and Adria, see G. A. Mansuelli and R. Scarani, *L'Emilia prima dei Romani*, Milan, 1961, pp. 264ff.; G. A. Mansuelli, 'Formazione delle Civiltà Storiche nella Pianura Padana Orientale: Aspetti e Problemi', *Studi Etruschi*, XXXIII, 2nd series, 1965, pp. 3ff.

29 Alfieri, Arias and Hirmer, op. cit., pp. 21f.

30 Cf. Devoto, op. cit., pp. 61ff.; more recently G. Devoto, *Origini Indoeuropee*, Florence, 1962, pp. 133ff., 148ff.

31 The Etruscan speakers, even when they appear to have been—on the evidence of their names—Veneti, nevertheless spoke Etruscan: so Ambrose Josef Pfiffig, 'Spina—Etruskisch oder Venetisch', *Die Sprache*, VIII, Vienna, 1962, pp. 149ff.

32 Hellanicus apud Dion. Hal. I, 28; Dionysius's own version, I, 18.

33 Justin, XX, 1, xi; cf. Diod. Sic., XIV, 113, i–iii.

34 Pliny, *N.H.* III, 120. On Diomede as an oecist in the Adriatic, cf. Bérard, op. cit., pp. 368ff.; also Brelich, op. cit., p. 137.

35 Strabo, *Geog.* V, 1, vii.

36 On Adria-*atrium*, see M. T. Varro, *Varro de L.L.* V, 161; and Fest., s.v. *Atrium*; the earlier name of Adriatic was the Ionian sea, after Ionius, the hero-leader of the Illyrians, and son of Adria, the eponymous hero of the town. The name was probably changed late in the sixth or early in the fifth century; see Giulia Fagolari and Bianca Maria Scarfi, *Adria Antica*, Venice, 1970, p. 17.

37 Strabo, loc. cit.

38 There are wares graffitoed both in Etruscan and in Greek. See Aurigemma and Alfieri, op. cit., p. 10.

39 This was noted by A. Maiuri, *Arte e Civiltà nell'Italia Antica*, Milan, 1960, p. 51.

39a C. A. Burney and G. R. J. Lawson, 'Measured Plans of Urartian Fortresses', *Anatolian Studies*, X, 1960, pp. 177ff.

40 See pp. 29, 133.

41 See above, p. 48.

42 II, 1267.

43 F. Castagnoli, *Ippodamo di Mileto e l'Urbanistica a Pianta ortogonale*, Rome, 1956, pp. 71ff. Martin, op. cit., 15f., 103ff.; Wycherley, op. cit., pp. 17ff.

44 J.-P. Vernant, *Mythe et Pensée*, Paris, 1966, p. 173. The book must be consulted generally on Hippodamus, his relation to Cleisthenes before and Plato after him, as well as his dependence on Pythagorean teaching.

45 Lines 995–1009.

46 So R. E. Wycherley, *The Birds*, 995–1009 in *C.R.*, 1937, pp. 22–31, esp. p. 28.

47 So A. von Gerkan, for instance, *Griechische Städteanlagen*, op. cit., p. 51ff.

48 Martin, op. cit., pp. 103ff., 274.

49 Herodotus refers to Sesostris, *Senuseret*, I; however, the deeds attributed to him appear to be those of Ramses II and several other Pharaohs.

50 Herod., II, 109. So also Serv. in Virg. III *Ecl.* 41.

51 Nonnius, in explaining the term *groma* (Aurel. Aug. *de Civ. Dei*. 63, iv and v) discusses two archaic uses of the verb *degrumari*: by Ennius (Tac. *Ann.*, Bk. XVIII, fr. 439) as *Degrumare forum;* and Lucillus (Macrob. *Sat.* Bk. III, fr. 96–7) as *viamque/degrumavisti ut castris mensor facit olim.* Carlo de Simone examines the word in his *Die Griechischen Entlehnungen im Etruskischen*, Wiesbaden, 1968–70, II, pp. 286ff., and hypothesises on an Etruscan word *crumu* from which the Latin *groma* would have derived directly. Cf. also Clemen, op. cit., pp. 54f.

51a See above, p. 50, n. 66.

52 Claude Lévi-Strauss, *Anthropologie Structurale*, Paris, 1958, p. 241.

53 Cic. I, *de Div.*, 16.

54 Cato, *de R.R.*, 54; of Col. *de R.R.*, i, 8 and xi, 1.

55 The phrase is Dumézil's, op. cit., p. 126.

56 *Improbare, refutare omen*; it would simply be done by hiding one's face.

57 As in many known cases of *haruspicinium* or general *extispicium.*

58 *Abominari: omen obsecrare* of Cicero.

59 Cf. above, p. 33.

60 Varro, *de L.L.*, VII, 8.

61 Pliny, *N.H.* XXVIII, 4; see also Val. Max. IX, 12; and Varro, *de L.L.*, V, 41.

62 Mircea Eliade, *Images et Symboles*, Paris, 1952, pp. 33–72; also *Traité d'Histoire des Religions*, Paris, 1953, pp. 339–49. Cf. also René Guénon, *Le Symbolisme de la Croix*, Paris, 1957, paragraph 16; *Symboles Fondamentaux de la Science Sacrée*, Paris, 1962, pp. 84–141; also Musée Guimet, *Symbolisme Cosmique et Monuments Religieux*, Paris, 1957.

63 G. van der Leeuw, *Phänomenologie der Religion*, Tübingen, 1953, p. 573; also P. Sartori, 'Bauopfer' in *Zeitschrift für Ethnologie*, 1898, p. 4, n. 1. The literature of the civilizing hero and his place in religion is considerable: cf., e.g., E. Durkheim, *The Elementary Form of the Religious Life*, New York, 1961, pp. 321f. However, the great myths had more than one dimension. In a recent paper, René Martin, 'Essai d'Interprétation économico-sociale de la légende de Romulus', *Latonnus*, XXVI, April–June 1967, interprets the myth as a 'heroized' account of the passage from a primarily pastoral to a primarily agricultural organisation, which seems to support the interpretation I have advanced here.

64 Cf. Durkheim, op. cit., p. 31, n. 22.

65 Hyg. Grom., *de Const. Limit.*, ed. Thulin, p. 123.

66 Hyg. Grom., *de Munit. Castr.*, 18; and Flav. Veg., *Epitome on Strategy*, I, 23; see Hesselmeyer, op. cit., 133–4.

68 Pliny, *N.H.*, XVIII, 331.

69 Hyg. Grom., *de Const. Limit.*, p. 133; also Hesselmayer, op. cit., p. 147.

70 Fest. s.v. *Decumanus;* cf. also Serv. in Virg. I *Geor.*, 126.

71 Pliny, *N.H.*, loc. cit.; also Hesselmeyer, op. cit., p. 148.

72 Hyg. Grom., *de Const. Limit.*, p. 132f.

73 Julius Frontinus, *de Limit.*, ed. Thulin, pp. 10–11.

74 See above, p. 57.

75 See p. 65 n. 116.

76 See below, p. 98.

77 Also known as the temple of Jupiter Victor.

78 Varro, in *Sol.*, I, 18.

79 With his consort, Caca; Serv. in Virg. VIII *Aen.* 190. Cf. Dion. Hal., I, 32 (ii); Wissowa, op. cit., pp. 141f.; also *R.E.* s.v. Caca, *Cacus*. On the Hero Cacus, see also Solinus, I, 8; cf. Emeline Richardson, *The Etruscans*, Chicago, 1964, pp. 222f.

80 Dion. Hal., I, 56 and II.

81 Tac. *Ann.* XII, 24.

82 Lugli, op. cit., pp. 400f.

83 Aul. Gell., XIII, 14, ii.

84 Trepollius Pollio, *Scr. Hist. Aug.*, de Salonino Galieno.

85 Varro, *de L.L.*, VI, 34.

86 Ovid. *Fasti*, II, 36off.; Plutarch, 'Life of Romulus'. Cf., too, R. Lanciani, *Ruins and Excavations of Rome*, London, 1897, p. 131, n. 1 (with bibliography); Norman Neuburg, *L'Architettura delle Fontane e dei Ninfei nell' Antica Italia*, Naples, 1965, pp. 36, 219.

87 Fowler, op. cit., pp. 310ff. See also Wissowa, op. cit., p. 172f., pp. 483ff.; Latte, op.

cit., pp. 84f., 295f.; Dumézil, op. cit., pp. 340ff., 564ff.; A. Alföldi, *Die Trojanischen Urahnen der Römer*, Basel, 1957, p. 24f. A. Brelich, *Tre Variazioni*, pp. 64ff., 109ff. On the celebration of the rite at the end of the fifth century A.D., see E. Gibbon, *Decline and Fall of the Roman Empire*, II, chap. 36, p. 485.

88 Ovid. *Fasti*, II, 31; cf. Frazer's comment ad loc.

89 Varro, *de L.L.*, VI, 13; cf. Fest. s.v. *Februarius*.

90 Ovid. *Fasti*, II, 19ff.

91 Serv. ad Virg. VIII *Aen.* 343.

92 G. Piccaluga, *Elementi Spettacolari nei Rituali Festivi Romani*, Rome, 1965, pp. 46ff.

93 On the dog and goat sacrifice, cf. Plutarch, *R.Q.* 111. Cf. too Devoto, *Tabulae Iguvinae*, IIa, lines 15ff., for an Iguvian dog sacrifice; also Devoto, op. cit., pp. 318ff., 481f., and J. Pfiffig, op. cit., pp. 48f.

94 On Mola Salsa, see L. A. Holland, *Janus and the Bridge*, Rome, 1961, pp. 317f.

95 Aurel. Aug., *de Civ. Dei*, XVIII, 12.

96 Ovid, *Fasti*, II, 381.

97 Ovid, *Fasti*, II, 359.

98 Plutarch, *R.Q.*, 111.

99 Plutarch, 'Life of Caesar', 61; cf. Cic. II, *Philipp.* 84.

100 *Themis*, London, 1925, pp. 21ff. She had already pointed out the parallels between February and the Anthesteria in *Prolegomena*, pp. 49ff.

101 Cf. Mommsen, *Römische Geschichte*, I, 51.

102 So L. Preller, *Römische Mythologie*, Berlin, 1883, I, p. 126. On the other hand H. Jeanmaire, *Couroi et Couretes*, Lille, 1939, p. 574f., suggests a derivation from *lupus* and *hircus*; *hircus* being the Latin for he-goat and *ircus* the Sabine for wolf, so that the priesthood would really have carried a wolf-goat name.

103 Cf., however, Dumézil, *La Religion*, p. 341, n. 2.

104 Macrob. *Sat.* I, 10; Plutarch, 'Life of Romulus', 5; Plutarch, *R.Q.* 35.

105 Livy, I, 4; Plautus, *Epidicus* III, 3, 22; Cic. *Pro Mil.* 21.

106 Varro in Arnob. *Adv. Gent.* IV, 3; cf. Lactantius I, 20, ii.

107 Ovid. *Fasti*, II, 424; Valerius Flaccus VI, 533. Faunus is also, naturally enough, assimilated to Evander (Cincius Alimentus apud Serv. in Virg. I *Geor.* 10).

108 Cicero, *Pro Marco Coelio*, 26. His client was a plebeian, it may be worth noting against Dumézil.

109 As K. Kerenyi, 'Wolf und Ziege am Fest der Lupercalia', in *Mélanges Marouzeau*, 1948, pp. 309–17.

110 All such theories go back to W. Mannhardt's 'Schlag mit der Lebensrute' in *Wald- und Feldkulte*, Berlin, 1904, vol. I, pp. 266ff., 537ff.; vol. II, pp. 189, 195, 326, 343.

111 'Pontifices ab rege petunt et Flamine lanas/quis veterum lingua februa nomen erat . . .', Ovid II *Fasti*, 21f. Another pointer to this association is Mark Antony's offer of the crown to Caesar in the course of the race: Plutarch, 'Life of Caesar'.

112 Fabianii and Quinctii. On the two 'packs' and the origin of the Roman constitution, see A. Alföldi, op. cit.; also his *Early Rome and the Latins*, Ann Arbor, 1964, pp. 315ff.

113 On the meaning of the festival generally, see Brelich, loc. cit.; Fowler, op. cit., p. 316. On the blooding of the two youths (though I would hesitate to accept the Mannhardtian transference to the corn spirit) and on parallel customs, R. Eisler, *Man into Wolf*, London, 1951, a strange and very learned book. Further material on the dog sacrifice in M. Eliade, *Shamanism*, New York, 1964, p. 466, and on the priest of the Bloody Robe, Rev. 19, 13. Cf. C. G. Jung, *Symbols of Transformation*, New York, 1956, p. 104. Agnes Kirsop Michels, 'Topography and Interpretation of the Lupercalia', *Transactions of the American Philological Association*, LXXXIV, 1953, pp. 35–59, asserts that the *Luperci* did not run round the Palatine, but up and down the Via Sacra. She also assimilated the Lupercalia into the commemoration of the dead generally. Her interpretation, however, rests on an eccentric reading of Varro's 'gregibus humanis cinctum' which takes no account of the pastoral nature of the festival; she also neglects its agonal nature and consequently the topographical relation between the Lupercal, where the rites started and finished, and the Via Sacra. There is an inherent topographical difficulty in the Tacitean account which should be mentioned in conclusion. If the Luperci really ran *round* the shrine of Consus on the *meta* of the Circus Maximus, it would mean that the runners climbed over the *meta* itself, which seems highly improbable. It is therefore worth reiterating that it was the people rather than the ground which were purified.

114 On the Salii see Livy I, 20; Ovid. *Fasti*, III, 259; Plutarch, 'Life of Numa', 13; Serv. in Virg. VIII *Aen.*, 285. Cf. Dumézil, op. cit., pp. 152f., 237, n. 1; 274f.; Latte, op. cit., pp. 113, 115ff.

115 Plutarch, loc. cit.

116 Serv., loc. cit.

117 Serv., loc. cit.; and Virg. II *Aen.* 325.

118 Serv. in Virg. VII *Aen.* 385, 603.

On the possible Mycenaean origin of the shields see M. W. Helbig, 'Sur les Attributs des Saliens', *Mémoires de l'Institut National de France*, Academie des Inscriptions et des Belles Lettres, XXVII, 1906, p. 2, 205ff.

## Guardians of Centre, Guardians of Boundaries *(between pages 97 and 162)*

1 Ennius apud Fest., s.v. *Quadrata Roma;* Plutarch, 'Life of Romulus', p. 9; Dion. Hal., I, 79; Tac. *Ann.* XII, 24; Solinus, I, 18.

2 Above, p. 91 and below, p. 98.

3 A. von Blumenthal, 'Roma Quadrata', *Klio*, 1942, pp. 181–8.

4 *Birds*, 995–1009; see above, p. 87.

5 Herod. I, 96ff. on 'Ecbatan'; cf. G. Perrot and C. Chipiez *Histoire de l'Art dans l'Antiquité*, Paris, 1882 et seq., V, 1890, pp. 769ff.

6 See H. P. l'Orange, *Studies in the Iconography of Cosmic Kingship*, Oslo, 1953, pp. 13ff.; also l'Hautecoeur, op. cit., pp. 24f.

7 R. Naumann, *Architektur Kleinasiens*, Tübingen, 1955, p. 216, fig. 258; and generally pp. 212–20.

8 Plato, *Laws*, 778. Cf. also P. Friedländer, *Plato*, London, 1958, I, pp. 319ff.

9 Generally, on the circular town problem, see Joseph Gantner, *Grundformen der Europäischen Stadt*, Vienna, 1928, pp. 96ff.; Lavedan, op. cit., I, pp. 22ff.; Castagnoli, op. cit., pp. 62ff. Another circular enigma is the planning of the timber Viking settlements, of which the most notable is the Trelleborg in Seeland: see, with bibliography, Müller, op. cit., pp. 102ff.

10 Although Commodus recut the *pomoerium* of Rome and renamed the city Colonia Commodiana. See Aelius Lampridius, 'Vita Comm'., *Scr. Hist. Aug.*, pp. 49 a and b.

11 See Arpad Szabo, 'Roma Quadrata' in *Rh. M.* vol. 87, 1938, pp. 160–9 and *Maia*, 1956, pp. 243–74; also F. Castagnoli, 'Roma Quadrata', Robinson, *Collection of Texts and Studies*, p. 389, n. 1. Cf. S. Ferri 'Quadratus' e 'Tetrâs' in *Opuscula*, Florence, 1962.

12 Ennius apud Fest. s.v. *Quadrata Roma;* Varro apud Solinus, 1, 18. Müller, op. cit., has made this notion the central thesis of his book, adducing much documentary material: see particularly pp. 36–45.

13 The passage comes from Fest. loc. cit. (quoting Ennius). Cf. here G. Lugli, *Roma Antica*, pp. 423ff.; also cf. J. A. Richmond, 'The Augustan Palatinum', *J.R.S.*, IV, 1914.

14 See below, p. 121.

15 Gjerstad, op. cit., IV, 2, pp. 349ff.

16 As, for instance, R. Bloch, *The Origins of Rome*, London, 1960, pp. 35ff., 83ff., 96f.; also H. Müller-Karpe, *Vom Anfang Roms*, Heidelberg, 1959 (*Mitt. Deutsc. Arch. Inst. Rome*, Ergänzungsheft 5), pp. 29, 31ff., considers the first Palatine settlement much earlier than the traditional date of the foundation of the city.

17 Gjerstad, op. cit., pp. 352ff., 495ff.

18 On the shrines of the Argei and their connection with the four regions, see Varro, *de L.L.* V (viii) 45. On the Servian institution see Dion. Hal. IV, 14, ii. For the political and economic implications of this institution see George Willis Botsford, *The Roman Assemblies*, New York, 1909, pp. 48ff.; cf. Alföldi, op. cit., pp. 127f. On the ritual significance of the change from three to four tribes, see Dumézil, op. cit., pp. 192ff. On the Argei themselves see Plutarch *R.Q.* 32; Dion. Hal. I, 38, iii; Varro, *de L.L.* VII, 44; Ovid V. *Fasti*, 621; Macrob. *Sat.* I, 11, xlvii; Fest. s.v. *Argeos, Sexagenarios* (de ponte). For studies of the material see Latte, op. cit., pp. 412ff.; Dumézil, op. cit., pp. 435f. Fowler, op. cit., pp. 54f. and n. 24, pp. 321ff., had already disputed G. Wissowa's reading of the rite in *R.E.*, s.v. *Argei.* as a late intrusion Cf. his *Gesammelte Abhandlungen*, Munich, 1904, pp. 221ff. The most convincing, if partial, recent interpretation is perhaps that offered by J. Gagé, in *Huit Recherches sur les Origines Italiques et Romaines*, Paris, 1950, op. cit., pp. 41ff.

19 Lugli, op. cit., pp. 598ff.; cf. Gjerstad, op. cit., pp. 41ff. on the archaic construction.

20 Livy VII, 14, xii; Cic. in *P. Vatin*, X, 24.

21 When the tribune C. Licinius Crassus moved the Comitia Curiata to the Forum: Varro, *de R.R.* 1, 2, ix; Cic., *Lael* 25, xcvi.

22 Gjerstad, op. cit., IV, pp. 366ff. There is still unpublished material in the Antiquario Forense. Several reconstructions of the orientated Comitium are shown by Giuseppe Lugli in his *Monumenti Minori del Foro Romano*, Rome, 1947, pl. II.

22a A discussion of the terms and their application in A. O. W. Dilke, op. cit., pp. 231ff. Cf., however, J. B. Ward-Perkins, *Cities of Ancient Greece and Italy*, New York, 1974, pp. 27f., 109, n. 10.

23 Aul. Gell. XIV, vii, 7.

24 Cf. Serv. in Virg. VII *Aen.* 153: 'Nor would the senate meet where there were virgins. . .'. Servius then says, however, that they could meet in the Atrium Vestae; this and his other brief remarks explain Virgil's use of *augusta moenia* and the *tectum augustum* of VII, 170, as well as the term *augurio consecrata; quod nisi in augusto loco consilium senatus habere non poterat.* . . . However, the Atrium Vestae whose ruins survive in the Roman Forum, a Neronian construction, was actually the place where the Vestals lived. This and his comment '*nam haec erat Regia Numae Pompolii*' are most convincingly explained if the term Atrium Vestae is taken in its presumed archaic sense to include the Atrium proper of later times, the regia and the adjacent buildings, which surrounded the temple. So E. Welin, *Studien zur Topographie des Forum Romanum*, Lund, 1953, pp. 207ff.

25 Dumézil, op. cit., pp. 307ff. So e.g. Ovid. VI *Fasti*, 267, 291f.

26 Cf. Serv. in Virg. III *Aen.* 134.

27 Aul. Gell., loc. cit. Nor could the Comitium be held on the *dies nefasti* when the *mundus* stood open: Fest. s.v. *Mundus;* Macrob. *Sat.* I, 16.

28 Plutarch, *de Isid. et Os.* XXX.

29 See G. Boni, 'Il Sacrario di Vesta' in *Not. Scav.*, May, 1900, pp. 164ff.

30 Boni was as guilty as any; for instance his attempts to equate the 'favissa' with the habits of the *Terramaricoli* does not seem to be warranted, op. cit., p. 165; and his insistence that the 'favissa' is orientated. The *cardo* and *decumanus*, op. cit., fig. 6, drawn by Boni on the published survey are over 10 degrees out of true (cf. the drawing, inspected by me in the Antiquario Palatino, which has the true orientation drawn in pencil). However, his suggestion that the 'favissa' existed to put the fire in direct contact with unworked soil (op. cit., pp. 171f.) has a certain attraction. The re-examination of the animal bones found embedded in the platform has suggested to some scholars a dog sacrifice as well as a possible *suovetaurilia* at the foundation. (Gjerstadt, op. cit., IV, pp. 384f.), though this is not particularly illuminating either about the goddess or her cult. The more interesting notion about the identity of the primitive temple with the hut-urn, suggested by Müller-Karpe, op. cit., pp. 87ff., with particular reference to Mycenean precedent, has more force in spite of the essentially life-bound character of the Goddess which has been underlined by A. Brelich, *Vesta*, Zürich, 1949, pp. 53ff.; cf. G. Dumézil, *Rituels Indo-Européens*, p. 32. If the shrine of Vesta is like that of Romulus in that both refer to a circular archetype of a house, it may well be that certain classes of persons would be buried in urns shaped like this archetypal house. Indeed, there would be good reason to consider the circular form an archaic, even anachronistic construction and such a shrine to have some common characteristic with burial urns.

31 On secret state cults, see Brelich, op. cit., passim.

32 Plutarch, 'Life of Camillus'.

33 Pliny, *N.H.*, XXVIII, 7.

34 *C.I.L.*, X, 8375.

35 Plutarch, 'Life of Camillus'.

36 Above, p. 59.

37 Aul. Gell., I, 12; G. Dumézil, *Tarpeia*, pp. 105ff.; Wissowa, op. cit., p. 143ff.

38 G. Lugli, 203.

39 F. E. Brown, 'The Regia', *Mem. Am. Ac. Rome*, XII, 1935, 67–88; and more recently, in *Entretiens sur l'Antiquité Classique de la Fondation Hardt*, vol. XIII, Geneva, 1967, pp. 45ff. On the male and female fire cults, see G. Dumézil, *Rituels Indo-Européens*, pp. 27ff. The antiquity of the hearth-stones in the main chamber of the Regia has been known for some time, but the exact date of the primitive structure has been difficult to establish, as was the relation of the structure to the underlying hut settlement. Recent excavations have allowed Frank E. Brown to establish a sequence of events, which he has kindly communicated to me: sometime in the last quarter of the seventh century, in the reign of Ancus Marcius according to the Livian chronology, the huts on the site of the building and its court were burnt and their remains 'buried' in specially constructed wells, perhaps analogous to the favissae in which consecrated building fragments were buried in later times. Over the site, so purified, a new pavement was laid. Although very little is as yet known—nor is much more likely to come to light—the outlines of the buildings of this period do not correspond to those of the republican Regia.

40 Ovid. IV *Fasti*, 252f.

41 Plutarch, 'Life of Camillus', loc. cit.

42 Livy, *Epitome*, XIX.

43 For the putative documentation see Boni and Lugli, loc. cit. Most recently the evidence

about the Republican building, literary, numismatic and archaeological, has been discussed by Jane M. Cody, 'New Evidence for the Republican Aedes Vestae' in *A.J.A.*, 1973 (LXXVII), pp. 43ff.

44 Ovid. VI *Fasti*, 262ff.

45 Plutarch, 'Life of Romulus', 11; Dio Cass., fragm. 12; Fest. s.v. *Quadrata*. Cf. Virg I *Geor.* 498; Virg. IX, *Aen.* 259; Theodoret, *Ecclesiastical History* V, 11.

46 Lugli, op. cit., pp. 203f.

47 Livy, V, 52; Hor. III *Car.* v. 8–12.

48 Cf. L. Delroy, 'Le Culte du foyer dans la Grèce mycenéene', *Revue de l'Histoire des Religions*, 1950, p. 32, n. 1.

49 G. Dumézil, *La Religion Archaique*, pp. 317ff.; cf. Benveniste, op. cit., I, p. 317.

50 Aeschylus, *Eumenides*, 165–8; cf. Vernant, op. cit., p. 121.

51 Vernant, op. cit., pp. 97ff.

52 Cf. J. E. Harrison, *Themis*, p. 365.

53 Vernant, op. cit., pp. 99ff.

54 Hom. I *Hymn.* 'to Hestia'.

55 Hom. I *Hymn.* 'Aphrodite'.

56 Serv. in Virg. VII *Aen.* 678.

57 Plutarch, 'Life of Romulus', II, 7–14, relates the same myth to Romulus and Remus. On this and comparative Indo-European material, cf. Dumézil, *Rituels Indo-Européens*, p. 38f.

58 Brelich, op. cit.

59 Vernant, op. cit., pp. 98f.

60 Tacitus, XII, 24.

61 Fr. (Ex Libris Magonis et Vegoia Auctorum) in *Die Schriften der Römischen Feldmesser*, eds., F. Blume, K. Lachman and A. Rudorf, Berlin, 1848, p. 349.

62 Wissowa, op. cit., pp. 124f.; Dumézil, op. cit., pp. 203ff.; Latte, op. cit., pp. 64f.

63 Ovid II *Fasti*, 641ff.

64 A. B. Cook, *Zeus*, Cambridge, 1924–40, III, pp. 441f., 1067; cf. ibid., I, p. 17, II, p. 1090; Nilsson, op. cit., I, pp. 190f.

65 Illustrated in *The Athenian Citizen*, Princeton, 1960, fig. 35 (although it would be a mistake to attach too much significance to this relatively common turn of phrase).

66 Thuc. VI, 27f. Cf. M. P. Nilsson, *Greek Folk Religion*, New York, 1940, pp. 94, 122; E. R. Dodds, *Greeks and the Irrational*, Berkeley, 1964, pp. 190f.; also Jean Babelon, *Alcibiade*, Paris, 1935, pp. 130ff.

67 M. P. Nilsson, *Geschichte*, I, pp. 71.

68 Nilsson, op. cit., I, 190ff. On the significance of the phallic character, ibid., I, 107f.; also Harrison, op. cit., p. 364f. On the etymology of 'Hermes' and the worship of the heap of stones, ibid., I, 474f. On the herm as a tomb, ibid., I, 177.

69 Fest. 505; cf. Dion. Hal. II, 74; F. Bruns, *Fontes Iuri Romani*, Freiburg-im-Breisgau, 1889, pp. 10f.; also Dumézil, loc. cit., and Lex Fabia in *Corp. Agr. Vet.*, p. 264; and Siculus Flaccus, 'De Cond. Agrorum' in *Corp. Agr. Vet.*, ed. Thulin, pp. 104f. On the varieties of Roman boundary stones and their markings see extracts from Dolabella and other writers, 'De Terminibus', *Corp. Agr. Vet.*, op. cit., pp. 302ff.

70 *Kudurru* of the time of Meli-Shipak (third or Kassite dynasty of Babylon) in *Babylonian Boundary Stones and Memorial Tablets in the British Museum*, ed. L. W. King, London, 1912, pp. 7ff.

71 L. Delaporte, *Les Peuples de l'Orient Mediterranéen*, Paris, 1935, I, pp. 155f.

72 Sicculus Flaccus, 'De Condicionibus Agrorum', *Corp. Agr. Vet.*, op. cit., p. 104.

73 On the character of baetylic stones in general, see Eliade, op. cit., pp. 191ff.

74 Sicculus Flaccus, op. cit., p. 105.

75 Ovid., IV *Fasti*, 819.

76 Above p. 59.

77 Servius Ad. Virg. III *Aen.*, 134.

78 Lugli, op. cit., pp. 423ff.; above, p. 48f.

79 Fest., 126 (i).

80 *C.I.L.*, VI, 4 (ii), no. 2352.

81 Täubler, op. cit., p. 44ff.; cf. H. J. Rose, 'Mundus', in *St. M. St. R.*, VII, 1931, p. 123 though, of course, the *pomoerium* of the city was replonghed so many times later, that anyone of the other ploughs used may equally well have been deposited. J. A. Richmond suggested that the plough was the one used by Augustus in the rite after 27 B.C. (the Augustan Palatium, op. cit.). On the other extenders of the *pomoerium*, see below, n. 133.

82 Frank E. Brown, Emmeline H. Richardson and L. Richardson Jr., 'Cosa II, The Temples and the Arx', *Mem. Am. Ac. Rome*, XXVI, 1960, pp. 9–14.

83 Ibid., pp. 12f.

84 Ibid., p. 13.

85 Above, p. 117.

86 Herbam do, cum ait Plautus (fr. inc. 28) significat, victum me fateor; quod est antiquae et pastoralis vitae indicium . . . Fest. S.V. *Herbam do;* cf. Paulus in Fest. s.v. *Obsidionalis corona.*

87 Pliny, *N.H.,* VIII, 5; cf. also Serv. in VIII *Aen.* 76; and Pliny, *N.H.,* XXII, 4.

88 M. P. Nilsson, 'Die Traditio per Terram im Griechischen Rechtsbrauch', *Archiv f. Religionswissenschaft,* XX, 1920–1, pp. 330ff.

89 Du Cange, s.v. *Investitura, Scotatio.*

90 *La Cité Antique,* p. 154; Fustel de Coulanges bases himself on Plutarch, 'Life of Romulus', 11; and John Lydus, *On the Months,* IV, 73. He also adduces Dio Cassius, *Fr.* 12 (I take this to be Mai's *Fr.* 12, Dindorf's 37, which deals with the origin of the Lacus Curtius and cannot be used to support Plutarch without some reserve). Ovid. IV *Fasti,* 821 (also quoted by Fustel) is too general to support this specific point. In view of the similarity, as well as the apparent uniqueness, of the rite described by Plutarch to one which Pindar seems to echo in Pind. IV *Pyth.,* 33ff. (cf. above, p. 36), it might be worth noting here that Plutarch explicitly connects the rite with the *mundus,* which he spells in Greek μουνδος (*moundos*), a word for which he seems to know no exact Greek equivalent.

91 Fustel de Coulanges, op. cit., pp. 154–7; also above p. 59.

92 Serv. in Virg. III *Ecl.* 104–5.

93 Probably not the censor, but M. Porcius Cato Licinianus (Le Bonniec, *Culte de Cérès,* p. 176) quoted by Fest., s.v. *Mundus.*

94 Cf. Livy, XXXIV, 7, 9. Varro, de L.L., 129.

95 Ovid. IV *Fasti,* 820.

96 These are discussed by A. I. Charsekin, 'Zur Deutung Etruskischer Sprachdenkmäler, *Untersuchungen zur Römischen Geschichte,* III, Frankfurt-am-Main, 1963, pp. 77ff.; Charsekin's rather doubtful conclusions in A. J. Pfiffig, *Die Etruskische Sprache,* (op. cit.), p. 12.

97 *R.E.,* s.v. *Mundus;* cf. H. L. Stoltenberg, *Etruskische Gottesnamen,* Leverkusen, 1957, p. 41; R. A. Staccioli, *La Lingua degli Etruschi,* Rome, 1969, s.v. *mun. muni.* The word has been discussed at some length by Ambros Josef Pfiffig, 'Etruskisches: 1. Zur lat. *mundus* und etr. *munθ',* *Die Sprache,* Vienna, 1962, VIII, pp. 142ff.

98 Apuleius, *Apologia.* Since Apuleius is defending himself on a charge of vanity (as being a philosopher who owned a looking glass: quoniam ut res est, maius periculum decernis, speculum philosopho quam Cereris mundum prophano videre?), it may be that, as some have thought, Apuleius is thinking of some form of *cista mystica:* by the time he wrote, the mysteries of Ceres had been assimilated to the Eleusinian mysteries of Demeter, and it may be that the *mundus* here is the Eleusinian cista.; cf. Victor Magnien, *Eleusis,* Paris, 1938, pp. 138f.

99 Paulus in Festum, s.v. *Manulem Lapidem*

100 Varro in Macrob. I *Sat.* 16.

101 Le Bonniec, op. cit., p. 51.

102 *C.I.L.,* X, 3926. On the meaning of the word Cereris, cf. Weinstock, op. cit.; Wissowa, op. cit., pp. 161ff.

103 Warde-Fowler, *Roman Essays and Interpretations,* 1920, pp. 24–37; also *J.R.S.,* II, 1929, pp. 25ff., developing suggestions made by K. O. Müller, *Die Etrusker,* II, pp. 100ff. Cp. F. C. Cornford, 'The *aparchai* and the Eleusinian Mysteries', *Essays and Studies presented to William Ridgway,* ed. E. C. Quiggin, Cambridge, 1913, pp. 153ff.

104 The priesthood may have been female. Le Bonniec, op. cit., p. 175.

105 Bernese Scholia on Virg. III *Ecl.* 105–6; Le Bonniec, op. cit., pp. 181–3. On *mundus* in general however, see also M. H. Wagenvoort, *Initia Cereris,* Leiden, 1956, p. 168.

106 J. J. Bachofen, *Versuch über die Gräbersymbolik der Alten,* Basel, 1925, eds. Bernoulli and Kluges, p. 128. Some rather unusual stone cinerary urns, carved into the form of a round basket with a domical cover in the archaeological museum at Aquilea, may be an oblique reference to the ideas described by Bachofen; on the other hand, it may simply be yet another form of the *cista mystica.* Cf. too E. Neumann, *The Great Mother,* New York, n.d. pp. 282.

107 Wissowa, op. cit., pp. 129ff.; more recently G. Dumézil, *L'Héritage,* p. 82.

108 Varro, de R.R., II, 1 (x); Dion. Hal., IV, 22; Val. Max, IV, 1; Livy, I, 44.2, 10 and XL 45. Cf. Inez Scott Ryberg, *Rites of the State Religion in Roman Art,* Rome, 1955, pp. 104ff.

109 Cato, de R.R.

110 *T.A.P.A.,* LXXXIV, 1953, 35ff.

111 *C.I.L.,* IV, 2104, v. 31ff.; 1, 2. The best commentary on this archaic hymn of the Arval

brothers is the second part of Norden's *Aus Altrömischen Priesterbüchern*, Lund, 1939. Cf., however, Wissowa, pp. 485ff. In its present form the hymn (I quote the lines of the second and third strophe which were repeated thrice) is known from an inscription A.D. 218 (reign of Heliogabalus) found in the Vatican, in 1778. Since it was first found its reading and meaning have puzzled historians of religion as well as philologists. I have used the reading of V. Pisani, *Manuale Storico della Lingua Latina*, Turin, 1960, III pp. 2ff., and the conjectural interpretation of the second half of the second line is that of Warmington, op. cit., IV, pp. 250ff.; cf. also A. Ernout, *Recueil de Textes Latins Archaiques*, 3, Paris, 1947, pp. 107ff. A very different reconstruction of the text is given by S. Ferri, 'Il Carmen Fratrum Arvalium e il Metodo Archeologico' in *Opuscula*, Florence, 1962, pp. 604ff. It is based on the assumption that the text, as it stands, includes both the text to be sung and the 'rubrics' governing the action. The verses quoted would, in Ferri's reconstruction, be reduced to *Ne velue rue(m) Marmar/Satur fu ferc(to Mar)mar*. It is worth noting that Ferri considers the *carmen* very ancient, a Sabine hymn composed before 1000 B.C.

112   1, 9, 23 March and 19 October of Latte, op. cit., 115ff.; G. Dumézil, *Religion Archaique*, pp. 151ff., 171ff.; Bloch, op. cit., pp. 138ff.; earlier discussions in Wissowa, op. cit., pp. 480ff.; W. Warde Fowler, *Calendar*, pp. 38ff.; N. Turchi, *La Religion*, Rome, 1939, pp. 71ff. There were also Salian Virgins.

113   Wissowa, op. cit., p. 482, n. 4.

114   On the *Ancilia* and Mamurius Veturius, see Dumézil, op. cit., pp. 151, 216f., 329; also G. Warde Fowler, op. cit., pp. 46ff.; also W. M. Helbig, 'Sur les Attributs des Saliens', *Mémoires de l'Institut*, Academie des Inscriptions et des Belles Lettres, XXVII, 1906, pp. 205ff.

115   Lugli, op. cit., Rome, 1946, pp. 212ff.

116   Wissowa, op. cit., pp. 131ff.

117   On the possible Villanovan/Mycenaean origin of this dress, see Helbig, op. cit.

118   So Quintilian, *The Institutions of Rhetoric*, I, vi, 40f.; for the surviving fragments of the *carmen*, Vittore Pisani, *Manuale Storico della Lingua Latina*, Turin, 1960, III, pp. 36ff. For its apotropaic character, see also W. F. Jackson Knight, *Vergil*, London, 1966, pp. 208ff.; and J. E. Harrison, *Themis*, 2, 1926, pp. 194f.

119   On the *dies religiosi*, Agnes Kirsopp Miller, *The Calendar of the Roman Republic*, Princeton, 1967, p. 64.

120   Lugli, op. cit., Rome, 1946, pp. 423ff.

121   Cf. Le Bonniec, op. cit., pp. 63ff., 90ff.

122   Above, p. 96.

123   Virg., V, *Aen.*, pp. 84–9, 90–4.

124   Eliade, op. cit., pp. 152ff. and 247ff.

125   K. Kerenyi, *Labyrinthstudien*, Zürich, 1952, pp. 61f.

126   See Täubler, *Terramare*, pp. 44, n. 3 and 45, n. 1.

127   As H. Müller-Karpe, *Der Anfang Roms*, Heidelberg, 1959, pp. 31–3.

128   See Thulin, *Disciplina Etrusca*, pp. 10–17.

129   H. H. Scullard, loc. cit., after S. Mazzarino; cf. M. Pallottino, *Etruscologia*[6], 1968, p. 430.

130   G. Devoto, *Tabulae Iguuinae*, Rome, 1954, p. 162ff.

131   See S. Reinach, *Répertoire de la Statuaire*, Paris, 1897ff.; I, pp. 351, 364, 393, 458, 460; II, pp. 522–6; III, pp. 148, 269; IV, pp. 330–4; V, pp. 261–2. The hermaphrodite terms found among them frequently seem interesting in view of their possible relation with the *deus sive mas sive foemina* to whom I referred earlier, p. 116.

132   A convenient list in L. Homo, *Rome Imperiale et l'Urbanisme*, Paris, 1951, p. 94, n. 1.

133   The following Roman rulers have left records of their extension of the *pomoerium*:

    (1) Servius Tullius (Livy I, 44; Dion. Hal., 13, 3).

    (2) Sulla (Seneca, *de Brev. Vit.*, XIII, 8; Tac. *Ann.*, XII, 23; *Aul. Gell.* XIII, 14, v; Dio Cass. XLIII, 50, i).

    (3) Julius Caesar (Dio Cass. and *Aul. Gell.* loca cit.).

    (4) Augustus, c. 25 B.C. (Tac. *Ann.*, XII, 23; Dio Cass., LV, 6, vi; *Scr. Hist. Aug.* Aurel., XXI, 11; numismatic evidence in Lugli, *Fontes*, I, 127).

    (5) Claudius, A.D. 49 (Tac. *Ann.*, XII, 23–4; Pomoerial *cippi* in Lugli, *Fontes*, I, pp. 128f.).

    (6) Nero (?) (*Scr. Hist. Aug.* Aurel., loc. cit.).

    (7) Vespasian, A.D. 75 (Pliny, *N.H.*, III, 5, lxvi f; *C.I.L.*, VI, 930; *cippi* in Lugli, *Fontes*, I, p. 129f.).

    (8) Trajan (?) (*Scr. Hist. Aug.* Aurel., XXI, 11).

    (9) Hadrian, A.D. 121. (Restores pomoerial *cippi*. List in Lugli, *Fontes*, I, p. 130).

    (10) Commodus. Coin reproduced here, fig. 107.

    (11) Aurelian (*Scr. Hist. Aug.* Aurel., XXI, 9 and 11).

134  Aul. Gell., XIII, 14; he is quoting Messala the Augur: *habebat autem ius proferendi pomerii qui populi R. agro de hostibus capto auxerat.* See also Tac. *Ann.*, XII, 23.

135  See R. Wycherley, *How the Greeks built their Cities*, London, 1949, p. 89f.; also Martin, op. cit., pp. 190–1; cf. also Vitruv. II, 8, xv; and P.-W. s.v. Abaton; cf. also M. P. Nilsson, *Griechische Religion*, I, pp. 67ff.

136  Jackson Knight, op. cit., pp. 112ff., 208ff.

137  Herod., I, 84.

138  Nissen, *Pompeianische Studien*, Leipzig, 1877, p. 474; cf. also De Sanctis, op. cit., pp. 179, 389ff. (though the *pomoerium* still had some importance in state ritual). So, for instance, magistrates crossing either the *pomoerium* or the brook Petronia (which marked the limit of the urban auspices) to the Campus Martius to hold Comitia Centuriata had to take Auspices; Tiberius Gracchus rendered the election of his successors void: they then resigned, after the senate and augurs had considered the matter. This was in 214 B.C. Cic. *de Nat. Deor.*, II, 4, xi; Cic. *de Div.*, I, 17, xxxiii. Tacitus, however (Tac. III *Ann.* 19) records the correct taking of auspices at the time of Tiberius on a similar occasion. Cf. Botsford, op. cit., p. 106f.

139  Above, p. 65.

140  Eliade, op. cit., p. 226. This is true for many cultures; maybe for most. For a male earth-archetype, see H. Frankfort, 'Analytical Psychology and the History of Religion', *J. of the Warburg and Courtauld Inst.*, XXI, pp. 166–78.

141  Levy, op. cit., p. 145; G. Papasogli, *L'Agricoltura degli Etruschi e dei Romani*, Rome, 1942, p. 19ff.; cf. A. K. D. White, *Roman Farming*, London, 1970, pp. 170ff.

142  *Handwörterbuch des Deutschen Aberglaubens*, Berlin, 1927–42, s.v. *Pflug*, VI, 1718–25, for this and some subsequent material.

143  *Handwörterbuch*, loc. cit. Cf. A. Dessenne, *Le Sphinx*, Paris, 1957, p. 18.

144  Quint. Curt., VII, 8; Plutarch, 'Life of Alexander'. Alternative versions given by Strabo (XVII, 1, VI); Flavius Arrianus (III, 2); Pseudo-Callisthenes, *Anabasis of Alexander* (I, 32).

145  G. R. Levy, loc. cit.; cf. also Serv. in I *Geor.*, 45–6.

146  In Lucani, *The Civil War*.

147  Or grandson (Fest., s.v. *Tages*) see above, pp. 28, 86; and Clemen, op. cit., p. 14.

148  G. Vitali, 'l'Aratro Votivo di Bronzo di Talamone', *Studi Etruschi*, II, 1928, pp. 409–17; illustrated here, fig. 106. A more primitive form of plough was also found among these bronze votive objects. G. Vitali, 'Gli ogetti Votivi di Talamone II', *Studi Etruschi*, IV, 1930, pp. 302f.

149  Macrobius comments on its antiquity: Macrob. *Sat.*, V, 19, 13f.; see also Thulin, *Disziplin* III, 8; on the significance of the use of bronze in this context see Frazer's commentary on Ovid's *Metam.*, IV, 48–9.

150  G. Säflund, *Terramare*, Lund, 1939, p. 224.

151  E. C. Curwen, *Plough and Pasture*, London, 1946, pp. 56ff. On the sacred plough generally of S. Mayassisi 'Architecture, Religion, Symbolisme', *Bibliothèque d'Archéologie Orientale d'Athenes*, Athènes, 1965, IV, I, pp. 21ff.

152  I do not wish to imply that the rite was a neat jigsaw-puzzle construction of ceremonies from different sources: that the ploughing bulls belonged to the original Mediterranean stratum, the quadration to the invading Indo-Europeans, Etruscans, or whatever. On the contrary, if there was one element which on the whole came from one ethnical stratum, it could only be grafted onto another foreign element if the older 'structure' was such that it could receive it. So if quadration was more important to the Indo-Europeans than to the indigenous Mediterranean peoples, it could only have amalgamated with their ploughing rite if the two civilizations shared some cosmological beliefs which would have had their corresponding rites among the aboriginal Italiots, rites which were modified, or reinterpreted, by the invading peoples.

153  Fest s.v. *Urbs;* Varro, *de L.L.*, V, 127, 135; Sextus Pomponius in *Digests* (*Corpus Iuris Civilis*, ed. P. Kruger, Berlin, 1928, vol. I) I, 8, xi.

154  Fest., loc. cit. (quoting Ennius).

155  Varro, loc. cit. This is taken literally by P. Kornemann, 'Polis Und Urbs' in *Klio*, 1905, 88ff.; for criticism see Thulin, op. cit., III, 3, 4; modern scholars derive *urbs* from *rus* (set against *arx*), so Ernout and Maillet, op. cit., s.v. another, and to my mind unacceptable etymology in L. A. Holland, *Janus and the Bridge*, Rome, 1961, p. 6.

156  Dion Hal., I, 88.2; cf. Lavedan, op. cit., I, 100 and Hautecoeur, op. cit., 77.

157  Bruns, *Fontes*, p. 123 (op. cit.): the law refers back to the prohibition against burials in the city in the XII tables (1, table X).

158  Pomponius in *Digests* (op. cit.), I, 8, i.

159  Above, p. 112.

160  Lydus, *On the Months*, IV, 50, pp. 85–6 (ad II Kal. Maias) see above, p. 61.

161 As Täubler, for instance, op. cit., p. 11.

162 Quint. Curt.; Plutarch, 'Life of Alexander', IV, 8, 6; cf. also Strabo XVII, i. 6; Arrian *Anabasis*, III, 2; *Pseudo-Callisthenes* I, 32. Plutarch, 'Life of Alexander', II, 486, like Strabo, does not give full weight to the importance of the barley flour.

163 Catapatha Brahmana, VII, 2, 2, 12; quoted by G. Dumézil, *Jupiter, Mars, Quirinus*, Paris, 1941, p. 60.

164 Extensive commentary on these rites in Stella Kramrisch, *The Hindu Temple*, Calcutta, 1946, I, pp. 14–36.

165 J. Ruud, *Taboo, A Study of Malagasy Custom*, Oslo and London, 1960, pp. 113–14.

166 A. van Gennep, op. cit., p. 20; cf. G. von Kaschnitz-Weinberg, *Die Mittelmeerischen Grundlagen der Antiken Kunst*, Frankfurt-am-Main, 1944, p. 17.

167 John, X, 1, 2, 9.

168 Plutarch, *R.Q.*, 27. See above, p. 65.

169 It isn't for me to tread this dangerous and contested territory, however lightly: see however E. Benveniste *Le Vocabulaire des Institutions Indo-Européennes*, Paris, 1970, II, pp. 187ff.

170 Varro, *de L.L.*, V, p. 143. 'Hoc faciebant religionis causa die auspicato, ut fossa et muro essent munitia. Terram unde exculpserant "fossam" vocabant, et introrsum factum "murum".'

171 Varro, loc. cit.; Thulin, op. cit., III, p. 5, n. 2.

172 E. H. Warmington, *Remains of Old Latin*, IV, London, 1967, pp. 162ff. Cf., however, Guido Mansuelli, *Mémoires de l'Académie Française de Rome*, 1972.

173 See Norden, op. cit., p. 166; or Nissen, op. cit., p. 474f.

174 Thulin, op. cit., p. 64f.; A. L. Frothingham, *A.J.P.*, XXXVI, 1915, p. 322. Cf. Holland, op. cit., p. 53, n. 12.

175 Serv. in Virg. I, *Aen.* 426.

176 Of Vitruv. I, vii, 1. Grenier, op. cit., p. 23; Clemen, op. cit., p. 54.

177 Latte, op. cit., p. 89; Wissowa, op. cit., pp. 99ff.

178 Macrob. *Sat.* I, 9, xvii f. For other sources and information, see Lugli, op. cit., pp. 82–5.

179 Gaius, *The Institutes*, I, 8, i.

180 Wissowa, op. cit., p. 94ff.; G. Dumézil, *Tarpeia*, Paris, 1947, pp. 98ff.; Latte, loc. cit.

181 Dumézil, op. cit., pp. 326ff. On Janus οὐρανός (*ouranos*), Lydus, *On the Months*, IV, 2.

182 B. Olzscha, *Die Agramer Mumienbinden*, Leipzig, 1939, p. 48; against this identification see Latte, op. cit., p. 135, n. 4; cf. also Hans L. Stolterberg, *Etruskische Gottesnamen*, Leverkusen, 1957, p. 29; G. Dumézil, *La Religion Romaine*, p. 658.

183 B. Hrozny, *Histoire de l'Asie Antérieure*, Paris, 1947, p. 211; Levy, op. cit., p. 24.

184 Cf. H. T. Bossert, *Janus und der Mann mit der Adler-oder Greifenmaske*, Istanbul, 1959.

185 Mart. Capella, *De Nupt. Merc. et Phil.*, ed. H. Grotius, Leyden 1599, I, pp. 41ff.

186 On Janus generally, see R. Pettazzoni, *L'Omniscienza di Dio*, Turin, 1955, pp. 243ff.; G. Dumézil, *La Religion*, pp. 323ff., and passim; Latte, op. cit., pp. 132ff.; and N. Turchi, op. cit., p. 163ff. The discussion in G. Wissowa, *Religion and Kultus der Römer*, pp. 91ff., is still worth consulting, however.

187 W. Warde Fowler, *The Roman Festivals*, London, 1933, pp. 280f.

188 On Janus as a moon-god see I. A. MacKay, *Janus*, Berkeley and Los Angeles, 1956 (University of California Publications in Classical Philology XV, No. 6), 157ff. On Janus as deified bridge (less probably), see Holland, op. cit., passim.

189 H. Th. Bossert, *Janus*, Istanbul, 1959. Cf. M. P. Nilsson, *Geschichte*, I, pp. 206ff. Cf. also Anna Maria Bisi, *Il Grifone*, Rome, 1965.

190 M. Delcourt, *Hermaphrodite*, London, 1961, pp. 17ff.

191 Holland, op. cit., pp. 85ff.; cf. also Inez Scott Ryberg, *The Rites of Roman State Religion*, Rome, 1955, pp. 21ff., 141ff.; and C. Barini, *Triumphalia*, Turin, 1955, passim. The various shrines of Janus are described by Lugli, op. cit., pp. 83f.; and located by Holland, op. cit., pp. 29ff.—not always acceptably, to my mind.

192 A. Dessene, *Le Sphinx*, Paris, 1957, pp. 18f., 183.

193 G. von Kaschnitz-Weinberg, op. cit., p. 23f.

194 G. Kees, *Der Götterglaube im Alten Ägypten*, Leipzig, 1941, p. 41, n. 3; Dessene, op. cit., p. 14; cf. H. Frankfort, *Kingship and the Gods*, Chicago, 1948, pp. 10ff. A psycho-analytical interpretation of the sphinx is advanced by G. Roheim, *Riddle of the Sphinx*, London, 1934, pp. 16ff. and 210ff. Cf. also A. van Gennep, *The Rites of Passage*, London, 1960, pp. 21, 57ff.

195 Cf. A. van Gennep, op. cit., pp. 30f.

196 Cf., however, E. A. S. Butterworth, *Some Traces of the Pre-Olympian World in Greek Literature and Myth*, Berlin, 1966, pp. 45ff.

197 A. Brelich, *Gli Eroi Greci*, Rome, 1958, pp. 274ff.

198 Paus. IX, 26; J. G. Frazer, ad loc.

199 Soph. *Oed. Col.*, 1515ff.
200 On the tomb of Oedipus see Paus. I, 28; cf. also M. de G. Verrall and J. E. Harrison, *Mythology and Monuments in Ancient Athens*, London, 1890, pp. 563f.
201 W. F. Jackson Knight, *The Cumean Gates*, p. 13ff.
202 Ibid. and Levy, op. cit., p. 156f.; cf. F. Neumann, *The Great Mother*, New York, n.d., pp. 173ff.
203 Cf. George Thomson, *Aeschylus and Athens*, London, 1941, pp. 190ff.
204 Jackson Knight, op. cit., p. 150ff.; also W. L. Hildburgh: 'Indeterminability and Confusion as Apotropaic Elements in Italy and in Spain', *Folklore*, LV, December 1944, pp. 133–49; and by the same author, 'The Place of Confusion and Indeterminability in Mazes and Maze Dances', *Folklore*, LVI, March 1945, pp. 188–92.
205 See in addition to above, Richard Eilmann, *Labyrinthos*, Athens, 1928 (with analysis of patterns and collection of texts).
206 Pliny, *N.H.*, XXXVI, 19, 84f.
207 Virg. *Aen.* V, 575ff.
208 Σ 590ff. Cf. Callimachus, *Delian Hymn*, pp. 308ff., for Theseus's labyrinth dance on Delos.
209 Eustathius, *Commentary on the Iliad and the Odyssey* 1166, 17 (commentary on the above).
210 *R.E.* XIII, 2059. Cf. G. van der Leeuw, 'In der Hemel is eehen Dans', *De Weg der Mensheid*, Amsterdam, x, 1930, pp. 25ff.
211 Dr. Ernst Krause, (Caros Stern) *Die Trojaburgen Nordeuropas*, Glogau, 1893—informative but highly unreliable; see for instance Willy Pastor, *Der Zug vom Norden*, Jena, 1906, pp. 39–52, on the Wisby maze.
212 The Tragliatella *oinochoe* has been frequently published and discussed. A detailed description by G. Q. Giglioli, 'L'Oinochoe di Tragliatella', *Studi Etruschi*, III, 1929, pp. 111–60. Cf. also Latte, op. cit., pp. 115f.; A. Alföldi, *Early Rome and the Latins*, Ann Arbor, 1966, pp. 280ff.; G. Karl Galinsky, *Aeneas, Sicily and Rome*, Princeton, 1969, pp. 121ff.
213 For the most recent discussion, Alföldi, loc. cit.; Galinsky, loc. cit.: Galinsky's curious dismissal of the association because more than a thousand years after the graffito was scratched on the *oinochoe* Stephen of Byzantium described Troy as a Χαρξ (*charx*) seems to me capricious.
214 Plutarch, 'Life of Theseus', XXI. On this passage see K. Kerenyi, *Labyrinth-Studien*, Zürich, 1950, pp. 38ff.
215 K. Kerenyi, *The Gods of the Greeks*, p. 170.
216 K. Kerenyi, *Labyrinth-Studien*, Zürich, 1950, p. 38; also *The Gods of the Greeks*, pp. 237–9.
217 Plutarch, 'Life of Theseus', 21; cf. Livy XXVII, 37; Kerenyi, *Labyrinth*, p. 38.
218 Above, p. 44. Cf. *The Sacred Books of China* (ed. J. Legge, op. cit.), pp. 52ff.
219 The comparison was suggested by Böhl in *Labyrinth*, p. 21; for the variant texts of the epic see *Ancient Near Eastern Texts*, ed. James B. Pritchard, Princeton, 1955, pp. 73ff.; cf. S. N. Kramer, *History Begins at Sumer*, London, 1961, pp. 240ff.
220 The material was collected by A. H. Krappe in 'Die Sage von Tarpeia', *Rh. M.* (N.F.), LXXVIII, 1929, pp. 249ff.; the biblical parallel he is concerned with is, however, that of Samson and Delila. A. Dumézil, *Tarpeia*, pp. 279ff., is concerned with Tarpeia's corruptibility; her fecund character, which he there demonstrates, is equally pertinent to my reading of the legend as to his.
221 Joshua II, 1–21; VI, 22–25. Cf. J. Gagé, op. cit., pp. 41ff.
222 See Krappe and Dumézil, op. cit.; also Udo Hetzner, *Andromeda and Tarpeia*, Meisenheim-am-Glan, 1969, pp. 64ff.
223 Fest., s.v. Scelerato; Plutarch, *R.Q.*, XCVI. A list of the Vestals condemned in this way is given by T. Cato Worsfold, *History and Origin of the Vestal Virgins of Rome*, London, 1934, pp. 62ff.
224 X. 1; above, p. 34.
225 Livy, XXII, 57, vi.
226 Jackson Knight, *Cumean Gates*, pp. 124–6.
227 Gaius Publius Caecilius Secundus (Pliny the Younger), *Letters*, IV, 11.
228 *Annals*, I, 49 in Nonnius, 378, 15 (Warmington, I, p. 16).
229 Livy, I, 4, ii; also in Dion. Hal., I, 76; Serv. in Virg. VI A.:. 777; Strabo, V, 229, etc.
230 Latte, op. cit., pp. 404ff. for the most recent literature; cf. also Alföldi, op. cit., pp. 239ff.
231 Symmachus, *Epistles*, IX, 147f.
232 *C.I.L.*, X, 797; cf. Varro, V, *de L.L.*, V, 144, Dion. Hal., I, 45, 53f., 55f.; II, 86; VIII, 366; Livy, I, 1f.
233 On the Laurentinians as the inhabitants of Lanuvium see most recently Alföldi, op. cit., p. 246, n. 3; though his more general conclusion seems far-fetched. On this, see A. Momigliano in *J.R.S.*, 1972 (LXII) pp. 212ff.

234 Serv. in Virg. II *Aen.* 296; Serv. in Virg. III *Aen.* 12; Macrob. *Sat.* III, iv, 11.

235 Jean Gagé, op. cit., pp. 66ff., 163, 197, 201ff.

236 On Perseus the founder, see E. A. S. Butterworth, *Some Traces of the Pre-Olympian World in Greek Literature and Myth*, Berlin, 1966, pp. 20ff.

237 The material was collected by E. S. McCartney, 'Greek and Roman Lore of Animal-Nursed Infants', *Papers of the Michigan Academy of Science, Arts and Letters*, IV, 1924, pp. 15ff.

238 John Lydus, *De Ostent.*, 2. Several other versions of the legend are told: see, e.g. Herod. I, 94; Strabo, V; Vell. Pat., I, 1; Serv. ad Virg. X *Aen.* 179 and 189. On Tages, see above, pp. 29, 133.

239 Livy, I, 42, iv.

240 Ovid. VI *Fasti*, 627ff.

241 Dion. Hal. IV, 2; Plutarch, *de Sort. Rom.*, 10; Pliny, *N.H.* II, 107, p. 259 and XXXVI, 27, p. 348; Arnob. *Adv. Gent.* V, 18. Cf. Val. Max., x I, 6, i; also A. Brelich, *Vesta*, Zürich, 1949, pp. 98ff.; A. Brelich, *Tre Variazioni*, Rome, 1955, pp. 34ff.

242 Serv. in Virg. VII *Aen.* 678; Solinus II, 9. Cf. A. Brelich, *Tre Variazioni*.

243 Of Tethys, otherwise unknown. An emendation was proposed long ago by Thomas Dempster, in *Etruria Regali*, Florence, 1723, I, 79, to Themis.

244 Cf. A. Alföldi, op. cit., pp. 190f.

245 Plutarch, 'Life of Romulus', 2.

246 Cf. G. Dumézil, *Rituels Indo-Européens à Rome*, p. 138; C. Lévi-Strauss, 'Rites et Mythes des Peuples Voisins', *The Translation of Culture: Essays presented to E. E. Evans-Pritchard*, ed. T. O. Biedelman, London, 1971, pp. 161ff.

247 Pliny, *N.H.* XXVIII, vii.

248 Varro, *de L.L.* VII, 97.

249 Fest., s.v. *Mutini Titini*; Paulus in Festum s.v.

250 Tert. *Apol.* 25; Arnob. *Adv. Gent.* IV, vii, 11; Aurel. Aug. *de Civ. Dei.* IV, 11; Lucius Lactantius, *On the Divine Institutes*, I, xx. 36.

251 Dion. Cass. LXXIX, 9; Herodian, *History of the Great Emperors*, V, 6, i–ii; cf. Aelius Lampridius in *Scr. Hist. Aug.*, 6, v. Comment on all these in Gagé, op. cit., p. 201, n. 2.

252 So Clemens Romanus *ad Corinth.*, 12; Origen, *2nd Hom. on Joshua*, Justin Martyr, *ad Tryph.*, 111, etc.

253 Both quoted in Dumézil, *Tarpeia*, Paris, 1947, pp. 253ff., 287ff.

254 *C.I.L.*, I, p. 309.

255 Dion. Hal. II, 40; cf. W. Warde Fowler, *The Roman Festivals*, London, 1933.

256 Varro, *de L.L.*, VI, 23; a somewhat corrupt passage. The *Flamen Quirinalis* officiated on only two other festivals: the Robigalia (25 April) and the Consualia (21 August). On his function see G. Dumézil, *La Religion Romaine Antique*, Paris, 1966, pp. 161f., also pp. 266f. On the harlot Acca Laurentia, mentioned by the Praenestine calendar (who left her fortune to the Roman people) see Th. Mommsen, *Römische Forschungen*.

257 So G. Dumézil, *Tarpeia*, Paris, 1947, p. 280.

258 Ausonius, *Technopaegnium*, VIII, 9; cf. Wissowa, op. cit., p. 187.

259 Ovid. III *Fasti*, 55ff.

260 Lugli, op. cit., p. 123.

261 Above, p. 45; cf. Gjerstad, op. cit., p. 384.

262 Dion. Hal. I, 87, ii.

263 Hor. XVI *Epod.* 13f.; and Sch.

264 Plutarch, 'Life of Romulus', XI.

265 Attus Naevius: the story of the moving of the fig-tree from its original place on the Lupercal, Pliny, XV, *N.H.*, 20; Tac. XIII, *Ann.* 58.

266 Livy X, 23.

267 Lugli, op. cit., pp. 423ff.

268 Several of these survive; v. S. Reinach, op. cit.; s.v. Ville, *Personification*; also T. Dohrn, *Die Tyche von Antiochia*, Berlin, 1960, pp. 9ff. On Hittite goddesses with mural crowns, see E. Porada, 'Battlements in the Military Architecture of the Ancient Near East' *Essays presented to R. Wittkower*, eds. D. Fraser, H. Hibbard and M. J. Lewine, London, 1969, p. 2.

The Parallels *(between pages 163 and 187)*

1 G. Tucci, *The Theory and Practice of the Mandala*, London, 1961, pp. 85ff.

2 Mircea Eliade; *Yoga: Immortality and Freedom*, London, 1958, pp. 219–27; cf. M. Eliade, *Images et Symboles*, Paris, 1952, pp. 66f. and Tucci, op. cit., pp. 42f. and 47f.

3 Kramrisch, op. cit., pp. 21 and 58f.

4 *Manasara*, VII, 71ff.; *Viśwakarma Vatuśastram*, xviii. In a note on *Manasara*, VII, 155,

Acharya provides comparative material from other architectural treatises as well as some comment on site divisions other than square.

5 From √*vas*, to dwell, to be in a place. Hence anything to do with construction: ground, building, vehicle, furnishing. *Architecture of the Manasara*, trans. K. P. Acharya, London and Bombay, 1933, I, 6; III, 3.

6 On *purusa* as 'man' in the general Indo-European context, see E. Benveniste, *Le Vocabulaire*, II, p. 155f. The more 'spiritual' meaning however is equally valid. Cf. *Brhad-aranyaka Upanisad*, I, 4, i (trans. Radakrishnan): 'In the beginning this world was only the self, in the shape of a person. Looking round, he saw nothing else but self. . .'.

7 The first meaning in Kramrisch, op. cit., I. p. 21; the second, with its mythical aetiology in *Viśwakarma Vatuśastram*, pp. xviiff.

8 Kramrisch, op. cit., p. 17; *Rig-Veda*, X, 89, iv; *S.B.*, VII, 1, 1, 37.

9 Kramrisch, op. cit., p. 22.

10 For a commentary on this ritual, and its Iranian and European parallels, see G. Dumézil, *Rituels Indo-Européens à Rome*, Paris, 1954, pp. 28ff.

11 On the *śastras*, see B. Rowland, *Art and Architecture of India: Buddhist, Hindu, Jain*, Harmondsworth, 1953, pp. 164ff. The Gupta period is usually dated A.D. 320–600.

12 Cf. *Manasara*, passim.

13 *Manasara*, V. 82.

14 *Manasara*, VI, pp. 23ff.

15 *Manasara*, XII, pp. 153f.

16 A parallel 'seeding'' with metal and stone in a Hittite ritual; see James B. Pritchard, 'Ritual for the Erection of a House', *Near Eastern Texts*, Princeton, 1955, p. 356. Cf. Rowland, op. cit., p. 171; *Viśwakarma Vatuśastram*, pp. lxv f.

17 Cf. *Viśwakarma Vatuśastram*, op. cit., pp. xxiiiff.; *Manasara*, VII, p. 254f.

18 Leo Frobenius, *Kulturgeschichte Afrikas*, Zürich, 1933, pp. 177ff. It is not quite clear whom Frobenius exactly meant by these Mande. There is a tribe of that name in Sierra Leone; but they are recent Mandingo immigrants into the territory and have occupied it only since the eighteenth century (C. Fyfe, *A History of Sierra Leone*, London, 1962, pp. 6, 399). Frobenius seems to be speaking here of the Mandingo peoples in general who live in the territories of the old Mali empire and beyond them, particularly to the south and west. Frobenius is perhaps a little overassertive in describing them as the descendants ('Epigonen') of the Garamantes of classical antiquity; see Charles Daniels, *The Garamantes of Southern Libya*, Staughton, Wisconsin and N. Harrow, Middlesex; more particularly p. 36ff. for their towns.

19 See also W. Müller, op. cit., pp. 16off.; C. G. Jung and K. Kerenyi, *Introduction to a Science of Mythology*, London, 1951; and Eliade, op. cit., p. 321.

20 Georges Dumézil and his followers would also mark a more surprising piece of borrowing: the ritual presence of the three classes, which, according to Dumézil is the distinguishing feature of archaic Indo-European societies. Moreover, the division into warriors, bards, workmen suggests that attributed by Dumézil to the Indo-Europeans.

21 Frobenius, p. 177.

22 It may be worth noting that the capital of the old Mossi kingdom was called Wagadigu; it is now an important town of Upper Volta.

23 Frobenius quoted in Müller, op. cit., pp. 16of., 256, n. 1f.

24 Frobenius, op. cit., p. 181. Cf. Daniels, op. cit., pp. 43ff.

25 Gilberto Freyre, *The Masters and the Slaves*, New York, 1956, p. 82.

26 Cited by Claude Lévi-Strauss, *Tristes Tropiques*, Paris, 1955, pp. 227–33.

27 Claude Lévi-Strauss, *Anthropologie Structurale*, Paris, 1958, pp. 156f.

28 Lévi-Strauss, op. cit., p. 158; cf. ibid., p. 163.

29 *Wasichu* is usually translated as 'paleface'.

30 John G. Neihardt (Flaming Rainbow), *Black Elk Speaks*, Lincoln, Nebraska, 1961, p. 198.

31 Neihardt, op. cit., p. 169; cp. pp. 24, 210.

32 Neihardt, op. cit., p. 186. Standing Bear's illustrations for Black Elk's story are rather fragmentary. But the fourfold division of the circle is amply and beautifully illustrated by the sand-drawings of the Navahos. See Leland C. Wyman (ed.), *Bautyway: A Navaho ceremonial*, New York, 1957, passim; but especially figs. IV, VI, IX, XI, XII, XIII, XIV.

33 J. P. Mountford, *The Tiwi*, London and Melbourne, 1958.

34 J. J. Rousseau, *Essai sur l'Origine des Langues*, Paris, 1969, p. 519.

35 Erich Neumann, *The Origins and History of Consciousness*, New York, 1954, p. 16.

36 Norman O. Brown, *Love's Body*, New York, 1966, p. 148f.

37 Ad. E. Jensen, *Mythos und Kult bei Naturvölkern*, Wiesbaden, 1960, p. 198; cf. e.g. M. Griaule, *Conversations with Ogotemêli*, London, 1965, p. 114ff.

38 G. de Santillana, *The Origins of Scientific Thought*, London, 1961, p. 8.
39 Aurel. Aug. *de Civ. Dei.* XV, 17; Brown, op. cit., p. 146.
40 Gen. IV, 17.
41 Cf. Ralph Patia, *Man and Temple*, New York, 1967, p. 152.
42 M. Granet, *Danses et Légendes de la Chine Ancienne*, Paris, 1959, p. 548, n. 2.
43 Ibid., p. 330, n. 1.
44 Ibid., p. 50.
45 Ibid., pp. 238, 297.
46 Ibid., pp. 173ff.
47 G. Nicolas, 'Essai sur les Structures Fondamentales de l'Espace dans la Cosmologie Hausa', *Journal de la Société des Africanistes*, XXXVI, 1966, fasc. I, p. 101.
48 Ibid., p. 69.
49 See below, p. 178.
50 See below, p. 191.
51 K. Sethe, *Die Altägyptischen Pyramidentexte*, Leipzig, 1908ff. Cf. A. Piankoff and N. Ramborn, *The Shrines of Tut-Ankh-Amon*, New York, 1955, pp. 22ff.
52 M. Griaule, *Conversations with Ogotemêli*, London, 1965, pp. 96ff.; cf. M. Palau Marti, *Les Dogon*, Paris, 1957, pp. 57ff.
53 The onion fields of the Dogon are indeed still divided into square paddies, and for certain purposes the village and individual houses are represented as a grid. Geneviève Calame-Griaule, *La Parole chez les Dogon*, Paris, 1965, pp. 518ff.
54 Griaule, ibid.
55 On the foundation of the house, Calame-Griaule, op. cit. She notes, too, prohibitions on sexual intercourse outside the house. Ibid., p. 337.
56 Ibid.
57 Cf. A. Ch. Lagopoulos, 'The semeiological analysis of the traditional African Settlement', *Ekistics*, XXXIII, 195, February 1972, pp. 142ff.; also Fritz Morgenthaler, 'The Dogon People (2)', *Meaning and Architecture*, eds. C. Jencks and G. Baird, London, 1969, pp. 194ff.
58 Griaule, op. cit., p. 17.
59 Marti, op. cit., p. 42; cf. Fritz Morgenthaler, *Die Weissen Denken Zuviel*, Zürich, 1963, pp. 69f.
60 Griaule, op. cit., pp. 30ff.; cf. Aldo van Eyck 'Basket—House—Village—Universe' op. cit., eds. Jencks and Baird, pp. 190ff.
61 Nicolas, op. cit., p. 72.
62 Ibid., p. 73.
63 Ibid., p. 76; cf. I Kings, XVI, 34f.; 'In his dayes did Hiel the Bethelite build Jericho: he laid the foundations thereof in Abiram his firstborn, and set up the gates thereof in his youngest son Segub, according to the words of the Lord, which he spake by Joshua the son of Nun'. Joshua's prophecy was made at the destruction of Jericho, and is recorded in Jos. VI 26: 'Cursed be the man before the Lord that riseth up and buildeth this city of Jericho: he shall lay the foundations thereof in his firstborn, and in his youngest son shall he set up the gates thereof'. See above, p. 152.
64 V. Pâques, *Les Bambara*, Paris, 1954, pp. 81, 99f.
65 Eva L. R. Meyerowitz, *The Sacred State of Akkan*, London, 1951, pp. 184ff.
66 Cf. Andrew F. Rutter, 'Ashanti Vernacular Architecture', *Shelter in Africa*, ed. Paul Oliver, London, 1971, pp. 153ff.
67 J.-P. Beguin, M. Kalt, J.-L. Leroy, D. Louis, J. Macray, P. Pelloux and H.-N. Peronne, *L'Habitat au Cameroun*, Paris, 1952, pp. 19 and 50.
68 L. Frobenius, *Kulturgeschichte Afrikas*, Zürich, 1933, p. 219f.
69 Op. cit., pp. 232ff.
70 Above, p. 176.
71 *Hung fan*, the Great Diagram, is not only the name of the diagram, but also of the commentary on it which is sometimes considered (by Granet, for instance: *Il Pensiero Chinese*, op. cit., pp. 122ff.) as the most ancient part of the *Shu Ching* (a title variously translated as 'Book of History', 'Ancient Records' and so on; see James Legge, *The Sacred Books of China*, Oxford 1879, vol. III of the 'Sacred Books of the East' series (ed. F. Max Müller, pp. xxiii, 137ff.). It also plays an important part in the *I Ching* (translated into English by Cary F. Baynes from the German of Richard Wilhelm, London, 1951, vol. I, pp. 331ff.; it is the ninth section of the first part of *Ta Chuan*, The Great Commentary. The Great Diagram in this ritual form is identified with *Lo Shu*, one of the two magical squares which the Yü emperor received from water animals: the *Lo Shu* from the turtle, the *Ho Thu* from a dragon-horse. On the place of these diagrams in Chinese mathematical thinking, and on their origins, see also Joseph Needham, *Science and Civilization in China*, vol. III, Cambridge, 1959, pp. 55ff. The Great Diagram

was also transcribed and commented on by the great Han historian, Sseu-ma Ts'ien in his *Historical Memoirs:* see E. Chavennes, *Les Mémoires Historiques de Se-ma Ts'ien*, Paris, 1895–1905, vol. I, pp. 101ff, II, pp. 219ff.

72 William Watson, *China*, London, 1961, pp. 16ff.; cf. C. P. Fitzgerald, *China*, London, 1954, pp. 26f.; and Herlee G. Creel, *Studies in Early Chinese Culture*, 1st series, Baltimore, 1937, pp. 97ff.

73 Granet, loc. cit.

74 A critical bibliography of this material in Creel, op. cit., pp. 1–16; William G. White, *Bone Culture of Ancient China*, Toronto, 1945, pp. 19ff., 51, 87ff. It may well be that the cruciform *Ya-hing* character, which appears frequently on oracle bones, is connected with the idea of the cruciform world-model, if not the 'Great Plan'. Cf. Carl Hentze and Ch. Kim, *Göttergestalten der Ältesten Chinesischen Schrift*, Antwerp, 1943, pp. 39f. Jean Gagé has pointed out strange Italiot cults of the tortoise, op. cit., pp. 64ff., 93f., 224ff., connected with Vulcan the smith. Particularly interesting in this context is the tortoise carapace parallel to the shield which Vulcan made for Aeneas; which was itself a world-model.

75 Granet, op. cit., pp. 77ff., 238f.; cf. B. Vuilleumier, *Symbolism of Chinese Imperial Ritual Robes*, London, 1939.

76 Wilhelm, op. cit., p. 81.

77 M. Granet, *La Religion Chinoise*, Paris, 1951, p. 17.

78 Paul Wheatley, *The Pivot of the Four Quarters*, Edinburgh, 1971, pl. 32; cf. E. A. Gutkind, *Revolution of Environment*, London, 1946, pp. 246ff.

79 Shu-Ching (*Book of History*) trans. Karlgren in Wheatley, op. cit., p. 421.

80 Shih Chi (*Book of Odes*, Mao Ode 50), trans. A. Waley (modified); cf. Wheatley op. cit., p. 426.

81 Wheatley, ibid.; cf. above, pp. 48, 166.

82 Wheatley, op. cit., p. 428.

83 Wen Wang yu sheng (Mao, Ode 244). I have used Ezra Pound's translation as far as I could, but modified it by comparison with Waley's and Karlgren's versions.

84 Cf. above, p. 37; Wheatley, op. cit., pp. 431, 435f. For the Altar of the Earth—and other platform altars—in recent times, cf. O. Siren, *The History of Early Chinese Art*, London, 1930, IV, pp. 7ff.

85 Granet, op. cit., p. 69.

86 Cf. B. P. Groslier, *Angkor, Hommes et Pierres*, Paris, 1956, passim; cf. L. Frederic (pseudonym), *The Temples and Sculptures of South East Asia*, London, 1965, esp. pp. 279ff.

87 M. Granet, *La Civilisation Chinoise*, Paris, 1929, pp. 284ff.; cf. Wheatley, op. cit., pp. 189ff.

88 On surviving earthen buildings, see O'Brien, op. cit., pp. 36f.

89 I.e., to organize the corvée.

90 *Book of Odes* (Mao Ode 237). My translation is again a conflation of Pound, Waley and Karlgren, using Wheatley's (op. cit., p. 34f.) commentary. The last verse is entirely as Pound does it.

91 Herlee Glessner Creel, *The Birth of China*, New York, 1967, pp. 227ff., 251ff.

92 The whole science of site inspection was later formulated (c. A.D. 1000) under the now familiar title, Feng Shui. Cf. a somewhat antiquated but very agreeable account, Ernest J. Eitel, *Feng Shui, or the Rudiments of Natural Science in China*, Hongkong, 1873.

93 On this parallel, see M. Granet, *Danses et Légendes*, pp. 428ff.

94 The ceremony is described by M. Granet, *La Civilisation Chinoise*, pp. 274ff., following the spring and summer annals, and the ritual commentary, the *Tse Chouan;* cf. Wheatley, op. cit., p. 435.

95 'A Chinese speaker, when addressing an audience of his fellow countrymen, will sometimes use the phrase "brethren (born) of the same mother". . .'. William C. White, *Bone Culture of Ancient China*, p. 5.

96 Above, p. 180; M. Granet, *Danses et Légendes*, p. 116; *Il Pensiero Cinese*, p. 77f.

97 M. Granet, *La Civilisation Chinoise*, p. 279.

98 Ibid., pp. 285f.

99 Above, p. 185. Recent excavation has shown that An-Yang is one, perhaps the last, of a series of Shang centres. See Chêng tê-k'un, 'New Light on Shang China' in *Antiquity*, XLIX, 1975, pp. 25ff.

100 Wheatley, op. cit., pp. 425, 435.

## The City as a Curable Disease: Ritual and Hysteria *(between pages 188 and 193)*

1 Sigmund Freud, *Works*, London, 1953–1966, XI, pp. 16f.

2 Ibid., p. 45.

3 Ernest Jones, *Siegmund Freud*, London, 1953, II, pp. 26ff.

4 Freud, op. cit., XI, p. 17.

5 E. Haussmann, a speech of 1864 in Françoise Choay, *Espacements*, Paris, 1969, p. 82.

6 Though he was well aware of this consideration. E. Haussmann, *Mémoires*, Paris, 1890–3, III, p. 55.

7 A. Breton, *Nadja*, Paris, 1949, pp. 105ff.

7a Though elsewhere Freud saw the 'dead' town of Pompeii as an image, almost as a means of integration. He set this out in his commentary on a short novel, *Gradiva*, by Wilhelm Jensen. See *Delusion and Dream: An Interpretation in the light of Psychoanalysis of Gradiva*, a novel by Wilhelm Jensen, New York, 1917; a more recent translation of the commentary only in S. Freud, *Complete Works*, op. cit., vol. IX. Elsewhere, however, Pompei returns as an image of repression (as in the case of the Rat-Man), S. Freud, op. cit., vol. X, pp. 176f.

8 On the rise of urban societies see Robert McC.Adams, *The Evolution of Urban Society*, Chicago, 1966.

9 A. Leroi-Gourhan, *Le Geste et la Parole*, Paris, 1965, I, p. 270.

10 Leroi-Gourhan, op. cit., II, pp. 139ff.

11 Leroi-Gourhan, op. cit., II, p. 148.

12 G. Clark and S. Piggott, *Prehistoric Societies*, London, 1965, pp. 69ff.

13 A reasoned description of this process in McC.Adams, op. cit., pp. 40ff.

14 The excavations have been described by D. Srejović, *Lepenski Vir: Europe's First Monumental Sculpture*, London, 1972.

15 Srejović, op. cit., pp. 62ff.

16 A. Badawy, 'Le Dessin Architectural chez les Anciens Egyptiens', *Annales du Service d'Antiquités de l'Egypte*, Cairo, 1948, pp. 57ff.; cf. above, p. 45.

17 A. Badawy, *History of Egyptian Architecture*, Giza, 1954, Berkeley, 1966.

18 S. Langdon, *Sumerian Grammar*, Paris, 1911, pp. 22, 301.

19 Cf., above, p. 180.

## Conclusion *(between pages 194 and 203)*

20 Badawy, op. cit., II, pp. 39ff.

21 See above, p. 79.

22 E. Minkowski, *Vers une Cosmologie, Fragments Philosophiques*, Paris, 1967, p. 191.

23 C. Clemen, *Fontes Historiae Religionis Germanicae*, Berlin, 1928, p. 43: 'Indiculus Superstitionum et Paganiarum', ca. 743 (?) confectus.

24 P. Sartori, op. cit., passim.

25 See George M. Foster, *Culture and Conquest*, Chicago, 1960, pp. 40ff., quoting largely L. Torres Balbas, L. Cervera, F. Chueca, and P. Bidagor, *Resumen Histórico del Urbanismo en España*, Madrid, 1954, which was not available to me.

26 George M. Foster, op. cit., p. 47.

27 F. A. Kirkpatrick, *The Spanish Conquistadores*, London, 1963, pp. 214f. On the 'New Laws of the Indies', ibid., pp. 256ff. Cf. also P. Lavedan, *Histoire de l'Urbanisme*, Paris, 1959, vol. III, pp. 469ff.

28 It was the cactus, *tenochtli*, which gave its name to the town. The sanguinary details of the myth were told many times.

29 See fig. 161. The Arms of Mexico are based on such an image. See also James Cooper Clark, *The Mexican Manuscript* known as *The Collection of Mendoza* and preserved in the Bodleian Library at Oxford; London, 1938, vol. II, p. 1f. Cooper Clark provides an alternative etymology: *Tenoch*, the great chief and hero-founder of the town; *titlan*, in, near. The name of the town then would mean in the place of Tenoch or the place founded by Tenoch. The two etymologies are suspiciously parallel to the various interpretations of the name of Rome.

30 The literature of the subject has been collected by Werner Müller in 'Raum und Zeit bei den Maya. Stadtplan und Richtungskalender', *Antaios*, VI, 1964, pp. 339ff.

31 The conquerors were very responsive to the splendours they had found. Cortes and his soldiers were astonished and highly impressed by their first sight of Tenochtitlàn; though according to Diaz, it was not the splendours of antiquity, but the enchantments of which they had read in *Amadis de Gaule*, that the great city evoked.

32 *Handbuch des Deutschen Aberglaubens*, 1922ff., s.v. Pflug, vol. VI, 1718ff.

33 Antonio Averlino detto il Filarete, *Trattato di Architettura, a cura di Anna Maria Finoli e Liliana Grassi*, Milano, 1972, pp. 100ff.

34 J. R. Hale, 'The End of Florentine Liberty: The Fortezza da Basso', *Florentine Studies*, ed. N. Rubinstein, London, 1968, pp. 518f., 525.

35 N. Rubinstein, 'Vasari's Painting of *The Foundation of Florence* in the Palazzo Vecchio' in *Essays in the History of Architecture presented to Rudolf Wittkower*, op. cit., pp. 64ff.

35a Another fresco actually showing the *Ploughing of the Boundaries of Rome by Romulus* was painted by Annibale Caracci for the frieze of the main *salone* of the Palazzo Magnani-Salem in Bologna about 1590. The frieze consisted of eight scenes representing the founding of Rome drawn from Livy and Plutarch. On this frieze, and the problems of attribution, see D. Posner, *Annibale Caracci*, London. 1971, pp. 59ff., and cat. no. 52.

36 Cf. L. von Pastor, *The History of the Popes*, Vol. XXX (Innocent X) London, 1940, pp. 370f., part p. 371, n. 6.

37 The legend is told by several ecclesiastical historians, as well as later pagan authors. The material is collected and interpreted by D. Lathaud, in *Echos d'Orient*, XXIII, 1924, pp. 289ff., and XXIV, 1925, pp. 180ff.; and John Holland Smith, *Constantine the Great*, pp. 217ff.

38 Philostorgus, *Ecclesiastical History*, I.M, 2, ix. (in Photius' *Bibliotheca*, II, 9.) cf. Hermias Sozomen, *Ecclesiastical History*, II, 3.

39 Cf. D. Lathoud, op. cit.,

40 See E. Freshfield, *A Letter to the Rt Hon. Lord Aldenham, upon the subject of a Byzantine Evangelion*, London, 1900, pp. 9ff.

# Index

Page numbers in *italic* refer to illustrations and their captions